It Was Better Than Working

With Best Wishes,

Jack Manning.

The extraordinary life of a Morecambe Bay fisherman

Written and Published
in 2010 and re-edited in 2016

by

Jack Manning

Flookburgh, Cumbria, England

j.mann@live.co.uk

I dedicate this to my wife, Margaret, for tolerating and supporting me throughout the sixty-two years of our marriage - also for her patience during the hundreds of hours I've spent preparing this book.

I wish to thank my friends David and Noelene Shore for their support.

Sincere thanks also to my cousin, David Churches, for his technical assistance with the publishing programme.

Introduction

I am the fourth generation of a family who have wrested a precarious living from the sands and channels of Morecambe Bay, gathering mainly cockles, mussels, shrimps, salmon and flatfish.

During the latter part of the 1980s and throughout the 1990s, I gradually put together my memoirs, first with a pen and paper then progressing to a computer. They were intended only to tell the younger members of the family, and those who follow, what my life has been like. It is also a record of some of the history of the fishing industry in which I worked all my life.

For many years I have regretted not paying more attention to what my grandfather told me about his life and work. It was for this reason that I decided to write down some of my life story so that my descendants may know of it if they so wish. Inevitably, some parts are my views with which not everyone may agree but, as the saying goes – that's life.

There is much small detail that may be considered irrelevant but I have no idea what may be of interest ten, twenty or fifty years hence. The document has been edited numerous times in the thirty years since I started writing but remains the same in essence. All dates given are correct unless I have expressed doubt about them.

The title, It Was Better Than Working, comes from a statement made by a fisherman and market gardener who, in the dark days of the depression of the 1920s, was said to be working virtually day and night to scratch a living when times were very hard. If he wasn't fishing or gardening for himself he was odd jobbing on farms to make a few shillings. When someone suggested that he was doing too much, he said: "Well, it's better than working", meaning, I suppose, it was better than working for someone else. At least he was his own boss and reasonably independent – as I have been.

There are been parts of the book where it may appear that I am boasting – which I certainly do not wish to do; I have tried to put down the facts as truthfully as possible. I suppose I could have employed a ghost writer but then it would not have been my own work or my own words – which is what I wished it to be.

Table of Contents

Pictures and Illustrations

Childhood

Nineteen thirty-two was not a good year from the economic point of view. The country was in the depths of the notorious depression which had brought much of the population to the edge of starvation. But, it wasn't all bad because it was the year that I was born. There were good stocks of cockles in the bay, and plaice that were feeding on the tiny cockles or wheat as they are known locally. These could be harvested in good quantities but they were worth practically nothing. Flatfish and shellfish were sent by rail to fish merchants at markets in various northern towns. Shrimps were also sent, sometimes without being ordered, simply in the hope that the merchant would send some money in return. This was known as "sending on spec" which I assume meant speculation, but most times no money arrived.

My earliest recollections of going out fishing are of trips over the sands of Morecambe Bay with a horse and cart along with my grandfather, Jim Butler when I was perhaps five or six years old. He would occasionally say: "Thou can gaa t't sand in't mornin' if it's fine." The colloquial expression for "Going fishing" has always been, and still is, "going to the sand" or in dialect "gine t't' sand." Throughout my working life, if anyone were to enquire as to my whereabouts when I was out fishing the reply would be: "He's gone t't' sand". This is in a dialect peculiar to this immediate district which was in common usage, especially by the fishermen, but was in general use until thirty years ago. Now it is spoken regularly by only a few people. I'm sorry to see it dying out and am pleased that at least some of the younger men, and especially those from fishing families, have retained parts of it. In 2008 I compiled a booklet of local dialect words so that they may be preserved.

If I were due to go fishing early with grandfather, I would occasionally sleep at his house which was next door but one to ours when he lived at New Cottage, which is now 72 Main St, and we lived at Fairfield Cottage, now 68 Main Street. I would go to bed full of enthusiasm and anticipation for the morning's expedition, but when he woke me the following morning at some unearthly hour, probably still dark, the prospect did not seem quite so inviting.

I can remember asking: "Is it a fine morning granddad?" Of course it was, otherwise he would not have wakened me. He was a quiet, happy and contented man and I was the apple of his eye. We would travel out to the nets which were staked out in the bay, perhaps three miles from shore, and he would do his work, taking out the fish which were trapped in the nets and I would help in my small way. The work completed, we would set off for home. He sat up on the front of the body of the cart on what was called the forrend with legs outside the cart and feet on the left side shaft, having already sat me in a front corner of the cart on a sack or something similar. If it was rather cold, which it often was, he would cover me with his jacket or oilskin which gave me the feeling of being in a tent and looking out of the door flap. He would sing quietly most of the way home, songs such as Danny Boy, The Rose of Tralee or perhaps a hymn. Whilst thinking back over these things it has just occurred to me that I cannot remember him ever raising his voice in anger to me.

Harold Manning & Jim Butler - unyoking horse, Tony c. 1952

Jim Butler and his wife Jane had adopted my father, Harold Mitchell Manning, when he was about two and a half years old. He was the illegitimate son of Nellie Manning (the same name as my mother), a domestic servant who lived in the Bristol area. Harold was born in a maternity home at 50 Southwell Street, Bristol, on the 26th of January 1906 and came to my grandfather and grandmother via an orphanage in Arnside. After adoption, his name became Harold Butler but because there was already a Harold Butler in the family (my mother's brother).To avoid confusion, when he married he reverted to his original name of Manning. Nellie's father had been a farm manager in Gloucestershire and in Somerset. He and his wife, Sarah, had five daughters, twins Nellie and Lizzie, Aileen, Bella, and Dorothy, who was born on an Indian reservation in Canada.

In adulthood, my father desperately wished to trace his birth family and made attempts to do so but had no success. In the early 1990s, my wife, Margaret, and I went to the records office, then at St Catherine's House in London, and made a determined effort to trace them. The only record we found was that of the marriage of Aileen to Ivor Walter Hendy in 1912. We found no more references to any of the family so we came to the conclusion that they must have emigrated.

During the last couple of months of the year 2006, our son, Stephen, searched the internet heritage sites and discovered some of father's family in America. It transpires that after my father came here, his mother and father married then emigrated to Canada. After only a few years they moved to America and settled in Detroit.

Harold's father was William Herbert Churches. He and Nellie had four more sons, Arthur, Robert, Cecil and David. One son was born in England when Nellie was on a trip home to Somerset, and the youngest, David, born back in Detroit in 1921. Strangely enough, my Great-Aunt Mary, grandmother Jane's sister, mentioned many years ago that my real grandmother, Nellie, came to Flookburgh only a short time after my father was adopted and wanted to reclaim him, stating that she was going to marry and emigrate. I assume she came to the orphanage at Arnside in the hope of taking him back but found he had been adopted. Obviously Jim and Jane would not part with him. We gave no credence to that story and really just dismissed it. At that time it was not easy, in fact almost impossible, for mothers to trace adopted children or vice versa.

Although my father's brothers had died when all this was discovered, I believe there were six of my full cousins in America at that time. I have been in touch with some of them and now so far as I know there is only one still alive. On the sixth of March 2007 I sent an e-mail to David Churches and his wife, Nancy, in Minneapolis and that was my first direct contact with any of my father's family. We were delighted when David visited us in May of 2009, spending three weeks in Flookburgh but taking a few days out to look at the ancestral region in Somerset. I found these discoveries exciting and yet very emotional because father had desperately wanted to find his family and even went down to Bristol by train in the 1950s but found nothing. Now, a century after he came to Flookburgh, we are in contact with them. How I wish he could have been here!

After adopting my father, James and Jane Butler had a son, Frederick, born to them naturally. Uncle Fred was a very mild man, easy to get on with and certainly good to me. Although he was raised in a family where almost all the males were fishermen, he served his time as a stonemason, building and repairing many of the large limestone houses in Grange-Over-Sands and the surrounding district until he became employed in the same trade on the railways with LMS and British Rail. He and his wife Nellie had two children, Frieda and James. I think it was in the 1970s that Fred and James set up a building company. Fred and Nellie lived almost all of their married life in a cottage in Flookburgh Square.

My grandparents with their son, David, in America

In my formative years father had little influence on my learning about fishing because just before the Second World War it was nearly impossible to make a living from fishing so for a time he worked at the Barrow Steelworks. Soon after the outbreak of war he was called up for service in the Royal Navy.

He served on the destroyer H.M.S. Calpé and after that, was posted to Iceland where he was shore based near to the town of Akureyri for three years. When father went to Iceland he found that some of the language was similar to the dialect spoken here in Flookburgh so he picked it up quite easily. This has been well documented, in fact, the writer and broadcaster, Lord Melvyn Bragg, mentioned it in a radio programme about language and dialects. When father left the navy, in 1945, I was about twelve years old and had spent quite some time fishing and gardening etc. with two uncles and with my paternal grandfather, James Butler.

My maternal grandfather, John Butler, was also a fisherman but he died in 1926, six years before I was born, so of him I know very little except that from photographs he appears to be a very dark, handsome man; rather dour in the picture but people did not smile in photographs in those days. Both of my grandfathers were called Butler; in fact, James Butler's father and my mother

Nellie's father, John, were brothers so my mother and my father's adoptive father were cousins.

John Butler

John's wife, Anne, known to all her clan as Ganny, was the epitome of the traditional English working-class grandmother of that period. She was a smallish woman who dressed in near ankle-length dark clothes and most of the time wore a flowery wrap round pinny, except when she was about her dirty chores. On these occasions she wore a large apron made from hessian sacking which she called a 'rough brat.' I remember her mostly as a very homely woman around whom the whole of her family of about thirty souls revolved and evolved. Her home was the headquarters for us all, even though of her family of five girls and four boys, all except Winnie (Winifred) had married and made their own homes. Even now, fifty-six years after her death I still remember her with great affection.

The thing that I remember most about Ganny is that although she seemed to do nothing but work, looking after the house, picking shrimps, tending her hens or stirring blood for making black-puddings at pig-killing time, she never seemed to think about or mention money. Today we have so many financial millstones round our necks such as mortgages, fitted kitchens, fitted carpets, all our electrical appliances, telephones, televisions, cars and a thousand and one other things that have become virtual necessities over the last forty years, that we are slaves to money. Perhaps it was the age in which she lived, perhaps it was her personal philosophical outlook on life or maybe it was what I saw as a child and that the fears and traumas of life were there, but kept hidden from young minds. I remember one particular day, almost certainly in the autumn of 1953, when I arrived home from shrimping with a very poor catch when everyone else had done well. I was somewhat downhearted but she simply laughed and said; "Well nivver mind, it'll 'appen be thy turn tomorn." This was a typical example of her philosophical disposition which I am trying to illustrate. Ganny was widowed in 1926 when she was fifty-four years old but because she had not paid into any fund she received no pension until she was seventy; she then received 10 shillings, (50p) per week.

Myself at about 6 years old

Back in the time of my father and grandfather, most men were given nicknames and were usually addressed by them; father was called Hunter and of my mother's four brothers, only Jack did not have a nickname. Jonathan was Uncle Jont to us, the family, but to his fellows he was Meffat, Bill was Pongo and Harold was Tarro, (pronounced Tar-o). Grandfather Jim was Shigger, his brother Thomas was Bull, William was Ganza, Robert was known as Clyde and Jack was Kayan (pronounced kie-an). There doesn't appear to be any logical reason for the nicknames – ladies certainly didn't have them. Grandfather Jim also had four sisters, Mary and Esther, who were twins, Margaret and Elizabeth.

It is difficult to research the Butler family because there are so many with the same first names. In the records there are many John Butlers, likewise Robert, James and so on. Also, there were two more Butler families in the village who were not related to us. One man whom I knew when I was young was always known as Jimmy-John. The reason being, I suppose, was for identification because there were at least six John Butlers in our small village during the 1940s and 50s. There are now none.

When attending funerals, all of the men wore bowler hats but never at any other time so far as I remember. We, as young people, might not have known that a funeral was due to take place but we certainly knew when we saw a number of men wearing bowlers going down the street in the direction of the church. This tradition carried on until about the end of the 1950s. Even today I could not attend any funeral unless dressed in a dark suit, black tie and socks and a white shirt. When I see other men at funerals in light coloured, casual clothes or in brown shoes I always think of Stanley Holloway's recording of the song, Brown Boots.

In the 1950s there were about fourteen men from the Butler family in Flookburgh, Allithwaite and across on the Furness Peninsula who were actively involved in fishing and half that number who had been fishermen but were then retired. I should think that the whole clan of men, women and children with the surname of Butler would then have numbered more than fifty. This being so, I used to think that the numbers must grow as families and branches spread.

There are now no Butlers who are full-time fishermen in Flookburgh and just one who fishes part time. As the old fishermen have died the new generations have not followed on but have taken other trades or professions and some have moved away. Many of the offspring were girls so of course the name changed when they married. My cousin, James Butler, the only son of the aforementioned Fred, who died at a young age, had three children but all girls so that branch of the Butler family came to an end.

All of the main fishing families in the village were related. The Shaws, Robinsons, Bensons, the Hills and the Butlers. I was related to them all one way or another, either through birth, perhaps down the female line, through marriage or both. The family tree is a complex web that I still do not understand and with which even the elders have difficulty. I suppose I'm one of the elders now but not long ago there were a good number of the previous generation around. For instance, I was probably sixty years old when I was speaking to my mother's cousin, Bill Robinson. In the course of the conversation, he told me that Harry Shaw was his cousin. I had known these two all of my life and had fished alongside both of them until they retired but did not know that they were both cousins of my mother. So far as I can work out, I was related in some way to all the men who fished here in the 1950s.

Great-grandfather, Harry Couperthwaite, was an old man and retired when I was born. He lived with his daughter, my grandmother Jane, and grandfather Jim. Harry was a smallish, stocky man who, when I knew him, didn't walk well, even with the aid of a stick. He used to sit out on the front of 72 Main Street and look after me when I was just a toddler and controlled me with the crook of his walking-stick. If my shoelace came undone, he would say: "Come

13

'ere while I fasten thi' wang." He was the only person I ever heard call a shoelace a wang although I feel sure it must have been a common word in the dialect at that time; in fact, the word is quoted in a dictionary of local dialect called A Flookburgh Glossary. This was compiled, with the assistance of some of the boys and young men of that time including my father, by Rev. Canon Samuel Taylor who was the vicar here around 1920. When the ice-cream man came, Harry would root in his trousers pocket, pull out a coin and say: "Here's a haup'ny (halfpenny), ga an' git thissel an ice-cream." If my reckoning is correct, I believe a pre-decimal half penny to be a forty-eighth part of a ten pence piece. What we now call ten pence would then have bought 48 ice creams.

Harry died in New Cottage in 1940 and I remember his last days, when he had gangrene in his toes. When he was on his deathbed he asked for a bottle of stout, which was given to him – but only after a hot fire poker had been dipped in it, for what reason I had no idea. When Margaret and I were at a dance at Cartmel Village Hall on a cold winter's night in 1993, I went to the bar for drinks and remarked to a man from out Kendal way that the beer would be very cold. He replied by saying that it could do with a hot poker sticking in it. When I asked why, he said: "Just to warm it up a bit." I suppose that was the reason for the poker in the stout.

At one period in their lives, James and Jane ran the village shop on the north side of Main Street that is now No.14. It is no longer a shop and has recently had the large shop window taken out. Grandfather was fishing as well as running the other business. At that time he was one of a number of men, including at least two brothers, Robert and William, who sailed boats out from Sandgate shore, westward across the estuary to the mussel beds off the southern end of the Furness peninsula, say a mile or a mile and a half east of Rampside or Newbiggin. The boats were loaded with mussels, sailed back to Sandgate shore and from there the mussels were transported by horse and cart to Cark Station to be despatched to markets in Yorkshire and South Lancashire. It was the very railway which carried the mussels away that caused the demise of the boat fishing in this region. After the railways were constructed, in the 1850s, silting of the estuaries occurred very rapidly. This was mainly due to the fact that the rivers were then fixed to one place where they passed under the railway and were then unable to meander as they had done previously. Due to the shallowness of the channels and the raising of sandbanks, the boating from our shore became too dangerous and ceased at about the beginning of the First World War.

Grandfather smoked a clay pipe or perhaps I should say hundreds of clay pipes in his lifetime because he regularly broke them in the course of his work. They would be used until dropped several times then abandoned when they got down to a couple of inches of stem. Most of the old men smoked pipes and chewed tobacco which was bought by the ounce and came in lengths like rope, to be cut off in sections, just enough for a pipeful, then rolled around between the palms of the hands to break it up. If it were chewed, then about an inch would be cut off and put straight into the mouth. Tobacco chewers used to continually spit out copious amounts of juice which was accumulated in the mouth. When this was ejected, the wise person made sure he was well away or upwind. Grandfather's particular brand of tobacco was Black Twist which was kept in a circular silver tin container. It was about three inches in diameter and an inch or so deep so it fitted nicely into his jacket pocket. The tobacco fitted inside the tin like a piece of coiled rope or a sleeping snake.

He only used one plate for his dinner. When finishing his main course he scraped the plate by bending his knife flat down on the plate and drawing it across, which left the plate absolutely clean. His rice pudding, eaten every Sunday and probably some other days, was then put on the plate and he ate this with the same knife, yes, with the knife, the pudding always being so stiff that the spoon would stand up in the pan or vessel in which it was cooked. He was always slim and once told me that he had never weighed more than ten and a half stones. I find this hard to believe, as I don't think he was a particularly small man. So far as I know we only have one photograph of him and this is of him helping my father to unyoke the horse, Tony, in about 1952.

Many of the local fishermen spent some time in summer, during the years of recession between the wars, haymaking over in the Yorkshire Dales and were hired at Bentham fair for the hay making season which would probably be about a month. I think the going rate was about £10, plus their keep, for a man and horse, not per week, but for the whole of the haymaking period.

Both father and grandfather went over to The Dales with one horse and cart. This was before my time so almost certainly in the 1920s. In the year 2004 I was speaking to Bill Robinson, (father of Cedric, guide over the Kent Sands) who was a few months short of his 100th birthday and he could tell me on which farms he had worked in various years and the names of the farmers. He could also tell me on which farms all the other local men had worked -all of which were in the dales around Giggleswick, Austwick and Horton-in-Ribblesdale.

Grandmother Jane frowned upon people who frequented public houses. One night, on returning home, grandfather said he had been singing in the pub. At this news she expressed her disapproval but he said: "It must have been good singing." She asked how he came to this conclusion. He said: "Well, everybody clapped." In fact he was a good, tuneful singer. In spite of her disapproval, my father went to the pub almost every night. Jane died in 1943 at the age of sixty-one. At that time I was attending Holker School and father was in Iceland. She used to bake the most delicious bread and would say to me: "Do you want a jam cake?" The answer was always in the affirmative, whereon she would coat the thickly-cut bread with a copious amount of butter and Robertson's Bramble Seedless jam (with the golliwog on the label). Jane was a rather nervous woman who, when left alone in the house, used to come to our house and always as she opened the back door said: "It's only me". My mother's mother and my father's father both died in the same week, in May 1954, and were, as I remember them, two of the kindliest people in the world and are both fixed fondly in my memory.

Mother at 80 years of age

Mother, nee Ellen Butler, but always known as Nellie, was one of nine children and was the last survivor of that family. I regret having always taken her too much for granted because when I was young she was my strength and shield and I could not imagine what I would have done if she had died or left us when I was a small child. I relied on her completely and I know I didn't pay her nearly enough attention or visit often enough, even though she only lived sixty yards away from us. In fact, the farthest I ever lived from her from the time I was born until the day she died, except when I was in the army, was sixty yards. The whole of her working life was extremely hard and mostly spent in poverty. We, as children, had no idea just how poor we were. In later years I came to realise, through what she said in general conversation, how hard times had been and I know now that she neglected her own well-being in order to feed and clothe us. Mother was 'in service' in the Manchester area during her teenage years, doing housework for rich families or certainly very rich by our standards.

Mother had to look after the family and pick (peel) shrimps, scalding them (washing in hot water) and cooling them by spreading them on the kitchen table which was covered by a cloth. This cloth soaked up the excess moisture so that the shrimps came off the table almost dry. At that time, we had no refrigerators so obviously no ice in which to pack them. Next, they had to be delivered to the railway station, perhaps late at night or for the first train in the morning. This was done by bicycle because we were still several years before the acquisition of a motor vehicle. Another job which had to be done by Mother in those days was lighting the boiler. The water had to be boiling ready to receive the shrimps at whatever time father came home.

Harold Manning (1942)

The boiler was fuelled by wood and coal so it took up to an hour to come to the boil so it had to be lit at the appropriate time, be it day or night. After we converted to oil fired boilers this was no longer necessary as they boiled in a few minutes so could be lit when the fisherman arrived home. All in all it was a hard life. Luckily, mother survived to a big age and was able to enjoy her retirement. She still picked shrimps most days until she was ninety-six, attended meetings of one or two organisations and played whist every Monday until she was well into her nineties. Although, quite naturally, in her later years she slowed down, I'm sure it is true to say that she had fewer illnesses than any of her extended family of two children, five grandchildren and fifteen great-grandchildren. In May 1993, at the age of eighty-eight, she had a hip replacement operation which gave her a new lease of life. One of the most gratifying things about my mother in her old age was that right up to the week that she died, at the age of

100 years and 3 days, her mind was still as agile as it had ever been and her memory perfect.

Father worked until he was nearly seventy and started to be ill in late 1975. He had undergone surgery for prostate trouble some months earlier but suspected that things were not right immediately after the operation. He had been operated on at least twice by Mr. Strachan, for small health problems. On each occasion he went into hospital full of confidence in the surgeon and was soon bouncing back to fitness. When I went to see him after the last operation he said: "I'm not right this time," and sure enough he was not. A couple of weeks later I went to see his G.P. and asked: "Is there anything that I should know?" He then told me that father had cancer of the prostate gland "but with medication, could last a good number of years". I immediately went to the hospital to warn them not to tell him what was wrong but was too late because he had asked Mr Strachan straight out what was wrong and he had told him. When I arrived he was rather upset for a while but never mentioned anything about it to me again to the day he died. The treatment made him so ill that he decided to give it up. A few weeks before he died he just said to Joan: "I'm not afraid of death" and asked: "Are all my things in order?" meaning his will etc., then not another word about the situation.

Life's Journey

For over sixty years I believed that I was born at No. 23 Market Street, Flookburgh, where father and mother lived for a while after they were married but my sister Joan says we were all born at Ganny's house, Hill Foot, now 73 Main Street. There were four of us, Father, Mother, Joan, who is almost three years older than me, and myself. There was another boy, James, who was born between Joan and I but sadly he died before he was two years old. We soon moved to 68 Main Street, then known as Fairfield Cottage, and it is there that my memories begin.

Until just before the outbreak of World War II there was no electricity in the house, or indeed in the village, so we had candles and oil lamps for lighting, an open coal fire in a range with an integral oven heated by the same fire for cooking. The only source of hot water, even for personal washing or baths was from an iron kettle which was placed directly onto the coal fire. It must be difficult for young people these days to imagine what it would be like to have no electricity. Think of all the facilities and activities that rely on an electrical supply that we take for granted, from domestic appliances to phones and computers. It is true that what you never had you never miss and as we didn't even know about such things, we certainly didn't miss them.

Once every week we bathed in front of the kitchen fire in a small bathtub. There were just two rooms downstairs, two upstairs and an earth lavatory outside behind the washhouse. There was no such thing as toilet paper, only torn-up newspaper. All the houses in the village had earth lavatories that were cleaned out by a man who shovelled the excreta into a cart along with the ashes from domestic fires.

We lived in the back room all the time, except for a few days at Christmas, when a fire was lit in 'the parlour' at the front. This was a most exciting time, when we lit that fire and the decorations were put up, almost as exciting as Christmas itself. At bedtime on Christmas Eve, Joan and I hung pillowcases on the end of the bed and tried to sleep, but for a long time no success. We could hear, or Joan told me she could hear and I absolutely believed it, Father Christmas ringing a bell as he went round Ravenstown corner, twenty yards from our bedroom window so we knew he would soon be here. Eventually we must have gone to sleep because the next thing we knew it was morning and the pillowcases were bulging with presents. The presents were usually a few fruits such as apples, pears and oranges (except in wartime when there were no oranges, bananas, coconuts or grapes etc.), a game such as ludo, chocolate coins in a sort of net stocking, perhaps one toy and some sugar mice. For Christmas dinner we had a cock chicken which was given by Ganny. This was the only time in the year that we ever tasted chicken so it was the height of luxury.

Whilst on the subject of Christmas I must add this little story. When we first acquired a colour television, I was off work suffering from flu or something and Lynn, then about six years old, was off school with some minor ailment. There were several women in the kitchen picking shrimps whilst Lynn and I were watching a women's magazine programme in which three middle-aged women of different social classes and backgrounds were describing their early Christmases. The lady from the lower class who lived in a rural community in Yorkshire related that her grandfather kept a few hens in his back garden and that he always gave them one of these for Christmas dinner. Next, she said she received as presents, some fruit, a board game, and some chocolate coins. She then stopped and the next guest began to speak. I said (to the television): "You've forgotten your sugar mice", She suddenly jumped back into the conversation and said: "Oh, and some sugar mice." It somehow seems sad or an indictment on our way of life nowadays that children appear to generate no more excitement from the great quantities of expensive and sophisticated toys they receive at Christmas than we did from the few small items we received. On second thoughts, perhaps it may be that one could not be more excited than we were as it was only at Christmas that we received any presents whereas now children have things bought for them all the year round.

It was about 1947 when we moved almost directly across the street to Dolphin House, now 57 Main Street, at the junction with Winder Lane. Father and mother lived there until their deaths in 1976 and 2005 respectively.

We never made any fuss over birthdays and only sent cards to close family members whereas these days they are sent to the whole extended family and a large circle of friends. Having said that, I must admit it gives me great pleasure when I receive more than a dozen birthday cards, even now in my late seventies.

I have always believed that I first went to school when I was three years old. This was backed up in 1995 when, in my 63rd year, I met a man with whom I went to school from the time I started, to the time we left the grammar school and he went on to university. He said: "Well, next year it will be sixty years since we started school". I should think that I started in the September -three months before my fourth birthday,

The infants' school was just up the hill on the right on leaving Flookburgh Square in the direction of Cark. In the first year we were in a wooden annexe at the back of the main building in Mrs Culley's class. I cannot remember learning anything but she used to play the piano and sing to us and every afternoon we went to sleep on small beds. I suppose it was very much as nursery school is today. In 1937, Queen Mary, the widow of George V, visited the area and we all trooped from school to the church to watch her plant a tree a few yards north of the cenotaph. The tree, a red-flowering hawthorn, is still there.

Every winter we sledged down the steep hill in Main Street, known as Sandgate Hill. Another favourite was the field known as The Heights, on the left hand side at the crown of the hill and sloping down towards Shore Lane and Ravenstown. Yes, we did have snow every winter when I was young and that was so until about the early 1960s. Since then, for some reason unknown to me, we have had very few falls of snow which were any good for sledging. We also swam in the beck on Sandgate shore regularly in summer and almost every day in the summer holidays.

I moved up to Holker School about the time of the start of World War II. The school was the last building on the left on leaving Holker coming towards Cark and practically opposite the last house in the row coming from the Holker Park gates. I try to clarify the position of buildings because on reading James Stockdale's 'Annals of Cartmel' I found references to buildings; the uses of which have changed and one cannot now locate them. For instance, he mentions a schoolroom at the east end of Flookburgh which would probably be just a room in a house. The book was written in about 1865 and there is now no evidence as to where the schoolroom was. Holker and Flookburgh schools became obsolete when the new one was built down Winder Lane in the late 1960s. The old Holker School has since been used for various businesses, none of which have lasted very long, and Flookburgh infants' school is now a house.

Immediately after the outbreak of war we were all issued with gas masks because during The First World War, the Germans had used mustard gas with devastating effects and it was believed that they would use it again. Thankfully, gas was never used as a weapon in World War II.

Some bombs fell in this district during the war. It was always during the night that the sirens wailed and we arose to go out and shelter in the corrugated iron roofed washhouse. I have many times thought that we might as well have stayed in bed. The only benefit of going outside was that there was less building material to fall on us. There was a little damage done in our village but more in Allithwaite and Grange-over-Sands. We always believed that the German bombers were destined for Barrow and the shipyard but dropped their bombs in this area by mistake. This supposition was proved wrong in the year 2000 when, on looking for old records from the parish for the centenary of our church, I discovered German aerial photographs and pilots' instructions for the bombing of Flookburgh Airfield. These were in the archives at Preston.

On the 12th of July 1943, a fine summer's day, when I was ten years old, I was on Sandgate shore when I heard a woman screaming and saw that she was waving her arms and obviously distressed. I ran down to the water's edge where she was standing and saw a girl struggling in the water. I lay down on the grass at the edge of The Beck (which dropped off to about eight feet deep) and hung out as far as I could over the water, grasped her hand and pulled her out. The woman was then shouting that there was another person in the water but I couldn't see him. The family was well known to me as they lived probably less than a hundred yards away from us. The girl, Constance Campbell, was in my class at school and was an evacuee from Salford, along with maybe a dozen or so others who had come to this area to escape the dangers from German bombs. Constance and her brother Malcolm were housed with Thomas Mayor and his wife, May, at 48 Main Street. May was the daughter of a fisherman, Richard (Dickie) Dickinson. On that tragic day, Thomas was drowned and his body was recovered when the tide went out. There were quite a number of people swimming in the tide at Sandgate, that day, but most were over by Cut Bridge, four hundred yards away from where I was and were oblivious of the tragedy. Thomas Mayor's name is engraved on the war memorial in Flookburgh Church along with those who were killed whilst serving in the armed forces during the Second World War but he died on Sandgate shore and is buried in Flookburgh cemetery. His headstone tells us he was 34 years old and a Gunner in the Royal Artillery. When I play The Last Post at church on Remembrance Sunday every year I think of Thomas.

It was about this time when Ganny asked my cousin Alastair Butler and me to take a hen to Mrs. Taylor at the large detached house called The Borridge. She said:"Mrs Taylor wants a clock-hen, will you take it?" She then put the hen in a Hessian sack and off we went, up the path across the fields towards the station then over a fence into the grounds of The Borridge. When we arrived, Mrs Taylor, a very nice lady who was several social classes above us said: "Ah, you've brought the broody hen. "Well, we looked at each other but didn't know what to say. On our arrival back home, Ganny asked if we had managed all right. We said: "She swore." Ganny asked: "Oh, what did she say?" We then replied: "She said: "have you brought the bloody hen?" Ganny rocked with laughter. We had never heard of a broody hen, they were always clock-hens or clockers. In those days hens laid eggs and chickens were the tiny young of hens. These days no-one speaks of hens any more, only chickens, and then it's always pronounced chickins.

Now, three generations later, the class distinction between our family and the Taylors has gone. After service in the Royal Navy during WWII, Mrs

Taylor's son set up a garden centre in the grounds of the Borridge which is now run by her grandson and his family. Her granddaughter has an excellent cafe on the same site.

I was about four or five years old when Mother worked for Mrs Taylor. I would occasionally go to The Borridge and can remember being shown into the nursery or children's playroom. To me, it was an Aladdin's Cave, the like of which I could never have imagined. It was absolutely amazing to see the amount of toys -the room was full of dozens of playthings. At our home, Joan and I would each have a couple of cheap toys. Grandfather owned the field at the top of the hill where my sister Joan and her husband, Jack, now have their bungalow, 110 Main Street. In the mid-1930s, a greenhouse was built in the middle of the field and a small section near the road was a vegetable garden which was tilled by hand or with a horse drawn plough and harrow. Various crops were grown and sold to local hawkers and market traders.

When I was about eight or nine years old we hatched seven Khaki Campbell ducks which were then kept in the field. These proved to be a Godsend in those austere times when food was scarce and I suppose eggs were rationed. They laid eggs almost the year round. We ate the eggs throughout the war years and sold some. One day my cousin and I came to the conclusion that ducks ought to have a swim now and again so we walked them to Sandgate Shore for a swim in the beck. On arrival there they seemed to be afraid of the water and tried desperately to escape. One duck dashed off up into the thick bushes which were along the eastern edge of the shore, with the result that we lost it. A week or so later it turned up at Cark from where we recovered it. It took a long time to live down that episode.

The war years were a dreadful time for everyone. There were shortages of almost everything but I suppose we were better situated to survive it than town dwellers. Eggs and meat were rationed but could be obtained because many families kept a couple of pigs or a few hens and there were at least a dozen market gardeners in Flookburgh. Obviously there were anxieties because it was not by any means certain that our side was going to win the war and then a fair percentage of the male population, including my father, were away in the armed forces and in many cases their whereabouts unknown. Inevitably, the worries of the adults were noticed by, and therefore transmitted to the children, even if they did not fully understand the implications of the facts, speculations and rumours. Even through the darkest periods of the war there was humour and for us children, life went on quite normally. We occasionally played at being soldiers. My cousin, John Jones, and I constructed an anti-aircraft gun out of wheels and axle from a pram and a length of iron down spout for the gun's barrel. We were exceedingly pleased with it and towed it behind a bicycle for miles. There were plenty of examples of this type of thing for us to copy as there were numerous soldiers down at the army camp which was a training unit for anti-aircraft shooting. There was also the aerodrome with many airmen and Women's Auxiliary Air Force personnel stationed there. All in all it was a very busy village. The pubs were packed, likewise the buses.

Several small aircraft crashed or made emergency landings in fields or on the sand, the first one or two of which we went to see as we had never seen an aeroplane at close quarters. One plane crash–landed in the river channel a quarter of a mile north of Plumpton Viaduct. It sank out of sight and I believe the pilot's body was never recovered. Among the first planes we saw were Tiger Moths, Lysanders and Avro Ansons.

As children we all roamed around freely, boys and girls, with never a thought about assaults or abduction, even with all those strangers around. Such things were practically unheard of. In the camps there were mainly British troops of course but amongst them came American, Canadian and Polish personnel. The cinema at Grange was well patronised and local dances, held in the Lower Holker Club, were full to capacity. Several local girls, including two of my cousins, married soldiers who were based here and inevitably there were some illicit associations involving local married women whose husbands were away in the forces.

In my first couple of years at Holker School, which I attended between the ages of seven and eleven, the aerodrome was still being constructed. This was more than just runways and associated buildings but also blocks of barrack rooms, messes, concert room, cinema and many other buildings which really made a small town. There was also an area known as The W.A.A.F. Site for female personnel. This was situated in the second field on the left on going down Moor Lane or, as we call it, The Mile Road. It was the field before Willow Lane. There were also R.A.F. buildings, including a cinema where the industrial site is now. Some of those wartime buildings are still being used. A constant stream of wagons travelled past the school, loaded with bricks, tarmac, timber and all manner of building materials. The whole set-up was built in a very short time, bearing in mind there were not the tractors and earth moving machines which are available today. Most of the materials were moved around the various sites by horse and cart.

I cannot remember much about the army camp being built but I do remember grand-father Jim working there – it was about the time that great-grandfather Harry Couperthwaite died. This camp also was large and had some excellent leisure facilities. There was a huge hall that was used as a cinema, ballroom and concert hall.

We used to go to the cinemas at both camps several times a week. At the small cinema in the R.A.F. base we were supposed to be accompanied by a serviceman. We just stood in the queue and asked any airman to buy our tickets which I think cost about three or four pre-decimal pence. We sat in the front row on what appeared to be huge leather-upholstered bus seats.

On V.E. Day (Victory in Europe) 8th of May 1945, my cousin and I yoked Dickie Dickinson's small black horse, Darkie, to cart material to help to build a huge bonfire in the village square. There was great rejoicing and dancing which went on late into the night. We all absolutely hated Adolf Hitler and I can well remember the things we promised to do to him if we could get our hands on him. Because of all the media propaganda which incited us to hatred, it was well known that he was an evil man but it became clear at the end of the war in Europe, when the atrocities were revealed, that he was far more vile and twisted in mind than we had ever imagined.

In the 1950s, the army camp was bought by Danny Latham who made it into a duck farm for a few years. Later he turned it into the Ponderosa Caravan Park. It is now owned by a large national company and is called The Lakeland Leisure Park. Danny also bought the aerodrome in the mid-1960s.

*

I really had no interest in schooling and although I qualified for, and progressed to Ulverston Grammar School, it was just a matter of putting on time for five years. Looking back, I feel truly sorry that I wasted the opportunity given to me. I now realise that I was privileged to be selected to attend a Grammar School and given the chance of a proper education. Perhaps there were some gains in what I did at Ulverston that I have taken in unnoticed, but were they of any advantage in the life that I have led? If I had achieved a better education I might have gone into a far different occupation – but then I might have wished I were a fisherman!

Whilst I was attending school at Ulverston, when father caught a cormorant in his nets he would chop off the head and I would take it (the head) to the office of the Ministry of Agriculture and Fisheries where I was paid a few shillings. It could have been three shillings or it could have been five. There was a bounty on the heads of cormorants because of the amount of fish they consumed. In either case it was the equivalent of the price of a hundredweight of coal or six pints of beer, perhaps twelve pounds in today's terms. In the first year at Ulverston I was top of the class in woodwork, perhaps because I had done some whilst at Holker. For that tuition we had to travel by bus from Holker school to what was known as the Cartmel Special Subject Centre which is now an old peoples' home. In the first year at Ulverston I was also top in French and physics and quite well up in one or two other subjects but so bad in maths that I came third overall. After that I went down and down in the ensuing years until I was almost at the bottom of the class.

There is no doubt that I had some ability at school but did not apply it. I only came to realise some of my potential when I went work at the Glaxo chemical factory in 1965 and saw people with whom I was at school. I knew they were no more intelligent than I, and yet they had quite good jobs in the laboratories etc. When I started work there as a process worker I was determined to learn as much about the job as I could and as quickly as I could. One started out as a class three process worker and could progress to class two and then, if good enough, and after passing a maths exam, up to class one. Each move up the ladder signified one's ability to take on more responsible tasks.

When I had been there about six months I started to work on the maths. This was nothing like 0-level standard in that it was simply what I would call mechanical arithmetic. I started to re-learn things like multiplication and division in decimals and fractions, of which I had forgotten what little I had known, and to learn about percentages and ratios. I looked at past exam papers to find out what sort of questions to expect, then worked on those lines. When I took the test, I gained 100% mark and that surprised me more than anyone. The man who told me the result said he had only known one other person achieve that mark. I know this was very basic maths, yet this was an achievement for me and it came about because I wanted to learn, whereas at school I had no interest.

To be a Class One process worker at Glaxo was really only like being a glorified labourer but I had now seen that things could be achieved with effort and a desire to achieve. More importantly, it gave me confidence to do other things – a kick-start to my self-confidence. For instance, I had sometimes thought that I would like to sing or perhaps speak publicly but hadn't the courage. After this time I forced myself to have go. Gradually I did more and more until I went from being very introverted to extrovert and some people would probably say too much the other way. When at school, I was so shy and insecure that it could be painful and restrictive. I never went to school parties, and even when I was in my teenage years I could never 'chat-up' girls unless within the security of a group. As teenagers, even if we were recognised as courting or paired off, we usually went around in groups rather than as couples.

One Saturday evening when I was about seventeen, father's old Aunt Esther, grandfather Jim's sister, was in our house as I was getting ready to go out when she said - in the local dialect: "Hesn't thou gitten a woman yet?" I replied: "No, I can't git yan." She then said: "Well, thou likely hesn't gitten't knack." It seems strange now to think that it was normal to address people as thee or thou, but it was always the way in the dialect of that time, very seldom would one say you.

Was the former person the real me, or is it the latter? I prefer the latter because it has given me the courage or confidence to make more of opportunities and to live a far more varied life than would have been possible if I had remained so introverted.

*

I was always a somewhat nervous child. Whether this was part of my make-up from birth or the way I was raised? I have no idea. When Joan and I were very young, father would occasionally come home drunk, at which time we would be fearful of him. He was never physically violent, it was more like a violence or frustration within him. I have often thought that it might have been the fact that he was adopted and could not find his roots or even that he was forced into a life of fishing that he did not particularly like. I was later told that he was not welcomed by some of the extended family into which he was adopted. Whatever the reason, he always seemed to be dissatisfied with his lot. He never showed us any affection whatsoever or certainly not to me. In later years, and particularly after his grandchildren came along, father mellowed. He found that he did not have the same control over them. They would disobey him, which we would never have dared to do, but he was good with them and as they became old enough they went fishing with him and were a good help in his declining years.

By this time, he and I got on very well and for a long time after his death I missed him immensely. This, of course, is all as seen in retrospect. I have to say that we thought nothing of the situation at the time; it was normality for us. Then, as children, we didn't feel neglected, nor were we conscious of any problems related to the things just described. Fathers were the bosses and we thought it quite natural. Having written those derogatory remarks, I have to say that he was an honourable and honest man in all his personal and business dealings.

In the decade prior to his death, father had only been catching flukes whilst I was shrimping most of the time. I would perhaps go out at two or three o'clock in the morning and he would turn out to tend his nets a few hours later, sometimes he would just be going out when I was on my way home but when he arrived home, and I was in the process of boiling my shrimps, he always came round to see what I had caught. We would discuss the events of that morning and any difficulties that may have arisen. When we discussed these things, we each knew and could picture exactly what had occurred as those events were described. This was what I missed most after his death, someone with whom I could converse about fishing and who understood instantly because he had experienced them himself and of course we used the same terminology and dialect. Every aspect of our bay, its landmarks and even continuously changing patterns have a unique language of names used among fishermen to describe them and I found that I could not discuss these things with anyone else at home.

Even so, it is true that in my childhood he never, and I mean never, sat me on his knee or picked me up at all and I think that if he had I would have felt uncomfortable. To be honest, I must say that in childhood we were somewhat afraid of him at times. If Joan and I were fooling around in the house or were being rather boisterous when father was approaching, mother would say: "Your dad's coming" and we would immediately sit down and be absolutely silent. Thinking about it now, I find it surprising that he was like that because Joan and I were, so far as he knew, his only blood relatives in the whole world.

*

On the day that I went into the army I caught the train at Cark for Euston then the tube to Waterloo and another train to Ash Vale, Surrey. I didn't have a bite to eat all the way down because I was so shy, unworldly and introverted that I couldn't go into the restaurant car on my own. When I alighted from the train at Euston, another lad who had travelled down on the same train was walking down the platform shouting: "Anyone going to Keggog barracks?" This proved to be a good idea because we soon gathered a group of about six or perhaps eight lads, all of us eighteen years old and going to Keogh Barracks at Mytchett in Surrey. This was about the sixth of May 1951 and the Festival of Britain had just opened on the South Bank of the Thames, near Waterloo Station. We had been sent rail tickets but as we arrived at the ticket collector, our leader said to him: "Schoolboys' trip to the exhibition" waved his ticket and we all trooped through. One big regret, I have had ever since that time was the fact that I did not visit the festival, having been so near it. Not being used to travelling, even the forty or fifty miles from Ash Vale to London seemed a long way. I remember this as if it was last week and the pictures of events are as clear as can be. What I also recall is arriving at Keogh famished and with a terrible headache which, on reflection, was probably migraine. The first meal on arrival was flounder which absolutely stank. This was at about four o'clock in the afternoon and I hadn't eaten since leaving home at six-thirty a.m. Even so, I declined the flounder and settled for bread and jam.

Having never been away from home before, I was terribly homesick, but then, so were most of the others. The thought of two years away seemed such a long time -as indeed it was. The perception of time increases in speed as one gets older. When I think how long it appeared to be between birthdays or Christmases when I was six years old compared with a year now, the difference is incredible. I had always thought this was because of the busy life until my mother, then in her nineties and who did nothing except read and watch television said: "Doesn't time fly."

Those two years really were wasted years because I hated every minute and did nothing at all which was of any use. We were paid 12 shillings a week (60p) at first and after two increases I know that in the final few months I was picking up 32 shillings or £1.60. After being kitted out and given some drill instruction for two weeks, we moved just a few miles to Queen Elizabeth Barracks at Crookham in Hampshire where all Medical Corps soldiers did their three months basic training. It was a hot summer and most uncomfortable doing drill in heavy khaki clothing. I had always lived near to the sea and constantly felt the need to see it and also, strangely, felt that it could not be very far away. I can remember climbing onto the roof of the wooden, single storey wooden barrack room in an attempt to see the sea. I must have had little idea of the situation of Crookham on the map of England or how far one could see from ground level. It was perhaps fifty miles to the south coast of England but I had no idea where or how far away was the nearest coast.

When the training period was ended, in August, I moved to Catterick Camp in Yorkshire where I spent the rest of my service. The Korean War was still going on although winding down but some of our group were sent there, some to Germany and some to Cyprus. At Catterick, I was told there were 32,000 troops of various regiments, but mainly Royal Signals and Tank Corps. I was based at the military hospital, supposedly as a nursing orderly, which was what I had trained for, but I did not do any nursing - the only time I went into the hospital was as a patient.

I had bought a Matchless motorcycle about six months before being 'called up' into the army so as soon as I settled at Catterick I took the bike over there. I could nip home any weekend that I was not on duty. Petrol was about two shillings and sixpence or three shillings a gallon (15p) but it was available from a certain army ambulance driver at 5/- per 5 gallon jerry can, including the can.

My room at Catterick was adjacent to a recreation ground where the Royal Signals Corps motor cycle display team rehearsed their routine. In one of the moves, about a dozen men formed a pyramid on two motor cycles. It was no easy feat for the last two or three men to scramble their way to the top, and often, to my amusement, they collapsed into a heap on the ground. When perfected it was quite a spectacle and must have provided great entertainment to thousands of people at shows. On the evening of Sunday the 23rd of December 1951, I was returning to Catterick after having been home for the weekend when I came off the bike on almost the highest part of the route between Ingleton and Hawes. It was about 11-30 pm, in fog and a light drizzle which one often finds up there on that high moorland. There were no other vehicles involved and I never really knew why I came off because I certainly

On a motor cycle at Catterick

was not going fast. I have thought since that time that I probably fell asleep. This was something I could not have thought possible at the time but have experienced many times since whilst driving a car. I had been out with the lads at a dance on the Saturday evening and, as usually happened; a gang of us had been to a cinema at Barrow on that evening so I was very tired. My face was lacerated in the accident, due to scraping along the gravel road, and my right hand was crushed because it was under the handlebar as it slid along the road. I did not know all this at the time because of course it was dark and I was badly shaken or probably only semi-conscious. I could see a light in a window a short distance back so I staggered or crawled to the house which, I was later told, was a gamekeeper's cottage. The occupants were an elderly couple, or so they seemed to me, who couldn't seem to grasp the fact that my hand was badly damaged because I was wearing big leather gauntlet gloves. They could see that my face was in a mess - none of us ever wore crash helmets then. Luckily, the man owned a car so he took me to Hawes police station, about eight miles away, where I felt certain that the duty policeman was drunk.

A doctor was brought and he did what he could, which included an injection of morphine to kill the pain. I asked if I could go to the military hospital at Catterick because that was my base. An ambulance was sent out but when, after a few hours it had not arrived, I rang the hospital myself and, knowing the staff at the other end, I said; "Please send another ambulance."

This eventually arrived and I sat in the front to guide them back to camp because I knew the road very well. We arrived at the hospital at about 5am on Christmas Eve.

Captain Thomas, a doctor whom I knew very well, came to see me and we exchanged a couple of jokes, after which he said: "I'm pleased to see that you can laugh at a time like this." I then said that I was feeling chilled but at the same time sweating. He said: "What does your nursing training tell you about that?" I then realised that I was experiencing the symptoms of shock which I probably would have recognised in another patient but not in myself. Captain Thomas said that at least one finger would have to be amputated as it was completely crushed. The surgeon, Colonel Skinner, (an appropriate name) came at about nine a.m. and said that he would amputate the whole of the middle finger of the right hand but try to save the index finger which was also broken in a few places and a lot of skin gone, thereby exposing the bone.

Although I was sedated I asked him to leave as much of the middle finger as he could because I was a trumpet player. He remarked that stumps could be a nuisance but he would do as I asked, although it might have to be removed later. After surgery I was put in a ward to awaken as Christmas celebrations of carol singing etc. were going on. I did not feel like celebrating. The facial damage was only superficial and had healed fairly well in a few weeks but I had to stay in hospital for several weeks for treatment to the hand and for another reason, which was that there was nothing else to do with a sick soldier in a place like that. I was still hospitalised when Joan and Jack were married on the 26th of January 1952 but was allowed to come home for the wedding.

*

That winter, several things occurred which were very memorable events now in history. There was the death of King George V1 in February 1952 and I can still remember exactly what I was doing when told of his death. The ship Flying Enterprise got into difficulty well out in the Atlantic whilst sailing from the USA to England. Gallant efforts were made to tow her to land through heavy seas. All the crew, with the exception of the captain, Kurt Carlsen, were taken off when the ship was listing badly and in danger of sinking. Despite pleas from the rescuers and probably from shore by radio, Carlsen refused to leave and stayed on board for several days until the ship was almost sinking. She sank on the 10th of January 1952. There were reports in newspapers and regular radio news bulletins which the nation awaited with bated breath. Captain Henrik Curt Carlsen was a real hero. He was Danish but it was an American ship so he was really fêted in the USA and honoured with the typical ticker-tape street parade in an open motorcade. If there had been television then it would have been compulsive viewing. Yes, there was television, but not yet for the masses, this came a little later, mainly spurred by the thought of a televised coronation.

It was also the year of the terrible Lynton and Lynmouth flood disaster. A little later, in January 1953, the car ferry Princess Victoria sank. The ship left Stranraer, bound for Larne in Northern Ireland on her regular run. A terrific northerly gale was blowing -so severe that it was said that the ship should never have left port. Not far out from Stranraer, the rear loading doors burst open, the sea rushed in and she sank with the loss of 133 persons. There have been two similar incidents with roll-on, roll-off ferries in recent times and yet, through all the coverage by the media about these incidents, the Princess Victoria has never, so far as I know, been mentioned.

On that morning, father and uncle Jont had been cockling and father told me it was one of the worst days on which he had ever been out. He said that the horses could hardly pull the loaded carts home into that very strong northerly wind, plus the fact that it was extremely cold. At Catterick Camp it snowed for about four days so that with the strong winds there were huge drifts which reached almost to the top of the door of the building in which I lived.

On the 31st of January 1953, a great flood swamped much of the east coast of England, killing 307 people. The death toll in The Netherlands was 1,800. This disaster was caused by the same storm that sank the Princess Victoria when the winds moved to the east side of Britain and swept down the North Sea. This funnelled water into the relatively narrow area between East Anglia and The Netherlands so as to build up a great tide that pushed water over the sea defences and onto the land.

I spent the rest of my army service at Catterick and was demobbed on the 6th of May 1953. It was about that time that my sister Joan and her husband bought one of the first televisions to come into the village. It was so unique that dozens of people crammed into their tiny cottage, 10 Main Street, to watch Blackpool win the F.A. cup. Stanley Mathews, the greatest footballer of his era and the first footballer to be knighted, received his only F.A. cup-winner's medal that day. It was also the year that the most famous jockey of his time, and perhaps the greatest of all time, Gordon Richards, rode his only Derby winner, Pinza. Gordon was knighted in that year, so far the only jockey to be knighted. He was champion jockey 26 times and his record number of winners in a season which stood for almost fifty years was only broken in the summer of 2002.

My first motorcycle was a 350 c.c. Matchless which I later exchanged at a dealership in Darlington whilst I was in the army, for a 500c.c. B.S.A. A7 twin-cylinder machine. It was on this bike that I had the accident. Before I left the army, I had ordered a new motorcycle from the motorcycle shop, James Walker at Kendal, and took delivery of the 350c.c.Matchless machine soon after coming home.

Jim Little, a man with whom I had done my training at Ash Vale and Crookham and where he and I had become good friends, had been posted to Cyprus but did not appear when most of our intake met up again at Crookham on demob day. On making enquiry I was told that he had stolen a motorcycle and taken a ride round the island as a sort of celebration a few days before they

Jim Little and I at Crookham in 1951

should have left Cyprus. For this he had been sentenced to 28 days detention. On a nice July day, two months after leaving the army, I thought Jim must be home so I decided to look him up and put a few miles on the clock in the way of running-in the new bike. On arrival at his home, which I still remember was 112 Common Road, Newton-le-Willows, I knocked on the door. A lady appeared and immediately she saw me she said: "I know who you are." I said: "Do you?" She then proceeded: "Yes, you're Jack Manning; our Jim has gone to your house. He's just bought a new motorcycle and thought he would ride up to see you and at the same time run-in the bike a bit."

There were very few telephones in homes then but I phoned to the local garage which was on Main Street, two hundred yards from my home, and asked the proprietor to pass the message that I would wait at Jim's house until he came back. After that time we spent a couple of weekends together in

Manchester, also here in Flookburgh, then lost touch. Jim was a very independent man who, unlike me, did not bother much about his roots and soon left for America, since when I have heard nothing from him. In the early 1990s, Margaret and I called at the house in Newton-le-Willows but the family had moved. We found an elderly lady living in the street who had known them and said that Mrs Little had gone to live with her daughter on the Wirral but knew nothing of the whereabouts of Jim. He was the only person that I met whilst in the army that I should like to have met up with again.

I believe it was 2013 when I mentioned this to my son, Stephen, which prompted him to start searching the internet for information about Jim. I sometimes wish I had not set that process in motion because the outcome was dreadful. He found that Jim had died in Vancouver as a down-and-out person in 1983. He would probably have been 51 or 52 years old. This was a real shock which saddened me tremendously – and still does. He was such a level-headed man, slim, very fit and seemed to me to be a person who would go on to achieve things in life. Perhaps he became an alcoholic? I'll never know! At the same time that Stephen found this information he also discovered that Jim's sister was still living on The Wirral. I didn't speak to her but I did speak to her daughter. She told me they knew he had died but knew little of his life or the circumstances of his death.

*

Just before I left the army, the fishermen at Flookburgh had started to harvest perhaps the greatest quantity of cockles ever seen in Morecambe Bay up to that time. So I came home at a time when we were guaranteed to make a decent living, for a while at least. We were receiving about six or seven shillings, (30 or 35p) per bag for cockles at that time and could bring home about 12 to 14 bags a day -about as much as the average horse could pull. They were one hundredweight bags, that is 112 pounds. This meant that we could make about £3 to £4 a day six days a week, (we didn't go cockling on Sundays) so shall I say over £20 a week when the average wage for a manual worker was about £7 or £8. I shall say more about cockles in a later chapter but just suffice to say that I had quite a good start which carried on until after I was married.

Margaret and I had known each other from being children but it was when we were both at school in Ulverston that I was first attracted to her and made my feelings known; she was thirteen and I was probably fifteen. From that time I believe we were always destined to be married. We both went out with others in the following few years but were always drawn back to each other. We were married on the third of April 1954, a most awful day of rain and wind. A small reception was held at Station House and our honeymoon consisted of a few days in Blackpool with Mr and Mrs Geraghty who were the parents-in-law of my cousin, Peggy Geraghty. For a while we lived with my parents at Dolphin House, now 57 Main Street. Stephen was born at the time that we were living there but he was actually born at Station House, Flookburgh, where Margaret's great uncle, Jackson Armstrong, was Station Master and lived in the Station House. Perhaps Margaret felt more comfortable to be with her own family for the birth.

Jackson Armstrong and his wife Margaret came from West Cumberland, first to Kents Bank station, then to Cark at about the beginning of World War Two. They had taken Margaret in, (not adopted) when she was about a year old because her father had undergone a serious operation which left her parents financially unable to cope. The problem was compounded by the fact that her sister, Doreen, was born just a year after Margaret, at a time when there was no National Health Service or Social Services. Nana and Gag, as they were always known, had no children but raised Margaret as their own. In her years with them she was

On a cruise in 2004

always well dressed and had a head of thick red hair which shone so that her appearance was that of the well cared-for child - which she certainly was. She was more disciplined than most children, which, although she probably didn't appreciate this, was for her own good. When, in early teenage years most of us stayed out until probably ten o'clock in the evening, she had to be in by eight-thirty or she was in trouble.

Whilst I am on this subject I want say more about Nana and Gag because they played an important part in my life and I was fond of them both. They moved to Keswick in about 1955 so Stephen was just a toddler but we used to go there several times a year, sometimes just for the day and sometimes to stay for a few days in their very nice detached Station House. When they came to stay with us they brought lots of small presents for Stephen and Wendy, and later for Lynn of course. They were never well off, nor were they ever on good wages but were exceedingly good managers. When Keswick station closed, they retired to Distington in West Cumberland where most of Nana's clan lived.

We built a house for them next door to us, 63 Main Street, but unfortunately Gag died in February 1980, five months before the house was completed. Nana, (pronounced as in banana) lived in that house for a few years, then with us for a while. She died at Bridge House old peoples' home on the morning of Easter Sunday 1991 aged ninety years.

I received the news of Stephen's birth as I was coming home across West Plain salt marsh with a horse and cart loaded with cockles and was greeted by a man who was standing there, waiting for his son, also a cockler. He said:"You have son". He had heard that Margaret had given birth to Stephen. All the family adored Stephen, as one would expect with the first-born child. He was born three months after Joan's son, Mitchell, so they grew up together rather like the Two Little Boys in the Rolf Harris song. At school, Stephen was always ready to join in any activity, including sport and drama. I started to teach him to play the cornet when he was only about six years old. He picked it up quickly and was very soon good enough to play in Flookburgh Band. He won his first junior solo competition when he was eight years old and his first Open Solo Competition at ten. He played with the band for more than thirty years then gave up because of work commitments. After leaving school, he served his time as a draughtsman with a company in Ulverston. He then decided to join the Royal Navy and did well to achieve the rank of Chief Petty Officer during his few years in the service. Unsurprisingly, fishing was in his blood and he was determined to follow in the steps of his forefathers. He has now been a professional fisherman for more than a decade and in that time has inevitably experienced the ups and downs of the industry.

Wendy was born on the twenty-first of April 1957, almost three years after Stephen. We had hoped for a boy when Stephen was born and then for a girl so of course got our wish on both occasions. I thought: "This is easy, they arrive to order." That theory was subsequently proved wrong because although we wanted another child after a further couple of years, Lynn didn't arrive until nearly eight years after Wendy. Wendy, as a baby, was very placid, slept a lot, and was always pleasant. She would smile immediately she awoke, whatever time of day, and has continued to be pleasant in her nature. All her life from teenage years she has been a hard worker, sometimes doing several jobs. She joined one or two organisations and took on various offices and generally gained in confidence through these activities. I think that, like me, she has developed later in life. In temperament, I liken her to my mother – calm and able to cope in difficult situations.

Lynn had a good imagination and even as a small child, would play in her bedroom alone for hours, dreaming up all manner of ideas. When she was able to write, she used to compose letters to people such as the bank manager. I think she could have been an actress and could sing tunefully at a very young age. She was easy to teach when learning to write because she was eager to learn and could concentrate for long periods. Unfortunately Lynn did not like to be seen to be forward and although I knew that she could have been top of her classes at Flookburgh school, she always came second or third so I could not understand it. Likewise most of the constructive work which she did at home was done out of sight. I had the feeling throughout her school years that she was not achieving her full potential. On one occasion, when she was over thirty years of age, we were discussing schooling or education in general when Lynn said that there were many times when she knew answers to questions at school but did not want to appear forward or draw attention to herself. This may now look as though I thought that Lynn was a genius or a child prodigy; I didn't, but I did know there was something holding her back. Now, in her forties, she has proved she has the ability to do well and has gained a degree at The University of Central Lancashire. Margaret and I were extremely proud as we accompanied her to the graduation ceremony. The degree was gained whilst she held a full-time job and managed her home and four children.

The three of them now have their own children who are all completely different from each other. Margaret and I adore them all and they give us immense pleasure. I find it strange that of our eight grandchildren there are not any two alike in their personalities. They are, Ryan, Tim, Danielle, Lauren, Matthew, Charlotte, Ben and Jack. All of Mother's twenty-two descendants live within half a mile of her old home so we are a close family, both spiritually and geographically. As I edit again, in 2016, it is almost eleven years since Mother died but the rest of the family are all still living in this community. It is pleasing and gratifying that the whole family gets on well, and in particular that our eight grandchildren and Joan's seven are all good friends and often socialise together.

We now have three delightful great-grandchildren. Lynn's daughter, Danielle, has two daughters, three-years old Ava, and Annie who was born in

November 2015. Danielle's brother, Matthew has one son, Riley, who was born on the 4th of January 2015.

*

Margaret and I moved to 72 Main Street in the summer of 1955, a year after we were married, and lived there until Christmas 1966 when we moved straight across the road to number 61. Throughout the years spent at number 72 I made a living mainly from shrimping with a horse and cart but had used a tractor for cockling from 1954 onward. When we moved into number seventy-two I was working hard at the cockles and also catching some salmon, especially at night, so I was having very little sleep but didn't feel as though I needed it. I was also getting used to doing without much food and,

Bearded in 1967

although physically fit, I was working nearly non-stop and felt unable to slow down. One day in the summer of 1955, Mother said: "You are going to have a nervous breakdown if you don't slow down." I told her she was talking nonsense, I felt as fit as a fiddle. She was right. It was probably the fact that we were newly married and moving into our own house with all the stresses which go with that, and the work, that it became too much and I virtually collapsed.

It all started when I was coming along Holker Mosses, two miles from home, in a Morris 1000 van, when I suddenly felt faint, as though I was about

38

to pass out. I stopped for a few minutes until I recovered then drove home. I felt ill and somewhat afraid as these attacks kept recurring. The following day, after a particularly bad spell, father took me to see Dr. Charlton at his surgery at Cark. The doctor said I had tachycardia which meant that my heart was racing. It then suddenly slowed down thereby causing these awful feelings. He said that there was nothing really wrong with my heart but that the rhythm control was haywire. It was one of the worst periods of my life as I was afraid and anxious all the time with the feeling that I was going to die at any minute. I was taken to Lancaster Infirmary for examination and observation for a week or so. My pulse-rate at this time was constantly about 140 per minute. The consultant said that I should go back to work and just rest if I felt ill.

I was 24 years old and up to that time I had been cockling, a very physically hard job, so I was very muscular, had very broad shoulders and bulging biceps. When I stripped for examination the consultant looked at me and said: "There's nothing wrong with your heart," I said:"How do you know?" He said that anyone with a faulty heart could not do the exercise necessary to build muscles like that. I continued to work but had some terrible times, especially if out shrimping when the attacks came on, particularly disturbing if I was out fishing through the night. Spells of palpitations started to occur and have continued up to the present time although less and less. As time went on I grew used to the awful feelings and eventually learned to ignore or accept them. When I was about seven years old, I had rheumatic fever which left a murmur in my heart. In the 1960's when Dr. Linklater became our doctor he said he could not hear any trace of a murmur so it must have corrected itself. As a footnote to that, I would add this. On the return journey from a holiday in Singapore, New Zealand and Australia in March 2007, I had a very painful infection in my lungs which I was later told was pneumonia. When I went to Furness General hospital for an X-ray, a senior nurse gave me a thorough check over and on sounding my chest she said: "You know you have a heart murmur, don't you?"

Through the winter and spring of 1964, whilst my brother-in-law Jack Rowlandson and I were working in Scotland, I experienced some feelings of illness and general malaise. Although I carried on working, these attacks persisted. When we came home to start shrimping again, I was often quite ill and my temperature raised. One week in particular when Margaret and I went to London for a few days holiday I can remember being at Heathrow airport where we had gone just to look at the place, and feeling so ill that I did not enjoy it one bit and in fact hardly knew what was going on.

On a nice morning in late May of that year I was out early, fishing for shrimps, but not feeling very well, when I saw a salmon ploughing upstream. Although the water was thigh deep I caught it, and shortly after that another one. I was wet up to the waist and had to ride home in that state which wasn't the ideal state for a person with a fever. On that same morning I had an appointment to see Mr. Strachan, a consultant surgeon, at the out-patients clinic in Ulverston. He examined me and asked some questions then took my temperature which proved to be somewhat raised. I was told to go home and stay in bed until further notice. Dr. Linklater came to see me and said that I must go into hospital 'for a couple of days' for tests to see what was wrong.

Those few days turned out to be fourteen or fifteen weeks. There were numerous blood tests and all the routine tests which occur when one is admitted to hospital. All of that time my temperature was between about 100 degrees and 102 and never returning to the normal 98.4. As the blood tests, which I think were at that time sent to Preston for analysis, came back with no positive results from which a diagnosis could be made, further samples were extracted and again were away ten or perhaps even fourteen days. Having nothing to do but lie there, (I was not allowed out of bed at all), time dragged unbelievably slowly and as we were awakened at about 5.30 A.M., days were like weeks.

I believe it was the 2nd of June when I was admitted to hospital. On Margaret's birthday, the 20th of July, Dr. Waind the consultant physician, came round with his entourage, stood at the foot of the bed and said these words which are still deeply etched in my mind: "I'm very sorry old chap but I have some bad news for you. You have a very nasty illness called a collagen disease which is incurable but with medication you will probably live to a ripe old age; unfortunately you will never work again." Naturally, at this news I was devastated. When Margaret came to see me later that day I broke down into tears. Margaret was then heavily pregnant and carrying Lynn but only missed coming to the hospital on about two days until Lynn was born which was the 19th of September. I can still remember the exact amount we received in sick money from the DHSS - it was £7 and 1 shilling, (£7.5p per week). I was thirty-one years old and just beginning to achieve some sort of comfortable or settled life, or so I felt then, although I now know that life is always a struggle to a greater or lesser degree. Nevertheless, all I wanted to do was work.

About two weeks later, as I lay there with nothing but depressive thoughts, and of course still feeling quite ill because nothing in my condition had changed, Dr. Waind came to me and said: "You're not very happy at what I told you are you?" I assured him that I was not. He said: "Neither am I; how would you feel about going to see Professor Platt, (or Black, I'm not sure which) he is the president of the Royal College of Physicians?" I remarked that anything was worth a try.

One of the worst things that happened to me was the administration of the steroid drug, prednisone. This was prescribed in large dosage with the result that my body swelled and I developed what were described as a bull-neck and moon-face. This was during the first stay in hospital and went on for several months. I remember telling our GP, Dr. Linklater, when I was at home, waiting to go to Manchester, that I was desperate to come off this drug. He said that I was under the control of Barrow hospital and he could not interfere in the treatment. Unfortunately the man who had control was on an extended holiday abroad so nothing could be done.

*

I came home for perhaps ten days awaiting an appointment at Manchester Royal Infirmary. The appointment duly arrived and my sister, Joan, drove me there sometime in mid-August. Before I left, the professor said: "I don't know at this stage what you have got but it certainly is not what Dr. Waind thought."

A letter subsequently came from him to the hospital saying that he was not sure what was wrong with me but the blood tests showed similarities to those seen in brucellosis, a disease usually caught from untreated milk. I had to go back to hospital for treatment which consisted of two months of injections and pills but this time I was allowed to move around the ward at will which was better than the last visit. I was more settled and able to read, which I could not concentrate to do on the first stay.

Lynn was born on the 19th of September of that year, 1964, but I was not allowed out to see her and Margaret was not allowed to bring her into hospital. When she was a month old she was brought into the outpatients' waiting room and I went there to see her. When I arrived home, which was towards the end of October, I can remember very clearly the impact of seeing the colours in the house after being in a hospital for so long where everything was white. After all that time and all the treatment I was in exactly the same state as I had been six months earlier. My temperature was still raised and I could walk only a short distance.

Sometime around my birthday, which is the 10th of November, my father and Jack Rowlandson were going out on a Sunday afternoon to set or tend to some whitebait nets. Although it was an awfully cold day with some big showers of hail coming from north-west, I decided that I would go with them. There were protestations from the family but I said: "It will either kill or cure me." We were out in the bay for about two hours during which time I just sat on the trailer and became extremely cold. On arrival home I checked my temperature, which I had done several times a day over all those months, to find that it was so low that it was almost at the bottom of the thermometer. I was suffering from hypothermia. After recovering from that trip, my temperature came up to normal and remained there after having been raised incessantly since late May - over five months. This was very much, to my mind anyway, like a miracle in that it was virtually instant in its effect following such a long period of unbroken fever. As I said earlier, I checked my temperature many times every day and even took my own thermometer into the hospital. One day, shortly after I went into hospital, an auxiliary nurse came into the ward on the T.P.R. round and marked my temperature on the chart as 98.4 i.e., normal. I knew this was not correct as I had checked it not long before. I told the ward sister about the mistake and added that the reason for the mistake was that the thermometer was not left in place long enough The sister simply backed up the nurse, saying that I had no way of checking. I then produced my own thermometer and, needless to say, it was promptly confiscated. After the trip on the sand I slowly improved but it was a long slog because I had been sedentary for so long that just to get my limbs into a reasonably fit state took many weeks. I started to do a little work in February of 1965 and gradually achieved complete fitness.

That Christmas, 1964, was probably the best I have ever experienced, just for the sheer joy of being reasonably normal again and able to enjoy the festivities and family atmosphere. I believed then, and I still believe strongly today, that if I had not made the move and forced myself to go out on the sands that day I would have been an invalid -or dead at an early age. I have done a lot of work and lived what I consider a reasonably good and varied life in the forty-odd years since I was told I would never work again. I have spent some time on these two episodes of illness because they were so awful, not only for me but also for all the family.

*

In the mid 1950's, at the time that we were harvesting cockles, I was also doing some shrimping which was still with a horse and cart. I used to enjoy going out over the sand alone at night -and better still to come home with a good load of shrimps.

I gained most of my knowledge about shrimping from my uncle Bill, Mother's brother, with whom I spent a lot of time in the 1950s when we worked together, mostly at night. We worked at night, mainly because it was easier to catch shrimps in the dark because they then came out to the edge of the water. He gave me tips about finding the way in bad weather and on dark or foggy nights. For example, the lines of small ridges left on the sand by the receding tide tell us in which direction the water has gone with the ebb-tide which, when one is familiar with that particular area, are almost as good as a compass.

We went out on some awful nights when it was absolutely black dark and not a glimmer of light from any source. In fine weather when visibility is good, fishing at night is virtually the same as working in daylight to the experienced fisherman. Then there are nights when one may not be able to see any coastal lights by which one would normally navigate and yet there could be a dim glow in the clouds above coastal towns such as Ulverston, Barrow, Morecambe and Blackpool. These are as good as compass points but I have, on some occasions, had difficulty in deciding which glow was from which town without reference to a compass. There are also the nights on which there is no light from any source when one has to draw on all the experience and knowledge stored up over the years. In the days of fishing with a horse and cart I used a compass quite a lot so with practice I could go anywhere in the bay. Even so, there are obstacles such as deep gullies and cliffs in the sand carved by running streams. The latter we call bracks and can be any height from a few inches to ten feet high. One would usually know when there was a likelihood of these being in the area but not exactly where, so care was needed and a torch was an advantage. Extremes of weather such as high winds or torrential rain can occur fairly suddenly and unexpectedly and out in the exposed terrain of Morecambe Bay can be frightening as I have found out on two or three occasions but without doubt the most difficult weather condition is fog. Out on the sand it is like looking at a wall. This is bad enough in daylight but in the dark it can be dreadful. I have had some pretty bad experiences in fog which I will write about in a later chapter. I worked with a horse and cart until 1966 although we also had tractors from 1954. There were numerous incidents involving horses, some of which, again, I will describe in another part of this book.

*

To carry on with my life story from which I keep deviating, I am now up to about the late 1950s and working on the cockles and shrimping, still with the horse and cart but tractors had now arrived on the scene. It was in the autumn of 1955 when I, along with several other fishermen, mostly of our family, were arriving home from shrimping at about 7am when Aunt Maggie Butler, uncle Jack's wife, told us that my cousin Tony Eisner had been killed in a motorcycle accident. Tony's mother was my mother's sister. He was seventeen years old. This was a great shock to the whole community but devastating to our family. It was the first of a series of about a dozen fatal accidents involving local teenage boys and one girl, with motorcycles and in cars. It is said that time heals sad memories but in all of these cases one can see the pain that is continually with these parents, and probably will be for the rest of their lives.

Sometime in the late 1960s I was invited by an organisation in Grange to give a talk on fishing which I duly did. Why they invited me I have no idea. Perhaps I was the best known local fisherman and had been seen on several television shows. I suppose the talk must have been reasonably successful because since that time I have addressed and shown slides to hundreds of meetings of organisations from Women's Institutes to farmers' clubs, business men and history societies, one as far away as Liverpool but mostly within a radius of forty miles. On one occasion I spoke and showed slides about fishing to an audience in a building in Rylands Park, Lancaster. The talk lasted just over an hour and at the end there was a short question time. After one or two questions had been raised and answered a man got to his feet and said; "I am having trouble with some begonias; the leaves are going brown, can you tell me what to do with them?" I was rather taken aback by this so just I said that I did not know anything about gardening. Afterwards, the chairman came to me and apologised. He explained that one or two people came down from the mental hospital and sat inside just to keep warm. In the 1970s and 1980s I was probably doing thirty talks each year. The figure is now about eight.

I should think it was the 1970s when we went to visit Margaret's family near Whitehaven, in West Cumbria, and when we were due to come home there was a really bad snowstorm. It was a Sunday evening and our daughter, Wendy, ought to have been going to work next morning but I decided we could not travel home in that weather in case we became stuck in the deep snow. We stayed the night, then, although the snow was deep, we set off for home. Travelling down the west coast of Cumbria, when we came through a small village called Wabberthwaite, there were several cars in the side of the road which were completely hidden in the drifts and people were digging them out. Except for the fact that people were digging them out, one wouldn't have known the cars were there.

Six months later I was in Wabberthwaite to give a talk. At the end of the show I was asked to judge a photographic competition in which some of the pictures were of those snow drifts and the cars being dug out. I told them that by sheer coincidence I had travelled down that road and witnessed what I was seeing in the photographs. The response was to the effect that that was impossible because the road was impassable - but it was true.

In the late 1970s we bought 76 Main Street which was in an awful state inside, having had nothing done to it since it was built, perhaps a hundred and fifty years earlier. We paid £5,500 for it, renovated it throughout and let it as a holiday cottage for two or three years then sold it, making a good profit. It was then decided we should build the house for Nana and Gag. Having started in the property business, we bought and sold several more cottages but I must confess that we made only small profit on them. One of those cottages was number 70 Main Street, Flookburgh which also had two quite large garages. We sold the house but retained the two garages that stood side by side on the land behind the cottage. We then bought a small area of land behind the garages. In the first few years that we owned the garages, perhaps eight years, they were used as storage for equipment and the garden was planted with vegetables and soft fruit. In the early 1990s we decided to apply for permission to build a house on the land. The first application was refused then it went to appeal where it was again turned down. We accepted that decision until dwelling houses were being built on either side when we again applied, pointing out the anomaly of the others being granted when we were refused. After a long struggle and parting with what then looked like a lot of money for changes to plans, planning permission, with conditions, was granted for a bungalow. I sat in the public gallery at the council meeting at Kendal town hall on the 4th of January 1996 where the decision went in our favour by just one vote.

The task of removing the old garages, which I started on the 14th of February, was a major operation in itself and the work on the bungalow commenced in February 1996. There were twenty-one days of digging out the site to lower the ground level before any foundations were laid. The reason for the excavating being so protracted was because we could not get a decent sized digger or dumper through the narrow entrance to the site. The construction was carried out by a company owned by our two nephews, Mitchell and Tony Rowlandson and I did whatever work I could. We moved in on the 2nd of December 1996 and have enjoyed living here since that time. We could have moved anywhere on retirement but chose to live here, near to our family. This may be a good point to say that I have lived in five houses in my life and yet the furthest I've lived from my present home is fifty yards.

*

As soon as I could read reasonably well it was expected by my father that I would become a chorister at Flookburgh Church -which I did when I was about seven or eight years old. I enjoyed the singing but not necessarily the long services which we had to attend at least twice every Sunday and sometimes more. Nevertheless, by sitting through all those services I learned something about the Bible, its Christian teachings and tenets, even if I did not always heed them. I was a member of the choir for almost twenty years until one day, as we processed up from the vestry, past the organ and round by the pulpit to the choir stalls, I had an awful feeling of doubt about my faith, a feeling of guilt and hypocrisy. From that time I continued to attend church occasionally but only when the mood took me. I continued to think about the church and although I could make and listen to jokes about religion I could not stand to hear people seriously ridicule or denigrate the Christian Faith so there must still have been at least a flicker of belief left.

In the 1960s I stood as a Godfather for a child but knew I would never be able to fulfil the promises I was making. An awful feeling of guilt prevailed on me throughout the ceremony, so much so that I swore that I would never be a Godfather again although I had stood for several children previously to this occasion with no qualms. A year or so later I was invited to stand for one of Margaret's cousin's children at Workington. I refused, but added that I would be pleased to attend the Christening but not as a Godfather. Margaret was quite angry with me, saying that I would only be the same as anyone else who might stand but I was adamant that I would not make promises that I could not keep. During those years in the wilderness as it were, I often wished that my faith was strong. Luckily, things did take a turn for the better and I did eventually come back to the church which has meant a lot to me.

When we were on holiday near Venice in about 1980 or 81, I read one of the gospels, I think it was St. Mark, which was in the hotel room, probably put there by the Gideon Society. This was not a complete bible, just the one gospel. On reading this I realised by the simple down to earth way it was written, and the detail contained therein, that the writer or his informant must have actually been there and witnessed the events described. From that time I started to come back to the church and decided that I should be more active in the life of the local church. When I was asked to be a member of the Parochial Church Council, after some deliberation I agreed. In 1995 I accepted the invitation, from the Rev. Nick Ash, to be a churchwarden. I was a warden for five years then resigned but have continued to attend and work for the beautiful church of St. John the Baptist at Flookburgh.

Until 1998 the cemetery at Flookburgh was in an awful state, rather like a miniature First World War battlefield with great undulations. It took a gang of people to cut the grass with whatever tools they could muster. There was a scythe and an old strimmer that took longer to start the motor than it did to cut the grass. I decided that it was time we levelled the site so that it could be mown much easier. Via a note in the Parish Magazine, I called a meeting of volunteers who might help to level the ground. Nine people turned up at the first meeting. Four of us were fit enough to do the hard manual work and the others gave moral support and in some cases helped to raise funds for equipment. Permission to carry out the work had to be sought from the Carlisle Diocese, necessitating a faculty or licence. This was granted so we started work in the spring of 1998, levelling mounds and filling hollows. Some of the ground had to be re-seeded and yet we did not have a fund of money even to buy a few seeds, it came out of our pockets. Whilst this work was in progress we appealed to the community for money with which to buy grass-cutting machinery. With public donations and a grant of £450 from Cumbria County Council's Neighbourhood Forum we bought a new self-drive, walk-behind mower – not very efficient for 1½ acres of ground. After that, Lord Cavendish donated a new strimmer.

The levelling took until the end of that year. We then decided that we must try to remove as many as possible of the kerbstones from around graves to further facilitate the mowing. This was a tremendously hard job as most of it had to be done by hand because we could not get a

The New Lychgate

decent sized machine through the lychgate and many of the stones weighed up to four or five hundredweights. Probably the biggest job after that was the filling and seeding of the holes where the stones had been, bearing in mind that in a large percentage of those graves, the area within the kerbs had been concreted. There were about 140 graves with kerbs and we cleared all except about half a dozen which families wished to retain. The kerb stones were sold for about £2000, which paid for a small tractor mower. After the work was completed we found that four men could cut all the grass in about two hours by strimming round the stones first, then mowing with the tractor. The clearance and levelling was a mammoth task undertaken by a gang of pensioners but the end result transformed the cemetery and is, I believe, appreciated by the community.

The lychgate was known to be in a bad state of repair but we hoped to renovate the old structure. On inspection it was found to be rotten in almost all the joints. I then took it on myself to raise funds to completely rebuild the whole structure including the actual gates. Estimates for the work were between £5,300 and £6,500. I applied to about ten charities for assistance and received £1,000 each from three of them. The parish council gave £1,500 and a family gave £750 in memory of their parents. I appealed to the community for funds via the Parish Magazine and just over £1,500 was collected in donations that varied from £2 to £100. A grand total of £6,765 was accumulated over a period of about six months. The new lychgate, which I considered to be our Millennium Project, was put in place in October 2000 and the vicar, the Revd. Laura Gibson, officiated at a short ceremony of dedication at the site on Saturday the 4th of November.

*

When Princess Margaret came to open Cartmel School, in October 1958, father and I escorted her, along with Mr. and Mrs. Richard Cavendish, to Chapel Island, they on horseback and we with a horse and cart. After the event we received a thank you note in which she said that it was the highlight of her stay in the district. In 1976 when she opened the Lakeland Rose Show at Holker, Margaret and I along with Wendy and her then boyfriend attended a ball at The Hall where I was presented to the Princess. We spoke for several minutes at which time I reminded her about the trip to the island. In the course of this conversation she enquired about my father. He had died just a month earlier.

Princess Margaret at Sandgate (1958)

On the sixth of August 1987 I received a phone call from Mr. Hugh Cavendish asking if I would take Prince Philip out on the sand. As it was between shrimping seasons there were almost no shrimps but we went to the Leven channel with a party of about six or seven people and went through the motions of fishing.

The film Moonsmen, a film about fishing with horse and cart, made by three amateur film-makers and featuring my father and I, was mostly shot in September 1963 but it was found that a few more scenes were required so we finished it in Spring 1964. It was entered in the documentary section of the Edinburgh Festival of that year and was awarded a Diploma of Merit. We were extremely lucky to make that film to be kept as a record because horses had gone from the scene two years later. It was shot on 16 millimetre black and white film and, as I will explain later, was transferred to video. When the film was completed, some stills were required for promotional purposes. A large print of one of those pictures has been on a wall in our house since that time. In 1972 the BBC made a programme called Fishermen of Flookburgh. Although I don't necessarily think it is a good documentary film, it is a nice record of some events in Flookburgh as the village was then. For me it is quite nostalgic. It was shown in February of the following year and then was not seen again until about 1989, since when it has been repeated four times. When it was first made I asked the director, Colin Morris, if it would be possible to buy a copy. He said he thought it would be possible at a price of about £90. Although that was the equivalent of five or six hundred pounds in today's terms I said that would like to buy a copy. When I wrote to the BBC, requesting the

With Matthew Kelly

film, I was quoted £450, which, to put it into context, was just half the price of a new Ford Cortina car or at least £6,000 in today's money so I declined the offer.

Two years later, Dianne Campbell, who had been Colin Morris's assistant, came back, this time as a producer for Tyne-Tees T.V., to make a programme for children's television with Matthew Kelly. On this one I did speak and enjoyed working with Matthew who is a very nice man and a much quieter man than his T.V. image. He said I was the only person with whom he had worked who could carry on a conversation on camera without stopping or hesitating. In fact, he was the one for whom we had to re-take because he

49

occasionally slipped in some South Lancashire dialect such as: "Shall we have us dinner now" at which the director would gently rebuke him down his earpiece radio link.

It was 1984 when assisting in the making of a twelve part documentary called The Living Isles that I asked the producer, Roger Jones, of the natural history department of the BBC in Bristol, if he could transfer Moonsmen from the 16mm film to video. He said that was easily done. I then mentioned the programme Fishermen of Flookburgh and he said he could obtain that also on video if it was still in the BBC library, which he did. (There were no video machines when the show was first broadcast). We were thrilled to receive it as I had written to the BBC asking if they were planning to repeat it and they said they were not. By the time I received this film, several people who were featured in it, including my father, had died so it was particularly poignant and nostalgic.

A still from the film 'Moonsmen'

The programme has been shown on television at least four times since then. Margaret and I visited Roger and his wife, Lesley in May 2015 and were made very welcome in their fine Cotswold home. Roger gave up his job as a film producer and is now a very successful professional artist.

Circa 1979 I was invited to be involved in a short film to be produced by Michael Cole for a children's television series called Stop-Go. On this I didn't speak but there was a commentary by a lady. I remember the making of this film so well because on the day that we were due to film, the weather was beautiful but the tractor's steering system came adrift at Sandgate so we had to abandon it until the next day. I was so annoyed and embarrassed. The following day brought torrential rain so we sat around for several hours waiting for an improvement, not knowing if we were going to do anything at all and the crew were booked to do another sequence up in the lakes the day after that. The weather did improve at about 2pm and we went out with just enough time to make an entertaining little film. It has been shown many times on programmes for schools.

On the eleventh of November 1987, the TV personality Russell Harty was making a programme in the district and I was one of his guests. I went out shrimping in the east at about 6 am having the previous day given instructions to his researcher as to where to find me when they came out a few hours later. The weather was pretty awful with heavy, cold showers, with the result that they could not find me. I kept a lookout whilst working and eventually saw them about a mile or so to the south. When I caught up with them they were extremely relieved because they had no idea how to get back to shore. The crew did some filming out there but Russell did the interview back on shore. He asked some inane questions and I often wished I had had the courage to say what one of his former teachers said to him in another programme. She said: "Don't ask such silly questions, Russell".

Five days later, on the 16th and 17th of November 1987, five members of Flookburgh Band went to Lakeside Station, at the south end of Windermere Lake, to take part in a film called Without a Clue with Michael Caine and Ben Kingsley. I spent some time talking with Ben who was extremely nice and had no edge at all. This was about the time when he had just starred in his famous role as Gandhi. Michael was already

With Ben Kingsley at Lakeside Station

an award winner – perhaps even an OSCAR winner and received preferential treatment on the set such as a stand-in for long shots.

It was the 19th of September 1989 when I was one of a number of local people invited to be guests of Sir Harry Secombe in his programme, Highway. I think that was the only time that I was filmed whilst hauling a good catch.

51

On most occasions a producer or researcher rings up to request to do some filming and the odds are that it will be out of season for the particular job they wish to film.

I think all of these invitations to participate in the TV programmes came about because I had helped the various companies with news items in the district and particularly regarding incidents in the bay. Anyway, I believe that TV companies must have lists of people in the various regions on whom they can call for information on local events so whenever they wanted to film the fishing or anything related to this area, I was the man on the list. These films together with the videos I have made myself make a nice little library to leave for future generations.

I officially retired in 1997 but in the last two or three years of my working life I was in virtually the same position as my father was in his last years, that is, just catching flukes and a few salmon. I had developed problems in both shoulder joints which gave me hellish pain, so bad that I could not riddle shrimps by hand or even pull the long rope back onto the trailer. The last time I went shrimping for myself was in July 1994. In 2007, 2008 and 2009, I set nets and caught flukes and a few mullet and sea bass, just for the pleasure and I really enjoyed it. As my father said many years ago: "When fishing, every day is different and one goes out full of anticipation." I continued to occasionally set nets out on the sands until I was eighty years old then burned or took to the refuse tip almost all my fishing gear. I must confess that I kept one net so that I am be able to go out and catch a few fish for our own consumption if the mood takes me. Never say never!

Holidays

When I was young we didn't have holidays away; in fact, the only place I had ever been before I went into the army was to Southend Farm, Walney Island, where I stayed for a few days with my mother's sister, Edith, and her husband Herbert who were the tenants. Only middle class people had the traditional annual seaside holidays – or so it seemed to me.

The first holiday Margaret and I had, and the first real holiday for me was in 1959 when we stayed with Margaret's Great-aunt Ida and Uncle Clifford at Bologgas Cottage just west of Penzance on the main road to Lands End. It took us two days to travel the 440 miles. The main routes at that time (no motor-ways) went through the centres of towns and cities so the journey was very slow. Stephen and

Aunt Ida and the Morris van (1961)

Wendy must have had a weary journey, sitting in the back of the van. On the first day we progressed as far as Somerset where we stayed at what I have always believed was the Red Ball Inn, near Wellington. For almost forty years I was convinced it was the Red Ball Inn but when on holiday down that way in about 1996 we went to look for it and all we could find in that region was The Blue Ball.

That was quite an epic journey for us in 1959, having never been away before. We spent a very pleasant ten days or so, exploring the picturesque villages and countryside. We covered 1300 miles and the total cost of the petrol was £5. I remember this very well and yet still question it -but the answer is always the same. The van did 42 miles to the gallon and the price of petrol was somewhere in the region of three shillings or 15p per gallon. We again went to Ida's in 1961 in another Morris 1000 van which was the first brand new vehicle we ever bought. The price of the van was £420 and the colour was Pearl Grey. This time I think only Wendy came with us.

Incidentally, the next time I went to Barrow on a train was when I went to collect a new car in February 2015 – fifty five years later.

On the second trip to Cornwall we called at Torquay to look for Arthur Wopling, a man with whom I had spent some time in the army at Catterick. We went to the post office or the library to look through the electoral rolls of the area and somehow found his sister working in a shop in Torquay. When we eventually found Arthur and his wife, Gloria, known as Cindy, we stayed there for a few days and looked around the region at places of interest such as Cockington, Brixham, Dartmouth and Dartmoor. Arthur was a simple country lad like myself. He did not know anything about music or singing so when we were together at Catterick I had taught him to sing a little and to sing parts to songs such as Early One Morning and, appropriately, Widdecombe Fair, which really pleased him. He had never heard of the song Glorious Devon although he had lived all his life in that county. Surprisingly, when we met again he still remembered the tenor parts of those songs. I had also told him a story about Dickie Dickinson who is mentioned elsewhere in my memoirs and one of the first things he said to me on this visit was: "How is Dickie Dickinson?" We have kept in touch with Arthur and Cindy and visited them several times.

On Sunday the 22nd of March 1965 we went to stay with Arthur and Cindy for a week or so. Flookburgh Band was playing in the Congregational Church at Grange (now United Reformed) in the afternoon so we set off in the evening. We drove down the M6 in three or four inches of snow and stayed the night at an hotel near Stafford. When we arose next morning, the snow was turning to slush as we set off in the direction of Bristol in a milder, hazy, drizzly type of weather. (The M5 had not been built then). As we progressed, the weather improved all the way and was quite nice throughout our stay in Torquay. On the day that we came home, on the following Monday, just eight days later, the weather was glorious. We ate our picnic lunch on the roadside somewhere up through the chalk downs of Dorset, having been round by the Bridport-Gundry factory at Bridport to buy nets. When we were back on the M6 I phoned home to let them know we were coming and when father answered I said: "What's the weather like?" He replied; "Very warm; about 70 degrees." This was the difference in eight days.

*

In 1967, at the time that I was working at Glaxo, we went to south-west Ireland, taking the car ferry from Holyhead to Dublin then driving down to Limerick, Tralee and Killarney. At Tralee we stayed in a boarding house in the town where one morning I was awakened by a strange noise. On looking out, I saw that we were directly opposite a dairy and donkey carts were coming down the street one after another and drivers shouting at the donkeys something like "Gwarn," which I suppose was "go on". Later, as we drove out into the countryside, we saw donkey carts coming to the dairy from places many miles out. One evening there was a famous pop group of the time, The Searchers, playing at a venue just outside Tralee. I didn't fancy it so I pushed a shrimp net down a channel in the bay at ten or eleven at night whilst Margaret went to the show and I joined her there near the end of the show.

One day whilst driving down a country road on the Ring of Kerry, we came across a young boy with a donkey which was saddled with a pannier on each side. They were just standing on the side of the road. In one of the panniers was a dog which looked rather cute. The next day we went on the same road again and there was the boy with donkey and dog but also a bus load of tourists taking photographs. On the return journey I stopped and spoke to him, whereon I found that this was all he did, i.e. pose for tourists who gave him tips. I had thought him to be a poor little peasant boy but when he told me that he owned ten donkeys and how much he was making on average each day I was absolutely amazed, it was something like six times what I was making at that time. Another mile up the road on that return journey there was a gypsy type of man with a herd of perhaps thirty goats, a couple of which had cockerels stood on their backs and he was on the same game.

We went down a country lane, which was little more than a track, to a beach where I had heard that there were cockles and mussels. On the way down the lane the whole length of exhaust pipe fell off the car. I stopped to pick it up but found that it was too hot so decided to leave it until we came back. We did not see a soul down that mile long track, only a couple of donkeys, nor were there any houses, but on returning, perhaps twenty minutes later, the exhaust pipe had gone. On arrival home, the holiday photographs were developed to find that out of about forty snaps, more than half had donkeys on them.

It was 1968 when we first took a holiday in a static caravan. This was at Blue Anchor, near Minehead. The weather was beautiful and we thoroughly enjoyed it. We have several photographs from that holiday including one of Wendy on a horse. Lynn was three or perhaps four years old.

One year I bought an old caravan just to go on a holiday in North Wales. At the end of the holiday we sold the caravan to a site owner and bought four boats as I think I have described in the chapter on the boats business. Since that time we have been caravanning in most parts of mainland Britain and in the first few years of retirement we went away four or five times a year, visiting places we had always wanted to see.

In about 1980, Margaret and I took a touring caravan to Paignton where the weather was atrocious during the whole of our stay. Although we were parked within a hundred yards of the beach we were unable to spend any time there. It was then that we resolved to go abroad in future.

Because I was terrified even at the thought of flying, we drove to the south of France to a caravan site called Prairies de la Mer, near Port Grimaud, just across a small bay from St. Tropez. Wendy and Lynn came with us. We drove to Lyon then east to Grenoble and down through the lower French Alps, touching Sisteron and Grasse. We were quite thrilled with the whole holiday including the drive down through the diverse scenery.

In the Mirror dinghy near St. Tropez

On that first trip to the south of France I took a Mirror Dinghy on the roof-rack with a launching trolley on top of the dinghy. As we were going across the Thelwall Viaduct over the Mersey, a wheel came off the trolley. On looking in the rear view mirror I saw the wheel bouncing along the road. I continued to the far end of the bridge, parked the car, then walked all the way back to the north end, which must be nearly a mile, crossed both carriageways and walked back along the other side. There was no sign of the wheel so I assumed it must have gone over the edge and into the river or to the boggy ground along its banks. On the site in France I found that I could leave the boat on the beach so the trolley was not necessary anyway. I tried windsurfing on that holiday but could make nothing of it. We saw some of the sights along the Cote d'Azur, such as Cannes, Nice and Monaco.

The following year Margaret and I went to France again and although we did not plan on staying at the same place, it eventually worked out that way. We had not booked, as we had done on the first time, but having looked around and not found anywhere as good, we headed for Prairies again. That year I took a Topper dinghy which I was able to sail in rough seas when everyone else was blown off the water. On the site were a couple from London who had a windsurfer each so they let me have a go on them and they sailed the Topper.

After many attempts, my bones were aching and my knees were sore from clambering back on board after falling off.

As we were on our way back to the caravan late one evening I said to Margaret: "I'm never going to master the windsurfing and even if I do, I don't think I'm going to enjoy it." She said: "You're too old anyway, you don't see anyone else of your age windsurfing." The very next morning I went down to the beach at about 9 am, a time when the water was almost always dead calm, and took the board out. As the first light airs came along, I found that I was away. I sailed across the bay and back without falling off and from that time it was just a matter of practice. As soon as we arrived home I bought a second-hand board and sailed it at Sandgate and Old Park for a couple of summers and thoroughly enjoyed it.

Our third trip abroad was by coach to a hotel by the Adriatic Sea about ten miles north of Lido de Jesselo. The saga of this trip is worthy of a book of its own but I will stick to some of the "highlights." The coach departed from a place near Luton so we travelled down there on the evening before and stayed in an hotel close to the departure point. The next stop was at Victoria coach station in London where other parties joined us from all over the south of England until we were two coach loads. On arrival at Dover it was discovered that a driver had failed to collect someone at Wolverhampton so a car was dispatched to bring them. We carried on across the channel to Calais but then went along the coast to Boulogne to await the missing party who arrived after we had waited four hours. This delay threw the whole itinerary off schedule with the consequence that pre-booked meals on route were missed. For food, we had to grab a snack at any comfort stop. There was no overnight stop, just straight through to Italy over a day and a half. On the motorway after darkness fell, somewhere north of Paris, the headlights on our coach failed so we roared at about eighty miles an hour down the autoroute with only sidelights on but tucked in behind the other coach. As we neared Paris, in darkness, the traffic was held up for quite some time. The reason became obvious when we eventually passed a coach on the hard shoulder, which was burnt to a shell, its passengers with their luggage were just standing around. It was early morning and cold in the Alpine valley when we arrived at Aosta, having just gone through the Mont Blanc tunnel and over the border from France into Italy. By this time there was some panic amongst the drivers because they were running over their permitted working hours.

All of our travelling companions were going to hotels in Lido or to camp sites in that area. Long before we arrived at Lido we remarked to our courier that an hotel we had just passed looked very much like the one at which we were to stay, having seen a photograph in a brochure. He said; "No, you're all right, I know where you are going." Several miles further on we again expressed some doubt as to whether we were on the right route because we knew we should have been ten or more miles from the others. The courier then turned quite nasty, asking if we knew his job better than he did. It was no good saying any more because with all the hassle, tempers were already rather frayed. It was only when we had dropped off all the other people that the courier realised that he still had two passengers with nowhere to go. We were then dispatched by taxi back up the road to the hotel which we had passed two hours earlier.

The hotel was very good although rather isolated except for a new touristy village close by, but we were there specifically to see Venice, which we did. We went down the Grand Canal in a gondola, walked in St. Mark's Square and had coffee on the Piazza. I went up the famous Campanilla or bell tower but having arrived at the top I was terrified on looking out. The view across the lagoon was magnificent.

Our biggest worry was the thought of the journey home. Although I was afraid of flying, I would have done anything to avoid that coach ride. Enquiries were made about a flight home at whatever cost but it was said that there were no available seats so we did come home by coach which proved to be a little less stressful than the outward journey.

*

I realised that if we were to continue to go abroad and to see distant places I had to conquer my fear of flying. It was decided that we would fly on a shuttle from Manchester to Heathrow and, if I could stand it, back to Manchester, if not we would come back on a train. When the day arrived, Margaret was ill with flu so Lynn came with me. It was a cloudy, calm, February morning when we took off from Manchester and we were soon above the clouds in bright sunshine. Although I sat by the window there was really not much sense of height because we were not far above the clouds. As we came to London the cloud broke a little so I could see some buildings and the Thames and thought it was a fantastic sight. We had a snack at Heathrow then flew back.

Having achieved this breakthrough we then booked a holiday in Sorrento and duly flew to Naples. It was a nice clear morning and when we took off and I sat by a window watching the ground receding as we went up very steeply to 33,000 ft. This was quite a shock and my stomach turned over but after levelling out I was all right until landing time when there was a queue of planes waiting to land so we had to circle round for a while. In the mountainous country around Naples I could see the hills coming up then disappearing and my hands were sweaty with anxiety.

One evening, soon after we arrived at the Sorrento Palace Hotel, on returning from a walk to the town, we took a shortcut via the rear entrance, and suddenly I could smell pigs. Having been used to tending pigs at Ganny's and later having our own, I was certain in my mind what the very strong foul smell was. I had several attempts at finding them but with no success. After a few days it dawned on me that something was missing -the sound of

At the Trevi Fountain in Rome

pigs which are always noisy at feeding time even if at no other period. This baffled me for a while until I realised that the smell was from the sewers. When walking round the town of Sorrento, one could often get a whiff of the drains. Someone told me it was because there are no traps or U bends in the drainage and sewage systems. Surprisingly, having been warned that Venice was a very smelly city, we found no problems of that nature there.

Whilst at Sorrento, we went on a coach trip to Rome. It was a long way and although we set off at six o'clock in the morning, we didn't have many hours in The Eternal City. We did see some of the highlights and said we would like to go back to spend more time there but we never managed it.

Since that time, we have flown to various European countries and to America four times. As part of our Golden Wedding celebrations we went on a cruise on the Mediterranean Sea with visits to cities in France, Italy, Spain, Greece and Turkey. In March 2007 we flew to Auckland, New Zealand and boarded a cruise liner to sail round New Zealand then up to Melbourne and to Sydney. There was a two-day stop-over in Singapore on the way out and three days on the return.

As well as these, we have been on several holidays on The Continent with the caravan. Countries visited were France, Belgium, Luxembourg, Liechtenstein, Germany, Austria and Switzerland. We spent three weeks touring with the caravan in France in June 2000 and again in 2001. Those trips were very enjoyable, particularly the second one when we went from Calais to the Mediterranean, staying a few days at various places such as the Dordogne and the Loire. We also stopped off at places of interest, a memorable example of which was the great cathedral at Chartres.

Margaret and I really have enjoyed our holidays together. Luckily, we are compatible in what we like in our holidays and leisure time. Together we have always decided what we would like to do or see and have gone for it. Now that we are both in our eighties and having some health problems, we are finding that air travel is not easy so we may have to be content with holidays in Britain.

Fishing Methods
Shrimping

Let me say at the start of this section that I know that the word shrimp can be singular or plural. My American cousin speaks in terms of 'lots of shrimp', whereas we have always used 'shrimps' as the plural, so that is the case throughout this book.

As we catch, or have caught, various species, so have we used a wide variety of methods to catch them but most are still those traditionally used by my ancestors with just a few changes in recent years.

For shrimping, the actual shape of the net or the way in which it catches shrimps has never changed at all, only the way of propelling the net over the seabed has changed. The trawl has varied in size over the years but now seems to be set at about 15 feet wide, the mouth being about 15 inches high. Shrimps are on the

Bill Butler going out shrimping

sand under the water and as the trawl comes along it causes the water to surge up over the beam taking the shrimps back into the net. At present, the net has a regulation minimum mesh of 20mm. The bottom beam, which travels along the sand, was traditionally of a hard wood, weighted down by length of flat iron bar of about 1½" wide and 3/8" thick, bolted on top almost the whole length of the beam. Since about 1960 we have mainly used iron piping but I have also tried box iron simply because it is easier to weld on the necessary parts. The nets used for catching shrimps are exactly the same with the tractor as with the horse except that now we use two nets so twice the width of ground is trawled with the tractor.

When we used horse and cart, the net was placed length-way on one side of the cart with three feet or so going forward over the horse and several feet protruding beyond the back of the cart. On nearing the stretch of water to be fished, the trawl was placed across the rear of the cart ready to be lowered into the water as the horse was driven to the starting point. The net, with 10 or 12 metres of tow-line, was then dragged downstream. The towing line was never actually fastened to the cart by a knot, but by an easy release system. It came up from the trawl, over the rear of the cart, over the front or forrend, passed down, round under the right side shaft and back up into the body of the cart. A small section of the long length of spare rope was simply tucked under the main towing section as it came over the forrend so that it was trapped and held by the tension on the rope created by the drag of the net. In this way, if the net became fastened on any obstacle under water or if there was a small section of quicksand or if the horse went into a deep hole in the water and had to swim, the rope could quickly be released and some spare line let out to ease the load on the horse until the danger was past.

The distance trawled would depend on several factors such as how much seaweed there was around, how many shrimps there were or one could even arrive at the end of a particular channel. Being in there with the net, at least one had an idea of what was happening by the tension on the towline and the boil or disturbance of the water caused by the quantity of shrimps in the net. If there was a substantial amount of anything just in the tail or cod-end it would show a boil or disturbance in the water only at that point but if there was seaweed up the wings of the net then there would be a disturbance showing in the water over the full width of the net.

When working with the tractor, if the channel is shallow enough one can sometimes drive the vehicle with the trailer still attached, dragging two nets. More usually, the trailer is released from the tractor and a rope of up to three hundred yards will be between the tractor and the trailer with the tractor travelling down the edge of the channel and the trailer, with the steering turned so that it runs off to the side, away out in the channel which may be up to eight or nine feet deep. Having said that I must say that most of our shrimps are caught in three to six feet of water. One can shorten or lengthen the rope to suit the circumstances such as variations in the width of channels.

When we first started shrimping with tractors, we used heavy wire ropes between the tractor and trailer. These were awful to pull back on to the trailer as they were heavy and after having been dragged over the sand for a few weeks or months the outer strands became frayed and stuck out like needles which stabbed one's fingers. It was almost impossible to work without heavy gloves. It was perhaps the late sixties or even into the 70s when we changed to polythene or other synthetic rope. Again, when tractors were first used, after having one drag down a channel, we used to tow the trailer back to the top again by the long rope. In doing this, one could not see exactly where the trailer was going and what was in its path, with the result that the trailer would sometimes go over a small cliff or brack in a dyke or gutter and the nets would fall off or perhaps even damage the trailer. Remember, the rope was up to three hundred yards long. Harold Couperthwaite once sent his trailer through the middle of a row or band of my father's stream nets because he misjudged the situation. Another hazard was that when the tractors were out at night and there were still horses and carts around, we, with the horses, could hear the tractors coming up the sand so we had an idea where they were but had no idea where the trailers were. If we were in the line between the tractor and trailer it was possible that we could have been hit by the rope which was dragging between the vehicles at sand level or just above it. After a period of perhaps a couple of years, someone had the brilliant idea of using a short rope of about five metres or so with which to pull the trailer when simply moving from one place to another. The steering is still turned a little so that the trailer runs along to the side and slightly to the rear of the tractor. The long rope, still fastened to tractor and to trailer, drags behind in a great loop.

Cockling

Flookburgh fishermen throughout the ages and perhaps until the 1990s, only used one method for gathering cockles and that was with the jumbo in conjunction with either a craam or alternatively a rake or drag and a cockle basket. The jumbo is simply a flat board of about 5 feet long and 14 inches wide and

Jumbo, Cockle basket and Craam

handles reaching upwards from the board to a comfortable height to allow a person to rock the board back and forth. The action of the board turns the wet sand to liquid or quicksand and the cockles, being lighter than sand, float to the surface. There used to be a regulation maximum length of 4ft.-6ins for the jumbo but I believe there is now no limit on length. Until the last few years the jumbo was unique to Morecambe Bay but cocklers who came here from other places took the idea away with them. In August of the year 2000 I saw men working with jumbos on the Solway coast in Scotland near to Southerness. Cockles are just under the sand because they dig themselves there but are lighter than sand so when the sand is turned to liquid they float to the surface and can then be collected. Cockles are never more than about half an inch under the sand, because they have to syphon water through the feeding tube.

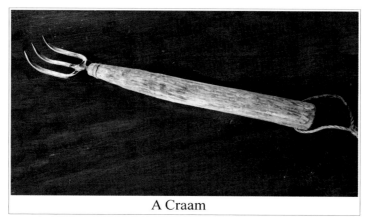

A Craam

If they were scarce they were picked up into a basket individually with the use of the craam which is a small three pronged fork with the last inch of the prongs bent over at right-angles and a handle of about a foot in length. If plentiful, they were raked up, put into a riddle to shake out the sand and undersized cockles, then tipped into a basket. The cockle basket was designed for this purpose and made by the oak basket makers or swillers, of whom there were quite a number around Haverthwaite and Lowick. Three baskets of cockles were put into one bag which was about a hundredweight, they were never weighed. To all local fishermen the cockle basket was an indispensable tool for perhaps more than two centuries. It was also used for collecting fish from nets and for removing shrimps from the boiler. The basket makers were called swillers and the craft completely died out in about 1960 but one man has started to make all manner rustic things from coppice wood, including baskets.

I took a photograph of a cockle basket to him and he made kindly made a new one. It is not quite as the old ones but good enough for my purpose. In the last few years, cockles have been gathered into net purses then tipped into buckets as a measure but not riddled at all. A bag of cockles was always about one hundredweight (112 pounds) but now they are mostly bagged in 25 kilos.

Cockles spawn in summertime then the tiny spawn settles on the sand and if it falls on suitable ground it will start to grow and will take about two years to reach marketable size. We have always called the tiny cockles wheat but now it is referred to as spat. I never heard of this word until I was more than sixty year old. If in one or two years none are spawned for any reason whatsoever, there will be no cockles to be harvested in subsequent years. This does happen quite often so there are years, sometimes several years, when there are no cockles in the bay. In about 1994 to 1996 there were no cockles at all. I used to send samples to Heysham Power Station for testing and at that time I could not get the two pounds of cockle meat needed for that sample. In the new millennium there have been two terrific harvests of cockles, all of which, except for the few sold on local markets, so far as I can tell, went to markets in France or Spain. It is written in a document in my possession that in 1880 there were about 180 people from this district who went cockling. This figure would include men, women and children because at this time I believe schooling was not yet compulsory. Cockles could, at that time, be collected much closer to shore as is shown on an old photograph of cocklers working not far out from Grange promenade.

Flukes (flounder)

It has been suggested many times that the name Flookburgh was derived from the name of the fish but such is not the case; it was almost certainly from

Holes made by flounder when digging out their food

the name of a Viking or Norseman. What we call flukes are really flounder although many customers ask for dabs which are different again, these having skin that is rough, like sandpaper.

The same methods were used to catch plaice but since the 1950s we have seen virtually no plaice at all so I write specifically about flukes. All the methods we use for flukes, bar one, involve stationary, fixed nets of various types.

The only one dragged through the water is the draw or seine net which was used quite regularly before the second world war but very little since then. Two types of staked nets have been the main ones used for as long as anyone knows; these are the baulk, and stream nets. I was almost certainly the last person who would ever set a baulk net. There is too much work involved in setting them compared to the modern tangle nets. With these, one simply strings out a net on wooden stakes or iron bars which takes very short time and no skill whatsoever and they will entangle any fish that swim into them.

One can often see on the sand, signs that flukes have been feeding in a particular area but on other occasions the marks will have been washed away

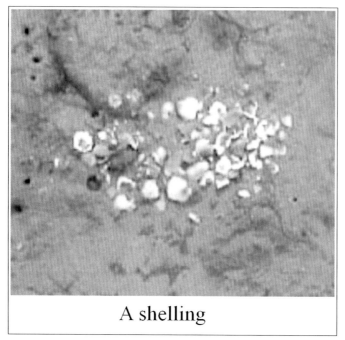

A shelling

by a strong flow of water or stormy tide. The signs consist of circular holes in the sand that are about four inches in diameter and perhaps an inch deep. The fish made the holes when they dug the small shellfish out of the sand. These small molluscs or macoma balthica, to give them their scientific name, are the size of a fingernail and very often the same pinkish colour as a fingernail or sometimes white. The flatfish crush the shells in their mouths, digest the meat then the shells pass through the gut. The broken shells are excreted onto the sand in a nearly circular cluster, which is three or four inches in diameter and called a shelling.

Baulk Nets

These, when set for flukes, are usually at least two hundred yards long and sometimes three hundred yards. They are set on five feet long stakes of ash or hazel, of which half of their length is worked into the sand about four yards apart and then hammered with a wooden mallet whilst still working them in. This is not so much to knock them into the sand but to make them firm as the hammering vibrates the sand around them thereby making it set hard.

Baulk nets were traditionally in lengths of twenty yards (for several years I have used thirty yards), tied together by the cords along top and bottom and the nets laced together at the ends so that one could add sections or take them away to make any length of baulk to suit any given situation. The net is hung on to stakes by knotting top and bottom cords to the end stake, then simply putting one turn of only the top cord round each stake at about knee height but both top and bottom cords on every seventh or eighth and at all corners or changes of direction in the net.

A spar or thin stick of hazel is then twisted into both top and bottom cords near to each stake where the net is fastened to the stake only at the top. This allows the bottom of the net to lift except where it is fastened at both top and bottom, thus allowing fish to pass through as the tide comes in.

Top and bottoms are very important as these prevent the bottom of the net from swinging over

The Baulk Net

the top of the stakes after high water rather than falling back to the sand on the front side. Put simply, they allow the bottom of the net to lift as the tide comes in, but prevent it from rising too high thereby allowing it to fall back over the top as the tide ebbs. As the bottom of the net falls back down on the ebb it is kept on the sand by pressure from water flowing against the spars.

Traditionally, baulks were set in an arc, formed by a series of straight lengths with slight changes of direction at any top and bottom. These nets were often set on great flat expanses of sand so the idea was to "surround" the fish or aim to turn them in from the ends to the centre of the net. A turnpike or small maze was formed at each end, which baffled the fish and prevented them from going round the end.

Baulk nets will, on occasions, catch large quantities of flukes if there are plenty feeding in the area. After a few tides, when all the fish in that place have been caught, the whole thing has to be pulled up and moved to another area where it is thought or it can be seen that fish are feeding. I have seen more than two tons lying in front of net. One could never sell that many but once the net is set it is just chance as to how many it catches. When moving net, the distance moved may be miles or only a few hundred yards. There are many occasions where baulks are set, only to find that they do not catch any fish at all after having taken half a day to set them up.

Setting baulks used to be a two-man job but after the 1950s it could be seen that it was uneconomical for two men to work together. It took me about three hours to set a full baulk but if it had to be picked up and moved, then at least four or five hours. Two experienced men would have set one in an hour and a half but even at that, with travelling time, it would be a good half-day. If the net was set on flat sand with no stream or low spot along it, then the fish would be lying on the sand in front of the net or, more likely, in one of the turnpikes or small mazes that are constructed at each the end of the net. If it was set through a stream with a few inches of water left in at low-water, fish could be lying anywhere from the net to perhaps a hundred yards upstream. They were picked up with the craam and thrown into a cockle basket.

Stream Nets

For these we can use the same nets as for the baulk but in this case the stakes are set in straight lines and much closer together – about a metre or so apart because they are placed on the edges of channels where the ebb tide is very fast-flowing therefore they have to withstand a great pressure of water,

Harold Manning (with cockle basket) adjusting a Stream Net

especially if they are full of fish or seaweed.

In this case, a length of twenty or thirty yards of net is fastened (both top and bottom cords) to stakes at both ends; the top one at about knee high and the bottom cord at about six inches from the ground. The top cord is hitched round every stake but the bottom cord this time only fastened at the ends so that it is free to lift. The next job is to twist a short spar into the top cord then into the bottom cord, sometimes one in each space between stakes but can be every second stake. Cords must be kept very tight by putting extra turns of the bottom cord round some spars if necessary to achieve this. We now should see a net with the top cord eighteen inches from the sand and the bottom cord about a foot lower which will be six inches or more above the sand. This gape can be altered to suit conditions. The net forms a bag and the fish are actually trapped in it. Further lengths of net can be added as is felt necessary.

Stream nets catch best on high tides because they must have a strong flow of water through them to catch at all. Father told me one autumn day in about 1959 that he had taken 'seven score', that is 140 pounds out of one twenty yard length of net. The amount of flukes caught was always talked of in scores that is in multiples of twenty pounds weight. Several people have continued to set stream nets until the last few years and I used them right up to the time I gave up fishing. Whether they will ever be used again is doubtful. In 2008 I set a baulk net in mid-June, just to catch a few flukes. I continued to catch and sell flukes plus a few mullet and sea-bass until October, similarly in 2009 until the last week of September when I retired from fishing completely.

The Flue Net

This is used in conjunction with a small rowing boat in deep holes in channels which are scoured out by the action of the tide rushing round large obstacles such as rocks or the railway viaducts. The net, with floats on top, weights along the bottom and an anchor attached to each end, is wound on to the stern of the boat so that it will pay out as the boat is rowed across the water. When the chosen place is reached, the first anchor, with a marker buoy attached, is thrown over the stern and the boat rowed until all the net is paid out then the other anchor is thrown overboard. The net is now set and the boat is rowed forty or so yards away. If there are two men, one splashes with a pummer to scare the fish into the net whilst the other rows back and forth along and nearer and nearer to the net. To do this job alone is difficult, particularly if there is a wind blowing, nevertheless I have mostly worked alone.

The net containing the catch is hauled back into the boat, which is rowed to the edge of the channel and the fish removed. This whole procedure can be repeated as many times as it is felt necessary. A pummer is simply a disc of wood about a foot in diameter and perhaps 1½" thick with a 5 feet long handle fitted into its centre with which to splash down into the water causing not only a splash on the surface but an echoing thud or reverberation on the sea-bed which should move the fish. If this action is carried out properly, the reverberation comes back up and hits the bottom of the boat which shudders. With this action there is no doubt that fish do not all flee towards the net but in all directions. Some will be caught and occasionally one may catch two or three hundred pounds in one shot. Another day one might catch 20 pounds and have eight or nine shots. On one occasion there were so many fish that I had to pull in half of the net containing several hundred pounds of flukes, cut the net, take those to the tractor then go back for the other half.

On a beautiful but frosty morning in the 1990s, four people came from Manchester University to collect flukes which I assume students dissected and studied. We went to Plumpton viaduct with the boat and net and before I got into the boat to start work I gave my video camera to the young lady who drove the van. She had never used a video camera but did film the action. It was mostly shot from a distance because she didn't know about the zoom but I was so pleased with the film because it is the only footage I have of flueing.

Drop Nets

I suppose it was in the 1970s that people started to use the bigger meshed nylon and fine monofilament nets. It is simply a matter of stringing out a net on a few stakes or iron bars and if there are any fish in that region they become entangled in the net. Iron bars have now replaced wooden stakes stakes on which to set nets but in the days of horses and carts, wooden stakes had to be used. A load of a hundred wooden stakes would not weigh much more than a hundred pounds but that number in iron bars must be around 2000lbs. The iron bars weigh, on average, about 20 pounds. One certainly could not travel round the sands with nearly a ton of bars, plus the nets, with a horse. I usually had about sixteen iron bars to each drop-net and sometimes have had as far as nine nets set out at one time. A drop net that is set for flukes needs to have a good sized mesh of say 5" or more so that flukes tangle in it. If it is too small it will catch small fish but the larger ones will not tangle but will bounce off.

One does require a smaller mesh to catching sea bass and mullet. For this the mesh needs to be in the region of three and a half to four inches. I learned this the hard way. When I was catching flukes but also caught the odd sea bass. They were always four, five and six pounders but a couple were worth more than the lot of flukes. It was only when I decided to try out some small meshed netting that had been stored away for many years that I started to catch the two and three pound fish which are far more numerous.

Bag Nets

These were like short baulk nets but had a pocket or bag into which flatfish were guided by the shape of the net and the manner in which it was set. They were in common usage until early in 1900s, after which I have only seen two people set them. A man who was a railway signalman but was from an old established fishing family set a bag net very near to Red Hill at Sandgate, only a few yards off shore on the edge of The Beck so that his nephew, Jim McClure, and I could walk to it and collect the fish. Jim would be about twelve years old and I could have been nine or ten. My father used the bag net quite often in the 1960 and 1970s after he had a bad spell of health. I, along with two of his grandsons, helped him to set a net on Chapel Island so that all he had to do was ride there on the tractor and take out the fish every day. It would never catch great quantities but would catch forty to fifty pounds or even a hundred pounds when first set. Luckily I took some photographs of that net with the fish therein and have shown those slides regularly for many years. Until the 1950s, all of these methods of catching flukes in set nets were two-man jobs. After

Flukes in a Bag Net

that time it became uneconomical in that it would not sustain two men because flukes are so cheap compared with other fish. There is a similar situation at Morecambe where the shrimp boats always had two men on board, but since about 1960 there has been only one.

Whitebait Nets

Whitebait was caught here between the years 1963 and 1990. Being a completely new job, there was much experimentation over a period of two or three years until we settled on the type of net which was most effective for our purpose.

The net is, or was, simply a huge funnel which, for the first four or five feet from the mouth, was made of about 4" meshed, heavyish netting, then a complete shrimp net, and finally, a small meshed nylon cod-end. It was stitched on to ropes to make a mouth of about fifteen feet across and four feet deep. It was held open to that depth by a wooden pole at each end. A plastic bottle or buoy of three or four gallons capacity was tied to each end of the front of the net to float it because whitebait tend to swim near to the surface. A cable ran forward from each end of the net at an angle of 45 degrees to the front of the net and tied to a heavy iron bar driven four feet or more into the sand held it against the ebb tide. Another cable was fastened to the cod-end, again tied to an iron bar but leaving some slack cable to allow the net to lift with the tide, held it against the flood or incoming tide. One would try to arrive at the nets as the tide was going back but whilst there was still enough water in which to wash the whitebait before tipping them into a box or boxes.

There was huge frustration associated with whitebaiting. Firstly, the fish come and go without any obvious pattern or season so it is a matter of setting nets from time to time to see if there are any but it can be months before any arrive. Secondly, after arriving home with the catch it has to be cleaned, which means removing from among the whitebait all tiny foreign bodies such as small jellyfish, which come in their millions, to minced up pieces of seaweed and leaves etc. which are washing up and down with the tide and would be no problem with a larger mesh. Thirdly, the nets, being bulky, were vulnerable in rough weather and could easily break away and be lost. The end of whitebait fishing came when the markets demanded the product to be I.Q.F. or individually quick frozen, that is frozen so that one could pour from the package a required amount as one does with frozen peas, for example. We could not freeze them that way. We had always simply put a pound of fish into a plastic bag and frozen it as a solid block. It is

A Whitebait Net

doubtful whether anyone in this village will attempt to catch whitebait again. Perhaps if they could find a market that would take them frozen in blocks, it might be viable.

Lave Net

When licences to net salmon and migratory trout were first issued, we tried haaf nets which were then and still are used on The Solway and on the river Lune. This is a net on a frame of about twelve feet wide and four feet high which the fisherman holds stationary in the water until a fish is felt to enter the net then he simply lifts it out of the water. In our estuaries, fish are so scarce that one would probably stand a lifetime before catching a fish in this manner.

It was soon realised that one had to be mobile with a net in order to chase fish on the shallow bars. The lave net is used on the Severn estuary and it was this which was adopted for use in our rivers. It is simply a triangular frame with a handle with which to carry it and a net hung on the frame. We are able to chase and catch some fish on bars where the river runs wide and shallow but in recent years there have been hardly any suitable bars formed, especially in the Leven. If there are a few salmon around this is really now just a sport. Incidentally, 2008, was the first year in which I did not hear of any salmon being caught in either of the rivers, the Leven or the Kent.

Stephen with Lave Net in 1986, (note the fast-flowing water)

Before the arrival of tractors on the sands we used to walk out to the bars which would always be between two and four miles from shore. We were always bare-footed and although it was a summer job, the weather and water could be cold. To alleviate that we often wore several layers of clothes and a short oilskin coat.

One would often carry a wooden stake to put into the sand in the middle of the bar to which one could tie a hessian sack into which the fish could be placed rather than taking it to the edge of the channel which could be two hundred or three hundred yards wide. On one occasion I did exactly that and, unexpectedly, caught seven salmon of various sizes which were then too heavy to carry home. I had to deposit the sack of fish into the cart of a shrimper who was coming past on his return journey. Of course, the news of my success soon spread round the village so the next day there were four men standing on the bar alongside me.

The Fishing

I suppose it was inevitable that I would become a fisherman. As I said at the beginning, I used to go out with my grandfather at a very early age when he was coming to the end of his working life, plus the fact that at least three previous generations of our family had been fishermen. Just before the Second World War I went cockling with Grandfather once or twice, then, during the early 1940s I went out with him and Jim (Jape) Hill. Jim was his cousin and also my mother's cousin.

When the tide is in, Morecambe Bay is more than 120 square miles of water but when it goes out it is, from the fisherman's point of view, two separate estuaries, the Leven and the Kent with numerous subsidiary drainage channels of various sizes running into each of the river channels. Throughout this book, when I write about going fishing "in the east" it means somewhere out towards Silverdale or Morecambe or in other words, towards the Kent channel. "in the west" is obviously to the Ulverston or Barrow direction or generally westward into the estuary of the river Leven.

The shape of all of the channels is constantly changing. Sometimes there are dramatic changes in a matter of days and at other times a slow process of carving and erosion over several years, as was the case in the lower reaches of the Leven during the 1990s. It carved eastward for the whole of the decade until it came into Cowpren Point and along the West Plain salt marsh, taking away perhaps 100 acres of the marsh. The river continued to a point about 300 yards eastward of the south west corner of the caravan site at East Plain. It left that region in the last week of June 2006 to run on its more normal route down the middle of the estuary.

When setting nets I used to think of the times I went with grandfather and he would set the sixty or more stakes needed for a baulk net (about two hundred yards in length) and when the nets were hung on there was exactly the right length set and just the last stake to be put in, none to spare nor none short. He must have set those stakes at exactly the same distance apart every time without any measuring but through sheer practice. I can remember riding around the bay with the two old men, Jape and Grandfather, looking for a suitable place to set nets, transported by horse and cart. Both smoked clay pipes or chewed black twist tobacco and spat out showers of brown saliva. As we went along, they would be looking at the sand for signs that flukes had been feeding there but also scanning the whole scene as far as the horizon for other fishermen or prizes such as timber which could be washed up after having been lost from vessels at sea or from the launching of vessels at Barrow.

There were times when there were such quantities of flukes caught by baulk nets that they were picked up into the traditional cockle baskets and tipped loose in the cart until it was full to overflowing. I remember carts coming home so full that the horse was taken out of the shafts and the cart supported on blocks to keep it level, then the fish were off-loaded and washed. When I was shrimping with my Uncle Bill Butler in the 1950s, he once said: "Me and Herbert Benson (his brother-in-law) sometimes arrived home before daylight on a Monday morning with £50 worth of flukes." He was speaking of the 1940s when one could buy a cottage in Flookburgh for £300; a house with a stable, a barn and a garden at the rear might be £1,000. After that time, one could not catch that quantity of flukes and if a person did manage to catch that many, he certainly could not sell them all. On the assumption that he did manage to sell them, he would now need several hundreds of cartfuls of flukes to be able to buy a cottage in Flookburgh. A frightening thought!

Flukes and plaice were measured rather than weighed. The cockle basket held forty pounds or 'two score' so, if a man ordered four score of flukes he received two basketfuls. If a person asked for an odd amount, say 25 pounds, they were weighed using a set of trones. This was a device which was simply a shaped iron bar, with hooks on which to hang a basket underneath and another hook on top by which to hold or hang the contraption. The trones could be hung up or held up by hand. A pear-shaped weight was slid along the bar as a counter balance until the bar balanced horizontally and the correct weight was read off from the calibrated bar. I now believe that the proper term for the device to which I am referring is a steelyard. I searched at many car boot sales and antique shops for a steelyard and eventually found one at the 2001 Cumbria Steam Gathering.

For more than thirty years we regularly sold flukes and shrimps to a friend of ours, Ben Woodhouse, a trawlerman at Morecambe who also had a fish stall on Lancaster market. He could sell more than he could catch himself so we supplied him. On one occasion Ben had ordered some flukes and father had taken them to Morecambe. Ben's old assistant, Bob Tait, watched my father measure out the flukes with the basket and tip them into boxes. Ben was out at the time but when he arrived home, Bob said to Ben: "He didn't weigh the flukes, only measured them, and I think we got short measure." Ben, being certain that Harold would not sell him short weight said: "Go and weigh them then." After a while Bob came back saying that there was well over the specified weight. Ben said: "Well, are you going to ring him and tell him?"

During the Second World War the bay was used by the army for anti-aircraft shooting practice. Aeroplanes went up from the aerodrome and let out to the rear of the plane, a target at which gunners at the army camp would shoot. The target consisted of a strong wooden pole of hardwood, probably about five feet long, weighted at one end so that it towed vertically. To that pole was fastened a long length of red linen material and at the end of that a length of small meshed netting, the whole being perhaps thirty feet long. It was towed in the sky like a long flag, for the gunners to shoot at. We could sometimes see the hits, whereon the targets became tattered but some broke loose or perhaps the shots broke the wires and the whole target fell onto the sand and were often picked up by fishermen. The poles ended up as brush handles, although thicker than normal and the red cloth was used to make various things including oilskins which were treated with linseed oil for waterproofing. One was made into a Father Christmas outfit which Aunt Mary (Pongo's wife) made and used for a number of years. When the shooting was taking place, a red flag was flown near the army camp and on Humphrey Head as a warning to fishermen.

When I was young there were still some items of chandlery from the boats and huge iron mussel rakes or drags as they were known, lying around at 72 Main Street. This was the first house we bought when we were married and had belonged to Grandfather. The large mussel drags were used to rake up mussels from the sand or scar when the boat was afloat above the mussel beds. So far as I can gather, the boat would lie at anchor and a man would drop the rake head over the side, probably at the stern end of the boat, and walk forward pulling it by the long shaft, thereby loading the rake with mussels then lifting them aboard. This must have been extremely hard work because, as I remember them, the rakes were two feet or more across the head and made of iron almost half an inch in thickness and having teeth of six or eight inches in length.

There is a mussel rake in the Maritime Museum at Lancaster. When the water ebbed enough for the boats to sit on the sand, the men would walk out onto the scar and continue to load the boats. A small garden rake and a basket are all that are required to collect mussels when the tide is out. I have a photograph of two boats moored in the beck at Sandgate, probably taken in about 1910 and it is, so far as I know, the only photograph in existence of those boats. I find it amazing that such small boats, perhaps eighteen feet in length, rigged with what looks like a single lug sail, sailed across the bay and came back loaded with mussels. The boats were built by Crosfields of Arnside. It almost certainly came about because of the fact that there were quantities of mussels on the lower part of the Furness coastline and unless one went to live or lodge over there, the only way to harvest them was by boat. Having seen the picture of the boats, I do not believe they were large enough or sturdy enough for that purpose.

Boating came to an end after two accidents, in one of which, on the 7th of November 1912, three men were drowned. They were two brothers, Thomas and Edward Robinson and their cousin Frank. Thomas was twenty-eight years old and had one child. Edward was thirty-two and had two children and Frank was twenty and single. They were musselling near the southern end of the Furness Peninsula when bad weather sprung up.

The picture above was an old sepia photograph which was given to me by an aunt of my father; it was so faded that one could barely see the features on it. After enhancing it to the best of my ability I was extremely pleased with the result because so far as I know it is the only real evidence of the boating era. Importantly for me, it shows the type of boat used and the rig.

Out of the small fleet of boats which were there from Flookburgh on that day, only two set sail on the perilous journey home. The others headed for the lee shore at Baycliff to stay out the storm. One boat, owned and crewed by Thomas and Christopher Stephenson managed to arrive home but were so traumatised by the experience that they could never speak of it again. It was said that they could hear the desperate shouting of the drowning men but could not give assistance. The body of Frank was discovered on the sands off Baycliff by the fathers of the men and the vicar of Flookburgh, the Rev. John Fowler.. They had travelled by train to Ulverston then down the coastal road and onto the sands to look for them. The body of Edward was found by my great-uncle, Robert Butler, (Clyde), a mile out from Aldingham. My grandfather and his brother, William, were also fishing on that fateful day. Grandfather and Robert were summoned to give evidence at the inquest which was held at the Fisherman's Arms, Baycliff.

It was the 18th of November before Thomas' body was recovered in an area known as Heysham Lake and was picked up in the scoop of a dredger which was working to keep Heysham harbour open. What were the odds against a dredger picking up a body in an area of open sea -millions to one? It was reported in the local newspaper of the time that about 500 people attended the funerals at which the bishop of Barrow, as well as the local vicar, preached. For many years I had envisaged them as elderly men; I suppose this was because they were contemporaries of my grandfather, it was only when I started to write about them and to research some facts that I realised that they were relatively young men when they were drowned.

The main reason for the boating coming to an end was the rapid silting up of the estuaries that occurred when the railways were built. After the construction of the railways, the main channels were not able to meander around as much, thus not scouring away sandbanks in the upper parts of the estuaries as had occurred previously. The river was fixed to one point where it flowed through the viaduct and the whole length of the wall on which the railway runs made a barrier that restricted the tidal flow so sediments fell down and rapidly built up high sand banks. There are now great expanses of salt marshes which grew up in the 20th Century where men once fished and boats sailed just a lifetime ago. The salt marsh at Sandgate probably increased by a third between my childhood and 1976. In that year the channel of the river Leven carved its way into the marsh and reduced it again to less than I had originally known it. The river channel came along the railway

Musselling Boats at Sandgate, Flookburgh (about 1910)

embankment, east from the viaduct until it reached the man-made wall which runs southward to Black Scars then eastward, carving into the marsh all the way until it reached Sandgate. It then turned south, touching Red Hill and still hugging the shore past Canon Winder Farm and Cowpren, going S.S.W. for another mile or more until it finally went westward. It would probably have cut back to the railway embankment all the way from the railway viaduct to Cark shore but for the fact that there is a man-made wall a quarter of a mile or so east of the viaduct which runs south from the railway, down to Black Scars. On top of the wall is a narrow gauge railway track on which ran the bogies used to carry materials to build the wall. The carving of the channel all the way to Flookburgh took about three years in all because of the great volume of sand and marsh clods to be shifted. The brack or cliff carved out was sometimes about fifteen feet high. This was the first time that the Leven channel had been into Flookburgh shore in the 20th Century.

*

From before my time, a number of men went out round the countryside with horse and cart, hawking fish and their produce from the garden. Some went into the Lake District and some into Kendal. These would be working fishermen selling their own goods and also retired fishermen, some of whom had been the boating men who bought their wares for re-sale. In later years, say from the 1930s to the 1950s, they took their wares by train to the markets at Barrow, Ulverston and Kendal. (when I was young, one could still travel by train from Cark to Kendal, changing at Arnside). They wheeled their goods to the station on handcarts and into the guard's van of the train, they then hawked along the streets or to market at the other end. When they came off the train at Cark, at about 1pm, they parked their handcarts on the front of the Station Hotel, which was just across the road from the station gates, then spent the afternoon inside, drinking quantities of mild ale. This practice went on until the mid 1950s when all of the old-timers passed on and those remaining were going to markets or hawking by motor vehicle. There had been a few men, including two of my uncles, using vans for this purpose during the 1940s but most were old men who never progressed to a motor vehicle. When that older generation passed on it was the end of an era because they had been the last of the boatmen. It was certainly the end of an era for the Station Hotel because it then closed down -probably about 1956. I once reckoned up the number men who had been hawkers and market traders who had lived in Flookburgh in my time and found that there had been more than thirty. Almost all of these hawkers lived in Main Street and Market Street, the latter being a continuation of the former. As I edit this again, in 2016, there is now just one man carrying on that tradition with a stall in Kendal market on Saturdays only. With the price of petrol and the advent of relatively cheap food in supermarkets it became impossible to make a living hawking produce round the countryside.

*

In an almanac for this district, dated April 1911, it is stated that the quantities of shellfish have decreased in recent years: "But at the same time, owing to the care so many take of their gardens and sale of their produce and the demand for village apartments, we cannot say that the year has been too bad." It continues: "Several of the villagers still keep up the practice of taking baskets to Ulverston and Kendal (obviously by train) and driving their ponies to Hawkshead, Bowness and Ambleside with produce from the Cark Sands and with fish consigned to them by train. The aforementioned almanac gives lists of cockles, mussels, flukes and samphire that were dispatched by rail.

Stocks of cockles vary tremendously from year to year and there is perhaps more variation in the present age than at the turn of the century, and in that I mean the turn from the nineteenth to the twentieth century. In the second half of the 20th Century there were many periods when there were no cockles. Sometimes this might be for just for one year and sometimes there were none for several years.

All the men of my grandfather's generation must have made a very good living because they all bought properties. Most bought houses with outbuildings, stables and small parcels of land attached. Some of these properties have passed down two or three generations and grandsons and great-grandsons are still working from these same properties. My maternal grandfather had such an establishment with about 1½ acres with the house and outbuildings. These passed to my uncle Harold. His son did not become a fisherman and when Harold suffered a heart attack in about 1960 that property was sold outside the family. My paternal grandfather owned at least ten cottages in Flookburgh when I was young. Unfortunately none of those cottages had any land or outbuildings with them.

Many tons of cockles were dispatched by train from Cark Station every year up to the mid-1950s. There were sidings and loading bays on both sides of the tracks. Factories now stand on the site of the former sidings on the east side and just recently a Jehovah's Witness Temple has been built on the west side. Several goods wagons were to be shunted into the sidings and marked with their destinations such as Manchester, Darwen, Bradford, Leeds, Keighley, and Liverpool. Fishermen took their cockles and deposited them into the respective wagons.

	1888	1890	1891	1897	1900	1901	1902
Cockles & Mussels	1,616	3,161	2,749	2,011		1,250	
Flukes					34.5	14.6	7.9
Samphire						3.0	4.5

They were in one hundredweight Hessian sacks, which were stitched across the top using string and a sail maker's needle, locally called a packing needle. Locomotives, which were steam driven, were very noisy; they chuffed from the chimneys and hissed jets of steam that frightened many of the horses. When they were shunting and coupling up to wagons they made a great clanging noise unlike any other sound and quite distinguishable, even from a distance. With this commotion, a trip to the station with a horse and cart could be quite hair-raising; some horses rapidly became used to the sounds but others never did.

•

Cocklers going out into the bay - perhaps 1920s

When we had the great quantity of cockles that we started to harvest in 1953, Father sent off, by rail, wagons containing several tons destined for Hoylake. Unfortunately one consignment was lost en route and was eventually found in a siding somewhere in south Lancashire but the cockles were rotten. After that he bought a small wagon to deliver cockles by road. After a year had passed it was realized that a larger vehicle was needed and the transporting was taken over by Wearing Brothers, a local haulage company.

In February 1976, as the channel of the river Leven was coming nearer to our side but was still perhaps a quarter of a mile out from Red Hill, I went out onto the sand with a tractor and on looking down the channel to the south at about four hours after high water I could see a pole sticking up out of the water. This seemed odd because when a channel carves in like that it normally undermines everything in its path, thereby dropping objects into the bottom of the channel or floating them away. I knew then that the pole must be set down into hard ground. Later, I discovered that the channel was exposing the edge of a scar, (an outcrop of stony ground) which I had not known existed. There had been up to fifteen feet of sand over that area. We took Father out to the scar later that spring and set a net there. He was seventy years of age and this was the first time he had seen it although it appeared that he knew about it. He died two months later.

For most of his life he wished that the channel would come near to our side of the estuary so that he could catch fish without travelling so far out. Ironically, it came to our shore six months after he finished working but if he

81

had survived to fish that year it would have been the biggest disappointment of his life. In the two years or more after his death there were virtually no fish to be caught in our part of the Leven Estuary. There were plenty over on the sands in front of Baycliff and in the Kent estuary. Likewise the Kent was teeming with salmon, almost certainly the most ever seen -but none in the Leven. My salmon licence applying to the Leven, I did not catch any that year. In the year that the channel came close to shore, the summer was hot and we swam and sailed just off Sandgate. Father went into High Carley hospital and died there on the tenth of June that year, 1976. This became known as the long hot summer.

Several times in my life the channel had worked this way but had only once before come within a mile of Sandgate and that was in 1958. We assumed that the sandbanks had become so high that excavation by tidal action was so slow that the channel could never again come this far eastward. Incidentally, at the same time as this, the Kent channel moved over from near Grange, to Silverdale shore, for the first time in sixty years.

Through the 1940s, 1950s and half of the 1960s the Kent channel came along the shore all the way from Holme Island, past Grange and Kents Bank and along Humphrey Head rocks. We occasionally, in summer, used to cross the channel at Kents Bank or Cart Lane with a horse to catch shrimps, trawling past Kirkhead and Humphrey Head. In the 1940s, mussels were picked on both of these rocks. Many years ago, perhaps in the 1970s or early 80s, Ethel Tyson, who was from a fishing family and elderly at the time , told me that when she was young the channel was always on the Silverdale side of the estuary. I had never seen it over that side and I could not even imagine what this would be like but from the late 1970s until about the year 2007 is was there again. The last time that it ran along Humphrey Head rocks was in 1964 but after moving away then it has not returned and a huge area of salt marsh has grown up from Holme Island right round to Humphrey Head Point. When the Kent channel carved and eroded its way over to the east, it removed all the huge expanse of salt marsh which was in front of Silverdale that had grown there earlier in the 20th century. When I worked over there in 1962, it extended to about three quarters of a mile out from Silverdale shore. A lady called Mary Holmes, whose father, Jackie, had been fisherman (the brother of the aforementioned Dickie Dickinson), lived at Shore Cottages, Silverdale, and had in her cottage a photograph of a steamer moored at a jetty at The Cove, Silverdale, and was dated 1906.

In January 2003, I went to look at Silverdale shore and found that almost all the salt marsh was gone. The channel of the river Kent had recently been close into the shore but had moved out again. There was a quite large 'old spot' or a channel where the Kent had been and on the edge of the shore were the remains of an old wattle hedge fish trap with some wattling still in situ but very delicate and brittle.

In 1829 the Leven channel came to the Flookburgh side of the estuary, taking away many acres of newly reclaimed land. Although this was recorded by James Stockdale in his book Annals of Cartmel, I found this difficult to envisage. The book, first published in 1872, gives details of the event and even the amount of crops harvested on that farm. The land had only been reclaimed from the sea in 1808 but it only lasted twenty years until the sea defence was breached and the land flooded by tidal water.

*

In the year 2000 it was clearly demonstrated how the channel of the river Leven can come eastward and carve into West Plain marsh. The channel was running down the Furness side, past Canal Foot at Ulverston, and down as far as Wadhead Scar near Bardsea. It then ran just about due east to the massive scar almost a mile south of Cowpren Point. The southern end of that scar had been under about fifteen feet of sand which the channel then removed. Having passed the scar, it then ran slightly north of east and carved into the marsh out in front of Raven Winder Farm. On reading the account of how the channel came to our side in 1829, I had believed the great scar to be an outcrop of stony ground, detached from Cowpren Point, and that the channel must have come round the north side of it, between the scar and Cowpren, I now know that this was not correct. I found that the scar is a continuation of Cowpren Point and had always, in my lifetime, been completely covered by many feet of sand. When approaching the fish traps from Cowpren Point, the first things one sees are two large boulders, the larger of the two being a metre high. When I first saw the scar, in 1975, only the western edge was exposed but in the years 2000 to 2005 it was all exposed. It is something like 400 acres in size and on it are hundreds of metres of low stone walls and stakes which had supported wattle hedging. They have obviously been fish traps. To build those walls, put in the posts and hedges must have been a mammoth task but presumably worth the effort. The strange thing is that I had never heard mention of them through any of my ancestors nor in any written records. I first saw the whole scar in May 2000 and did not know what to make of the structures on it. It was another two years before I returned and started to look at it with different eyes. Having spent some time studying and photographing the scar in July and August 2002 it became obvious that at some period in the past the scar must have been exposed for long periods for it to be worthwhile for people to enter into the laborious work necessary to construct those traps.

There are the remains of about twenty varying constructions and I would have thought they were built over a number of years or even centuries. The distance between the stakes or posts is, on average, about 18 inches. I now know that the scar is called Cowp Scar and is shown on some old maps. I believe that the traps were put there by the monks at Cartmel Priory before the dissolution of the monasteries by Henry VIII, or that at least that the workforce was organised by them. It is recorded that after the time of Henry VIII, the fishery was rented out and the rental was more than for any farm in the district. I think it was December 2003 when, having written a small booklet about the traps and a subsequent report of it in the Westmorland Gazette, two people called at my house, requesting a copy of the booklet. Noelene and David Shore were very interested in the subject so we joined forces to measure and record the items on the scar. We sent a small section of a post to Oxford University to be radiocarbon dated. The answer came back saying that it was from about 1350 AD or no later than 1411. This strengthened my belief that the traps were first set up by monks from Cartmel Priory; I think they would be the only people who could summon the workforce to organise such a project. Whilst we were observing the ancient traps, I shot some video footage so that it is recorded for future reference.

●

Through the war years, Father was away in the Royal Navy but I did some fishing with uncles, Harold (Tarro) and Uncle Bill (Pongo). I use the nicknames simply to identify people but we always called them Uncle Harold, Uncle Bill or whatever. In the summer of 1944, I was working regularly with Uncle Bill and his brother-in-law, Herbert Benson. The men often worked above and around Plumpton viaduct so they would go to Old Park late at night, either by van or on a cycle, and walk down to the viaduct where they had nets set and a boat was moored. There they fished most of the night. On these occasions when we were going out early I slept at Tommy McClure's (Uncle Bill's brother-in-law) house and was awakened by Mrs McClure at about 2 am. I would then cycle the two or more miles to Old Park, catch a horse which was left in a field on the left at the end of the road, yoke it into the cart and proceed round the shore and across the salt marsh to the railway viaduct to collect the catch. This was all done in the dark when I was eleven years old – just before I started school at Ulverston. I certainly could not imagine any of our youngsters today being sent off like that now.

It was almost certainly in that same year that, on the evening prior to going on our once-annual day trip with Mother to Morecambe, Uncle Bill gave me a ten-shilling note (50p). I couldn't believe my eyes. I had never had money like that before and as far as I remember that was the only time I ever received any payment from him nor did I expect any because I enjoyed fishing and he was an extremely good fisherman from whom to learn.

*

When Father came back from the navy I went out fishing with him and soon started to go cockling alone but still going a few times with Grandfather. In my first season after leaving school, Father sometimes sent me off shrimping alone. On one such occasion it was dark when he sent me off to go shrimping, something which I could not imagine anyone else doing, but still, I learned quickly through necessity. That season, 1949/50 we caught a few shrimps through most of the winter and I went along with my uncles and others because Father was off sick with pneumonia. That was the last time or probably the only time we had shrimps all winter, although since that time I have caught some in all the winter months in various years, but only for short periods in very mild spells of weather.

I left school in August 1949 and had only been working for a year and a half when I was called into the army for two years on National Service. Whilst in the army I did some fishing if I was at home at weekends and in fact had a horse stuck in quicksand in November 1952, of which I shall recount in a later chapter.

In the early months of 1953, just before I was due to leave the army, the fishermen were starting to harvest perhaps the largest amount of cockles ever seen in Morecambe Bay up to that time. It was the largest amount because the beds covered such a huge acreage of sand. Although still below the legal minimum size there were so many that permission was given by the authority for them to be taken. Seeing that there was to be a good harvest, Father set off by train to look for orders and, by what means of contact I have no idea, he did find an order from a family of fishermen at Hoylake on the Wirral. The Triggs family, of father and about four sons, were fishermen who had worked cockles for many years but now had none on their own shore so wished to buy ours which they would cook and thereby fulfil their orders. Father and Uncle Jont started sending loads by train but after one lot was lost on route, father bought a small lorry and we delivered our own. Jack Rowlandson had been a heavy vehicle driver so he was the driver until I passed my test, then we took it in turns. We used to go out cockling early in the morning, working hard for five or six hours and then set off with the wagon to Hoylake, also to St.Helens and Southport where we had gained further orders. This meant we were on the road perhaps eight hours as there were no motorways then.

Sometimes of course when the tides were such that we were fishing in an afternoon we set off with the wagon in the evening and would arrive home at perhaps 3am. How we did this day after day I have no idea but we did, and fished every day except Sunday although we did deliver on Sundays. Eventually the transporting was handed over to Charlie Struckman who lived next to us, at number 74, Main Street. Before very long the job became too big for him and it was taken over by Wearing Brothers, a haulage firm in the village. We were then sending away about thirty tons a week. Thirty tons per week was a tremendous lot at that time, when fishermen were usually sending just a few bags to various fish merchants or fish shops in markets in the north of England, perhaps two bags or half a dozen bags. There were not the great buyers sending quantities into Europe as we have seen in the past few years. There were twenty to thirty local fishermen cockling and no outsiders at all.

On many occasions, particularly in the spring and early summer of 1953, when the weather was fine and the cockles were lying in a film of mud, even a moderate wind would blow them into heaps. One could see the piles of cockles shining in the sun from a long distance away. Some of these heaps contained just a bag or two but some were quite large and one could perhaps harvest half a ton from them. The cockles in those piles soon died and there was a pile of shells and only the ones at the bottom were able to dig themselves into the sand and survive.

Such was the quantity of cockles available that the only factors that governed how much a person made was the amount of cockles he could cart home with a horse or how many he could sell. In some years, two or perhaps even three men had been able to go with one horse and easily cart their cockles home. There had also been times when men could only pick a couple of stones in weight of cockles so they walked out with a basket and craam, carrying their day's harvest home. In the latter instance, perhaps up to the 1920s, cockles could be gathered much closer to shore as is illustrated on old photographs on which people are shown picking cockles close to Grange promenade. When the great lot of cockles were in the bay in the 1950s, each man had to have a horse and cart and could load it to capacity. We could bring home anywhere between half a ton and three quarters of a ton each, depending on the capability of the horse.

Uncle Bill Butler worked with his son Leslie, two of his brothers-in-law and a nephew. As they owned a tractor with which to work their several acres of land and market garden, they decided to try to use the tractor to haul cockles home. Nobody knew whether a tractor would travel over the sand as it had never been tried so on the first day they went out with one horse and cart, several men and a tractor and trailer. The tractor was left about a mile out from shore and the gang of men went with the horse to the cockle beds three or four miles further out. The cart was loaded and one man took the cockles back to the trailer while the rest of the gang continued to gather cockles. This process was repeated several times until they eventually came home with about three tons of cockles with the use of one horse and a tractor. Day by day the tractor went a little farther out until after only a week or so it was out to the cockle

Cockling in 2004. Grandson, Ben, nearest to camera.

beds and for that family the horse was obsolete on that particular job. Within a few weeks or months most people were using tractors -all were at that time petrol or T.V.O. Ferguson tractors. This led to many more men coming onto the job because any fisherman with a tractor could take on casual labourers. It didn't matter because there were plenty of cockles and in any case they only lasted a short time due to another factor as yet unknown.

The beds of cockles attracted immense numbers of oystercatchers which began to decimate them. The birds came in great flocks and could virtually clear beds of cockles in weeks. We knew that something had to be done or there would be no cockles left in a matter of months. A study was carried out by Durham University to monitor the situation and find out exactly what damage was being done. The flocks were photographed from the air and the birds counted. We were told there were a quarter of a million birds and by opening up random samples of birds it was found that each bird could eat as many as sixty cockles per tide. A committee sat to find what could be done to alleviate the situation by killing some birds by shooting, poisoning, netting or just scaring them away. The committee, chaired by Lady Tweedsmuir, said that the birds must be protected so as a result of that decision all the cockles were eaten and there were no cockles in Morecambe Bay for several years. One could not find a single cockle. I think most people would now agree that wildlife populations have to be controlled and even elephants are culled if they become too numerous.

The oystercatcher is the only bird which can open cockles virtually instantly, thereby enabling it to consume great numbers. Seagulls used to pick cockles up and carry them high in the air then drop them in the hope that they would break. Sometimes they did break and sometimes not but it was a slow, laborious process therefore limiting the numbers consumed. I have not seen a seagull taking cockles into the air since that time, sixty years ago. The reason must surely be that it was a skill passed on from generation to generation and with there being no cockles for several years there was a generation or more of birds which missed out on this so the skill was lost. The cockling on those beds lasted for two years but after the birds arrived en mass they only lasted perhaps six months. We were then all back to shrimping full time but now the tractor was here to stay and one or two men were experimenting in catching shrimps with a tractor.

Pre-1952 or thereabouts, in the autumn and winter months and then only on dark, moonless nights, we used to set fly nets to catch oystercatchers. These were nets with a quite large mesh and made from fine cotton twine -the only material available then. They would, however, catch by entangling, any birds which came along as they were moved from their feeding grounds by the incoming tide. When Father was in Iceland with countless hours of boredom he requested that balls of twine be sent to him with which to braid fly nets. I remember very well the time that he came home with a ball of netting of about 2ft. in diameter, rolled up like one would wind a ball of wool. Inside the ball of netting were numerous packets of Lucky Strike cigarettes and all carried inside a seaman's jersey used as a sack.

Knots (known locally as mice), dunlin, curlew, redshank and shelduck were caught, but it was mainly oystercatchers, many of which were eaten locally and some were sent away to be sold in fish and game shops. We ate them several times a year and I must say they were delicious when roasted with onions and stuffing. It was in about 1952 or 1953 that Jane Allsebrook, the daughter of Judge Allsebrook, who lived at The Green, Flookburgh, was riding her horse out on the sand when she came across a net in which were some live birds. She made a great outcry and the practice was stopped.

In chapter two of this book I told about taking the heads of cormorants to Ulverston and receiving money for them. When I was shrimping in the evenings in the 1950s and 60s, leaving home at perhaps six pm., a flock of cormorants gathered every evening on the sand about two miles south of Cowpren Point. The flock gradually increased in size until there were about two hundred (I counted them as near as I could), then for some reason they divided into two flocks, both of which stayed in the same area but quite a distance apart. There is at present quite a large flock of cormorants hanging around near to Chapel Island and roosting in the trees on the island at night.

Throughout the years of fishing in Flookburgh, families have in some ways lived like crofters, selling and eating whatever was available. I have mentioned oystercatchers which, incidentally, were always called the seapies. I don't think I ever heard the word oystercatcher until I was in my twenties. Anyhow, just recently I remembered something that I read about fishermen catching scoter ducks. Apparently the ducks, locally called dowkers, dived down to the cockle beds when the tide was in, swam along close to the sand and picked up cockles until their crops were full. The fishermen set nets that trapped the scoters and thereby gained another source of food. The question in my mind is, how did the ducks digest the meat in the cockles. Those shellfish are not easy to open without a knife - or the method long used by fishermen – screwing two cockles together, where one used one cockle as a lever to open the other.

When I was about ten or twelve years old there was a large pond near to our village where sometimes there were a few 'tarry dowkers' swimming around but couldn't fly. We thought the birds were covered in tar but of course we, many years later, realised they had been covered in crude oil. On the edge of the pond was a large galvanised drinking trough for the cattle that grazed the field. We commandeered the trough in which we then rowed around the pond, chasing the scoters. Only fun and games to country lads. I have never seen a scoter since the 1940s. The word dowker is simply a dialect word for diver. People in the north of Cumbria often refer to swimming trunks as dowkers.

•

Shortly after tractors first appeared on the job, my father said: "There'll soon be no horses on the sand." I disagreed, saying that there was no way that tractors could replace horses for shrimping because particularly in the daytime one has to trawl in at least three or four feet of water. Although I had been using tractors for several years I was the last person to use a horse for fishing. This was in 1966, about thirteen years after the tractor first appeared. At that time I was working at the Glaxo factory and had kept Tinker mostly as a pet and I suppose I was reluctant to see the end of the horse era. Father was proved correct in his prediction.

For better or for worse, the tractor was now here to stay and if nothing else it saved travelling time to and from the fishing grounds. There were times when I went shrimping with a horse and took two and a quarter hours to arrive at the starting place. I would then trawl down the channel quite a way, sometimes coming out a mile or more downstream or maybe trawling back with the flood tide to a point near to where I had started. This meant another two and a quarter hours homeward journey. Four and a half hours of travelling time and usually twice a day although the daytime trip might not be as far. The tractor will easily do this journey in half an hour.

The method of shrimping with the tractor and four-wheeled trailer was started by Alan Benson who was the son of a fisherman but had been, amongst other things, a jockey. At the time that people were starting to catch shrimps using tractors as the means of transport, we were also starting to use mechanical riddles to sieve out the small shrimps. One day in the 1960s, having just arrived home from shrimping with a tractor, I was putting some shrimps down the mechanical riddle when William Cowperthwaite came in to watch and to converse, not having been out fishing himself. He was, I suppose, nearing seventy years of age, had only ever used and was still using a horse and cart. During our conversation he said: "My family want me to get modernised." Knowing that he could not and never would drive a motor vehicle, I said: "What do you mean Will?" He said: "They want me to put rubber-tyred wheels on my cart." We had always used large wooden wheels with iron hoops or tyres round them but in the 1950s we had started to fit pneumatic-tyred wheels for hauling heavy loads of cockles. Will hadn't progressed that far yet but he did eventually manage to fit the rubber tyres and fished all his working life with horse and cart. He was a fine old man from one of the old fishing families who although he mostly appeared to be a rather staid or even dour man he was surprisingly witty. It was whilst writing this that I realised that Will was another cousin but this time on father's side – not blood cousins because of fathers adoption. William's mother, Mary, was my grandfather Jim's sister. You may have noticed that I have referred to the names William Cowperthwaite and Matthew Couperthwaite. They were brothers but William decided to change his name when their payments for cockles etc. went to the wrong person. That is the explanation I was given.

•

Shrimps were plentiful in the 1950s and 60s and in the autumn we could often catch fifty or sixty quarts and occasionally eighty, just with a horse and cart pulling one fourteen foot wide trawl. This meant quart measures of picked (peeled) shrimps, sixty quarts being about twenty stones of shrimps in shell. Later we changed to weighing picked shrimps, a quart being approximately one and a half pounds so now sixty quarts became 90 pounds. This change occurred when Youngs opened a factory at Cark in 1950, for the sole purpose of purchasing and potting shrimps. The pound weight was a fixed amount whereas quarts of dry measure, unlike liquid, could vary considerably depending on how high the shrimps were piled or pressed down inside the cylindrical container. Even so, old habits die hard and the fishermen of my generation carried on speaking of amounts in quarts. I don't suppose the younger people know what a quart measure is.

The arrival of Youngs brought changes in other respects also, in fact they completely transformed the fishing industry in Flookburgh. Before they came, fishermen sold a few shrimps here and there but no-one had any major orders and many shrimps were sent into markets by train only to receive nothing in return. On looking back now, although I was only young then and knew nothing about marketing shrimps, I realise that most of the shrimps which were sent would be, to say the least, past their best on arrival.

They were mostly sent on the mail train at 5-30am but might have to be changed to other trains somewhere for Manchester and then have to await delivery by British Rail van at the other end so it is doubtful whether they arrived in time for market on that day. When shrimps were put on the train they were almost a day old and of course we did not have refrigerators then so, being the worst things in the world for decomposition, I would say they had very little chance of arriving in good condition.

Add to this the fact that several people would be sending shrimps to the same dealer and probably some were sent from other places as well, the wholesalers would often be swamped. Now I can state categorically that shrimps were certainly sent from Southport as I have described. I have just read a book with the title 'Don' E Want Ony Srimps', which tells of the development of the town of Southport and the history of the fishing industry along that coast. The writer, Harry Foster, tells what was related to him in his research: "People put shrimps on trains for Wigan or Manchester and often we got nothing back for them. You'd get a card from the market saying 'No Sale'. Many did not arrive at the market swiftly enough and were condemned as "unfit to eat." Almost all shrimps caught here were sold peeled or picked as we have always called it. I say were, because now that picking machines have been installed in the premises of the local wholesaler. Some are still peeled at home perhaps it may be fair to say that most are sold in the shell. They used to be all picked by hand, in what was a considerable cottage industry. We used to take out to various houses either buckets or boxes of shrimps. Each house would typically pick say 6 to 10 pounds -that is of finished product. Some would sit all day, and if there were more than one person in the house they might pick 20 pounds, particularly if the shrimps were a good size. As I said earlier in this book, in the 1950 and 60s we could get peeled 100 pounds per day and more than that on a few occasions. I say we because Margaret was very much involved in the work. She would look after up to 10 people, mostly women, but not exclusively so, who came to our house, ensuring there was a pile of shrimps on the table and weighing off the peeled shrimps and removing the empty shells (husks) from time to time. She also had to take shrimps round the community or collect them at the end of the day if I was out fishing. In amongst all this she also picked as many as possible herself. Each fisherman had his own pickers and if he didn't do right by them they could easily change their loyalty and work for someone else.

*

When Youngs came to Cark, they said they wanted all the shrimps we could catch. We could not possibly conceive this to be true because we knew we could catch lots of shrimps and could not see how anyone could handle or sell all those. Sure enough it turned out to be true and they did eventually take all we could catch. Father and I helped Jim Mason, their first manager, to build the fridges and freezers and soon the system was in production.

Shrimpers returning to Sandgate - 1952

We do not normally catch shrimps in winter so the first winter that Youngs were here they offered 10 shillings (50p) per day to anyone who would go out and try to catch a few. I suppose 10 shillings was the equivalent of about £8 in today's money. If I say it would have bought three gallons of petrol or two bags of coal, it would make it more than the £8. Well, it was some incentive to at least try to catch shrimps. When they were properly organised and we were into the autumn season they did receive good quantities of shrimps occasionally half a ton of picked shrimps in one evening. This was wonderful for us because instead of shrimping once a day or just a few times a week we could now fish every tide if we so wished. Fishermen who had small orders here and there gave them up because it was so convenient to take them up the road, mostly between nine and ten in the evening when the day's picking was finished. In the early days we were paid out in the big white £5 notes of that time. This was something completely new - guaranteed payment for all the shrimps we could catch.

There is no doubt that the establishment of the company Youngs Potted Shrimps was a godsend for local fishermen and the community in general because apart from buying our shrimps they also eventually employed about twenty people. This went on quite nicely for about six or seven years until, in the late 1950s, the price of shrimps went down gradually until it was becoming impossible for us to carry on. We went on strike to try to force the price up, but to no avail. We then threatened to set up our own company. I now realise that it may have been the state of the markets nationally which forced the price down but at that time we knew nothing of such things. We now know that what we catch here has very little effect on national or international markets.

"Picking" shrimps in our kitchen (1962)

*

In 1959 we formed the co-operative society, Flookburgh Fishermen Ltd. Several meetings were held to discuss the setting up of the company and so far as I remember, all fishermen were in favour. Eventually we arrived at the time, at a meeting in the village hall in July of that year, when we had to put money down, which was £50 per person in the first instance. Surprisingly, only about fifteen out of twenty-odd men came forward with money, the rest withdrew and never became members. The company started production with the assistance of a loan from the Fisheries Organisation Society and a grant of £750 which was mostly to cover the manager's salary for the first year. We bought the ex-wartime buildings in Moor Lane from Harold Willacy who had lived in Flookburgh and married a woman from a fishing family but who at that time lived at Haverigg. All members worked on the site to turn it into premises suitable for processing fish. Luckily some were tradesmen and others laboured.

The first manager lost us a considerable amount of money and fled. Charlie Bartle who was a local man, a joiner by trade and general foreman for Postlethwaites builders of Grange, then took over. He was a splendid manager and a grafter who worked himself into the ground to make it into a very good company. There were considerable amounts of shrimps, scampi and whitebait going through the factory. The scampi was bought in 'in the shell' from

Scotland and Ireland then peeled and packed in Flookburgh. Charlie managed the factory, was van driver and travelling salesman. The company prospered although it never accumulated any great amount of money because nearly all profits came back to fishermen as dividend. The company was set up simply to market our own products and was, for over thirty years, a great success. As time went on, some members died and others retired so it came to the stage where the amount of product going in was not enough to sustain the business. There were plenty of orders for the products but, sadly, it had to close. The company was sold to Leslie Salisbury of Furness Fish and Game Supplies on the sixth of January 1995 but the sorting out and dissolution of the Co-operative society took exactly another year. Now Leslie has installed mechanical shrimp-picking machines, the first ever seen in this district, in what were the premises of Flookburgh Fishermen Ltd. The end of an era!

Most of the true, established fishermen, who had been brought up into the industry from leaving school were still shrimping with horses until well into the 1960s and. I enjoyed that time, working with the horse. We often travelled out in a procession of carts, sometimes riding on the cart, sometimes walking by the side of the cart and could talk as we went because there was very little noise from carts or hooves on sand. Because of this it was more sociable than today. There were some moments of antagonism and jealousy amongst us, as there is in most fishing communities, but if anyone was in difficulty out on the sands, all the other fishermen went to help. After we started working with tractors, all this changed in that we could no longer communicate with each other without stopping because of the noise of the engine. Very often one could be out all day in close proximity with others and yet have no vocal contact whatsoever.

We regularly cross the fast flowing main river channels. Sometimes one can trawl down either side of a channel, particularly if it is running straight, but more often than not the channel will be carving into one side or the other so we can only work on the inside of the bend. We cross the channel on bars or shallow places where the water is flowing very fast in what we call gillimers, that is to say coming down in rollers at a speed of perhaps fifteen miles an hour. We often cross at the earliest time possible so when working with horses, the water came well up into the cart, and in doing so one had to progress through the channel downstream at an angle of forty-five degrees to the flow of water, keeping the force of the water to the rear corner of the cart so as to let the corner of the cart split the water as would the bow of a boat. If one went straight across with the fast flow to the side of the cart it would push the cart over. This did happen on at least a couple of occasions. Imagine the cart and horse being pushed over and rolling downstream. Thankfully it didn't happen to me. If a tractor stops in a fast flowing channel, the current scours a hole round each wheel and in a matter of a couple of minutes the tractor is dropped down and stuck.

I enjoyed working alone, night or day, especially on fine nights when I could amble along sometimes talking to the horse or singing and I even enjoyed the challenge of shrimping at night in bad, dark weather and having to navigate by the compass. This was at the time when shrimps came out to the edges of channels at night so were often easier to catch and more concentrated.

One question to which I really would like an answer is why shrimps no longer come to the edges of the channels at night in the autumn when at one time it seemed to be an involuntary action built into their make-up. They have not done so since about 1984. I have mentioned this fact to several, people including one or two scientists, whom I've come across at meetings but nobody can offer any explanation. Is it because of pollution or some influence by man's activities?

Through working night after night and wandering all around the bay I became familiar with all the 'landmarks' such as small streams or gutters, as they are known, and built up a mental map which enabled me to know my position at all times. Having said that, there were times when I would trawl down a channel on a dark night and not know exactly where I was coming out and had to do some searching and wandering to find a bearing. I have been out alone in weather that was atrocious and sometimes absolutely black dark when, without the aid of a compass it would have been impossible to navigate.

When working at night in autumn, one could often see the quite beautiful but eerie phenomenon that we call foxfire. On very dark calm nights, particularly when working with horses, it gave a very spectacular display, unlike anything else I can think of. As the horse entered the water, say just a few inches deep, the water was splashed around giving the effect of showers of sparks. When the trawl was in the water there was a bright greenish sparkling glow showing around the outline of the net, especially so when we worked, as I have said elsewhere in this book, in shallow water down the edge of a channel. Likewise, when one was catching salmon by entanglement in nets, when the foxfire appeared in the water salmon would not come near the nets because they glowed. The nearest thing one could liken it to might be the fibre optics one sees on Christmas trees these days, but more concentrated. Foxfire is not in the water in spring or summer but usually appears in August.

On one occasion, probably in the late 1950s or early 1960s, about eight of us had been shrimping with horses in a channel we had named The Goldmine, on what eventually became a very nasty drizzly, wet night with poor visibility. We came out of the water to make our way home at about midnight and were travelling in line, one behind the other. The route home was due north so with the aid of a compass it should have been easy to find the way home. I was last in the line and was tidying up, sorting the boxes of shrimps, fastening the shrimp net to the cart etc., jobs one always did on setting off home, while the horse followed on behind the others. Nobody was speaking, so, having finished these chores, just for something to say, I asked the question: "Does anyone know where we are?" The answer came back: "No." I then said: "You're joking of course." "No" was the reply. I said: "Would you all stop, but stay in line" which we did. "Has anyone got a compass?" I asked. I had previously been fishing over on the Furness side and had left my compass on the cart over there. A voice that I recognised said: "Yes, I have a compass but I can't see it." I said: "Will you give it to me?" I took the compass, which was about eight inches in diameter, and although he had said he couldn't see it, I found it had excellent luminescence. The truth was that he had no idea how to read it or even in which direction we ought to be travelling. Looking up the line of carts as they stood, I could see we had been heading in a westerly direction when we should have been going due north. I took the lead and guessing that we had been going in that direction for perhaps a quarter of an hour, I headed a little east of north, hoping that the adjustment was about right. After about an hour, my horse's feet clattered on to the stones at the bottom of West Plain salt marsh, at a place known as The Cradge, just a few yards east of the old, well worn track over the marsh. I thought it was quite funny when the man who loaned me the compass said, "It must be a good compass." It was no good to him! A compass is not of much use these days as the metal on the tractor affects the magnetic field. Fishermen are now using global satellite positioning equipment.

In the first few years of using tractors, many shrimp nets were lost through the sheer power of the machines and not knowing what was in the nets. When working with the horse one was able to feel the weight on the towing line or the horse would show signs of strain when a net was becoming full of seaweed or sand and it could be hauled on board and emptied. With a tractor the net can become weighted down and sanded but is two hundred yards out in the water so one cannot tell exactly what is happening and the tractor, being so powerful, gives no indication whatsoever. Nets were pulled off beams or torn to bits and ropes broke leaving whole trawls or even a trailer and two trawls in the channel. When nets were pulled to the edge of the channel and were full of sand, it was a hellish job to clear the sand and free the net - even with two men.

On one occasion in the early days of tractors I was speaking to Bill Robinson, the father of Cedric, now the guide across the Kent sands, when he said: "Our lot haven't lost anything today". I said: "Well that makes a change." He then added: "Yes, but they haven't been fishing." With experience and probably by making things a little stronger, losses became less frequent.

Unfortunately accidents still happen in this respect but we have come to notice certain signs and can very often avoid losses. A net can have great quantities of shrimps in and still be sand free but the presence of seaweed and other rubbish gathers sand so that when the net comes to the edge of the channel it can be fastened solid and one has to recover it as best one can, sometimes needing assistance and occasionally tearing the net beyond repair due to the force one had to use to free it.

*

In the mid-1970s I was invited to go over to Middleton Sands, south of Heysham, to act as guide and transporter for a team of surveyors who were doing a study for the power stations. They wanted two tractors and trailers so I employed my mate, Alan McDougall, to drive the second tractor. The work was due to start in August or September and I explained to the company involved that this was the time when I made most of my money in fishing so they said that I must price the job accordingly. With this in mind I tendered a very high price plus provision for accommodation in Morecambe in case it became necessary to stay there overnight. As it turned out, the job was delayed until the beginning of November so I got the best of the fishing season in then went on to make an amazing amount of money at a time of year when I would normally have been doing nothing.

The main reason for starting to tell of this particular episode was that when we were working at Heysham, Alan and I also did some shrimping at night when we could fit it in. On one such occasion we were out through the middle of the night and not catching many shrimps so I suggested that we should go farther west into a stretch of water where no-one had ever been but where I believed we might catch a few plaice to eat. We trawled down for a few hundred yards then, without hauling the nets, trawled back up, whereon we lifted about four boxes between us of the biggest shrimps I have ever seen. Although it was a very dark night I knew by the feel of them that they were very large but on arrival home I knew that they were by far the largest I had ever seen. In fact I can well remember saying that I did not know that shrimps grew that big. One lady took several bucketfuls of these and picked 3¼ pounds per hour, (weight of peeled shrimps). That was the fastest rate I have ever known.

In general there were far more shrimps to be caught in the 1950s and 60s than there are now and we made a nice living although it was always the case that about 80% of our annual income was made in the months of September, October and part of November. After Youngs opened their factory at Cark and the market for shrimps was unlimited, I went out shrimping twice each day five or six days a week, particularly in autumn. On a typical day I would set off at say ten o'clock in the morning, be home around mid-afternoon, boil the shrimps, take some around the village to be picked, then perhaps do some repairs. Around six in the evening I would go to bed for a couple of hours then be up to prepare to go fishing again. I could be home from that trip at three in the morning, boil the catch and be in bed by five or six am. And so it went on, two fishing trips per day and no more than two or three hours of sleep between each one. The only time this didn't happen was if the weather was extremely stormy in which case I would forgo the night tide.

I also caught more salmon then, especially in the 50s, and just one or two years in the 60s. The most memorable year for salmon for me was probably 1958 because Father and I just had one baulk net set in what was called an 'old spot' or in dialect, an aad spot, (aad pronounced as in promenade) where the main channel had been but had moved away, leaving a quite large channel which dried out at low-water. From this net we took up to eighteen salmon and/or sea trout in a tide. There was sometimes only one fish but usually something.

Baulk nets will not stand high tides so it probably fished about fifty per cent of days through that summer. I often think about it now and know that if the fine synthetic nets of today had been around at that time we would have caught tremendous amounts. The modern nylon or mono filament nets, if clean, i.e. not cluttered up with seaweed etc., will catch fish almost anywhere.

It was always illegal to take salmon from that type of fixed net but it did happen. I think that in fishing one has to make a living by any means possible or whatever one is allowed to do and I feel sure this applies to all fishing communities. The odd thing is that we never thought of it in the same light as say robbery or other common or petty crime but simply as a job to be done in way of life which has continued since before the bylaws existed.

When we were haymaking in June 1966, after throwing up the last bale on to the trailer, I said: "Thank God for that" and struck the fork hard down into the ground. Unfortunately, my foot was in the way and the fork went straight through it and pinned me to the spot with at least five inches of prong through my foot and into the ground. I was rather shocked but pulled it out and later went to see the doctor. He said I had been extremely lucky as the fork had gone through without damaging any bones. The very next morning, although the foot was extremely painful and swollen, I went out on the tractor and had a ride up and down the edge of the Leven channel looking for salmon. On seeing one swimming quite a distance from the tractor I jumped off and ran as fast as I could with the lave net and caught it. Afterwards I remember thinking: "What happened to the sore foot?" Mind over matter I suppose. Anyway, I was off work from Glaxo for a month and caught quite a lot of salmon in that time, most of them in a baulk net a few hundred yards west of Chapel Island. It was one of the best years for salmon in the Leven.

*

It must have been back in the late 1950s when I took some men from the G.P.O. (General Post Office) out into the bay to look at the route over which they were going to lay a telephone cable across the bay from Heysham to Rampside. Stephen was perhaps five years old at the time and he came with us on an old TVO–fuelled Fordson Major tractor. It was a nice summer day in either June or July, and as we stood at the edge of the river Leven, a long way down in the bay, there were numerous salmon leaping clear out of the water only a few yards in from the steep bank of the channel where we were standing. On seeing them, Stephen said: "Look Dad, flying fish". If I had not taken those people out I would have been standing on a bar with a lave net, trying to catch salmon along with several other men. Seeing all those salmon leaping, I was rather perturbed that I was missing a day when there were so many fish around. When I arrived home I enquired how many salmon had been caught that day -the answer was none, nor were there any in the following few days. Where did those salmon go? It was an incident I remember so well because it was a one-off. I have never seen anything like it either before or since that day. I have seen many salmon leaping further up in the estuary – say between Chapel Island and Greenodd but never down at the bottom of the bay.

A meeting of fishermen and G.P.O. officials was held in Flookburgh Village Hall to discuss the laying of this cable when questions were raised about the consequences if the cable became exposed and fishing gear was entrapped or damaged. We were told that if our gear was fouled on the cable we should cut our towing lines and claim compensation. It was made clear that we must in no way damage the cable. It was also said that such an event was extremely unlikely because the cable was so heavy that it would sink down into the sand out of harm's way.

It was perhaps ten years later that I was trawling down the Mussel Hollow, a mile and a half out from Newbiggin, on the Furness side of the bay when the trailer became stuck in the middle of the channel. I tried all ways to free it but without success. The next morning I went with several men and a boat to see what could be done but still we could not free it. It remained there, two nets, a trailer and a long wire rope, lying in nine or ten feet of water. I believed it to be stuck in mud or perhaps trapped by large stones on the edge of the mussel scar. I just had to forget about it and make up a new set of equipment.

Fast-forward several years, to a day when a few of us were musselling on the stony scars near to that spot. The fisheries inspector, Grenden Harrison, came on the scene, having walked out from the Furness coastal road. Whilst he was strolling around, looking at mussels on the scar he casually said: "Here's the telephone cable". I pointed out that my gear was lost in the channel only a couple of hundred yards from where we were standing. It then dawned on me that my gear was fouled on the cable. Until that time we did not even know where the cable was lying. Obviously it could not sink into the hard stony ground. After having assessed what it would cost to replace it, I sent in a claim for compensation for the equipment. I think I worked it out at about seventy-five pounds which was really a ridiculous figure because to make up new trawls and build a new trailer would cost a couple of hundred pounds in time alone, even then, in the 1960s; I had simply priced for the raw materials. Having come up with that figure, I doubled it, knowing that they would want to argue it down. A while later I received a letter saying that the fisheries inspector, Mr Harrison, implied that the value of the lost gear would be about seventy-five pounds -and that's what I received. I thought at the time I should have said to the company "Well! you replace it". It would have cost them ten times what they paid me. At that time we knew nothing of compensation claims, today it would be a different story.

In 1959 there was a good run of salmon but they came late in the season. I had been fishing up at Old Park all summer and had done quite well. In August I had to start shrimping because the pickers (peelers) expected them and some would perhaps have started working for someone else. I left a very short baulk net set but 'hung up', a few hundred yards north of Park Head point. When a net was not required to catch anything, both the top and bottom cords were fastened near the top of the stakes and were therefore said to be 'hung up'.

Baulk nets could be two hundred yards long or three hundred if set seaward of a certain line well down the bay and were set on anywhere from sixty to ninety stakes. This one was set through a very narrow dyke and was only about forty or fifty yards long.

Unfortunately, Father's horse, Darkie, died from lockjaw about that time and he was devastated because he was really fond of that animal. While he was looking for another horse he decided to use my net as he could walk out to it. He said: "How many spars do I need to bottom that net." I told him six. "SIX!" he exclaimed: "It must be a funny baulk." It was just a narrow stream with steep banks on each side. A decent sized baulk would need at least forty spars (look for spars in the chapter on Fishing Methods -Baulk Net). He put the spars in the baulk so that it could start catching again and over the next week or two it caught quite a number of salmon. The thing that I still remember well was the fact that they were mostly 18, 19 and 20 pounders. The end of salmon season came, 31st of August, and he carried on taking fish from the net because he still had no horse. It was always illegal to take salmon from a baulk net whether they were in season or not. On a Friday night, about the ninth of September, the bailiffs caught him with salmon and booked him. The next morning we were going to Belle Vue, Manchester, on a coach trip to the National Band Open Contest, not competing but as spectators. He wasn't able to go because he was so down about his situation. I could understand this and sympathised with him, having been prosecuted for the same activity myself and being fined on each occasion.

In that year, 1959, there was the longest dry period that I have ever known. This was confirmed by the Institute of Terrestrial Ecology at Merlewood, Grange. The fine dry weather started in early July and went on until about the time that the clocks went back in late October. The days were mostly cloudless but not necessarily hot. With the dry weather, salmon hung around in the estuary all the autumn and lads at Ulverston kept catching them all of that time. I had my old horse Bob down the coast road on Peter Lord's farm at Goadsbarrow for shrimping on that side. There were plenty of shrimps and they were clean because of the fine calm weather but they were small. Breezy, changeable weather is usually best for catching shrimps. When we were at Jonathan (Stoker) Butler's funeral at Allithwaite in late October the weather had just broken. Nathan Shaw (another fisherman) said: "We've done quite well with shrimps but we'll do better now that the weather has changed." After that time the winds brought in the sea weed which was ripe and had been lying around outside our area with the result that it became difficult to work, especially at night, and in fact we then caught fewer shrimps than in the fine period. Over the years I, also, have made many confident forecasts about fishing and have been proved wrong time and time again. Whilst about the subject of fine weather, I would like to mention the phenomenon that my father called the 'fine weather breeze'. In very fine cloudless weather, the mornings usually start off absolutely calm then by lunchtime or early afternoon a moderate or even fresh breeze develops, probably caused by heat convection. The odd thing is that on these sort of days the wind moves round just in front of the sun as the day progresses. That is to say that as one looks at the sun, the wind will be coming from slightly to the right of it all the time as the sun progresses westward, (or appears to). There are of course fine days when there is a steady breeze or fresh wind all day and night but this is a different thing.

Another strange but true thing he told me about when I was quite young was that here, in the Cartmel peninsula, thunderstorms always come from the south-east. That is to say that if one looks across the bay and can see a thunderstorm over in the direction of Morecambe, Carnforth or Bolton-le Sands, it will soon be here. On the other hand, if there is a thunderstorm over the Furness peninsula, at Barrow or Ulverston, it will not come here but will drift away to the north-west. From my observations over many years I can vouch that this is true. I cannot say whether this applies at other places although I would like to know if that is the case.

On the tenth of November 1992 (my 60th birthday), I went shrimping in Ulverston channel at 4 a.m. on a cold, moonlit morning on which there were some heavy showers coming from a westerly direction with bright, moonlit periods between. I started trawling a short distance below Wadhead Scar and whilst I was having my second drag, at about 5.30, a full rainbow developed in the moonlight. It was a tremendous bow which stretched from just south of Humphrey Head point at one end and directly onto Heysham Power Station at the other and was down to ground level at each end. There were no colours in it, just white, but perfectly defined in its shape and outline. This was something which I have only seen on that one occasion and, until then, didn't know was possible although shortly after I had seen it there was a report in a newspaper of another person seeing one over on the other side of the country.

In the 1950s and perhaps into the 60s I used to very often see the Aurora Borealis or Northern Lights when shrimping at night in autumn. Sometimes there were only shafts of light shining vertical, low down in the northern sky and sometimes quite spectacular displays of changing colours and lights well up into the sky. I even saw the Northern Lights from the backyard when we lived at number 72; in fact it was from just where the gates to our bungalow are now placed. Since that time I have never seen them at all. Is it that there are no displays now or that in recent years we have not been out fishing at night in the autumn as we used to. Is it that there is so much light pollution now that it obliterates the phenomenon?

*

In February 1962, I received a phone call from Syd Triggs at Hoylake, asking if we could supply cockles again as we had done in the 1950s. We doubted whether we could because although some men were cockling they were only getting a couple of bags or so per day but we said we would see what we could do. At the first opportunity, Jack Rowlandson and I set off on an old Fordson T.V.O. (paraffin fuelled) tractor, crossed the Kent channel at Cart Lane and headed down towards Morecambe. After searching for some time, we found a bed of cockles two miles or more south-west of Silverdale. It was probably the best I had ever seen in that it was many acres in size and the cockles were touching each other from almost one end of the bed to the other. I had just made arrangements to go to Ireland to try to buy a horse or horses so we decided to wait until I came back.

I drove to Liverpool where I met some of the Triggs men to discuss prices etc. A price of seven shillings a bag (35p) was agreed and I think this would be the 120-pound bag which we had supplied some years earlier. Late in the evening, and pretty well intoxicated, I embarked on the ferry to Dublin, arriving there fairly early next morning. Soon after my arrival home, Jack and I went across to Silverdale with the tractor and started to work the cockles. We raked up about twenty to thirty bags a day and stacked them on Silverdale shore to be collected by wagon every two or three days. After only a couple of days or so, Jack Butler and Bob Dickinson came over, first with a horse and cart but soon acquired a tractor which they lost in quicksand just off Silverdale shore only a few days after arriving over there.

The reason for working from Silverdale was that the channel of the Kent was running close to Grange shore and continued to hug the shore all the way to Humphrey Head Point. If one worked from Flookburgh it would be six hours after high tide before one could cross the channel then another half hour to travel to the cockle ground. From Silverdale, we could be working on the cockles no later than three hours after high tide.

One Saturday morning in May when I was going out from Silverdale alone because Jack went to Keswick market, Tim Proctor, who was I suppose about twelve or thirteen years old and lived at a farm close to the shore, decided to come with me. We went out and raked up about fifteen hundredweights but as we were returning we met a young man walking out about a mile from the shore. I approached him and warned him that the tide would be coming back in an hour or so but he didn't even acknowledge me. On the Monday, Jack and I went to Silverdale where we found that there were a number of policemen walking along the shore. Apparently there had been a motorcycle left there for two days but no sign of the owner. We went for our load of cockles and on our way back found the body of the man about a mile and a half out from shore, still wearing his spectacles and a haversack on his back. We went back to shore and reported to the police who came out with a coffin on the trailer to collect the body. A month later I was summoned to attend the inquest at Carnforth where, after giving evidence, the clerk asked if I had any expenses. After working out what I had lost in earnings and travel I came up with a figure of about six pounds but thought that sounded too much so I said three pounds. The clerk said nastily; "That's more than I make, you'll have twenty-six shillings." I decided then that if I ever found another body I would say nothing but when it did happen twenty years later I could not do that.

*

We worked those cockles until the warm weather came then went back to shrimping for a few months and I suppose I would be catching salmon for a while. In the late autumn we started cockling again but by now Edwin Kershaw of Southport, whom we had supplied in the 1950s, also asked us to supply him with cockles. By purchasing cockles from other fishermen we were able to keep both orders going for a while. Eventually Kershaw increased the price above that which Triggs' could match so they decided to come and gather their own. When we were in full swing we sent away something like thirty or forty tons per week just to Kershaws.

The winter of 1962/63 was the hardest winter that I have ever seen and probably the coldest of the twentieth century and with that the cockles were all killed by the beginning of March. There was hardly any snow here but very hard frost day after day for many weeks. Windermere was frozen to the extent that cars were driven across and water pipes were frozen underground for up to twelve weeks. We were working from Silverdale shore and apart from the agony of cockling in such conditions, one of the worst things I remember was driving back to shore into the cold east winds which prevailed almost every day. By then we were using two tractors, of which I always drove one and Jack Rowlandson the other. At least the other men could shelter under oilskins with their backs to the wind as we travelled. Nevertheless it was absolutely terrible working in those conditions but we were making good money so had to carry on. Eventually the frost killed all the cockles because if the tide went off at say eleven PM they were exposed to extreme frost all night and frozen in the sand. I developed shingles in early March so was unable to work at the latter end of the winter but the other men found a few cockles near Morecambe. They went there for a couple of weeks until that small bed was cleared up and then there were none anywhere in the bay.

There were three Kershaw brothers. Tom and Norman had set up their own company and Edwin was on his own. When cockles became scarcer there was a price war between the two companies which resulted in price rises sometimes every few days. I used to ring Edwin and say: "Your Tom has put the price up again so we are having difficulty buying enough." He would simply say: "All right, put it up another two or three shillings a bag." The severe weather conditions prevailed throughout northern Europe so cockles became very scarce. The following winter we decided to look elsewhere for cockles.

When we first went to Kershaw's at Scarrisbrick, the three brothers boiled all their cockles in a tiny wash-house at the back of their father's terraced cottage. When we went back in 1964, Edwin had built and moved into a large, luxurious bungalow with acres of ground on which he built a cockle-processing factory. He had large flower gardens, a gardener to tend them and altogether a fine establishment. There were lines of vans in which gangs of men went out selling cockles round pubs as far away as The Midlands. When I last saw Edwin he had branched out into making prepared meals such as chicken dinners and was in a big way. He said to me: "I wish I'd stayed small, I now turn over a huge amount of money and have ten times the worry but no more profit." Edwin, who was one of the easiest and most pleasant people to deal with, retired to the Isle of Man.

At the beginning of December 1963, Edwin rang to say he had heard about some cockles on the Isle of Barra in the Outer Hebrides so would we like to go and look at them? He said he would share the cost of the trip so off Jack Rowlandson and I went, sailing from Oban via various small islands on a nine hour crossing to Barra. We stayed for a few days with a family in a small cottage while we looked around. The cockles were on a small area of sand at the north end of the island on which aeroplanes landed on a regular service. There was an old man cockling but they were so scarce that it was difficult to believe that it was worth doing. We tried to explain that we were looking for a place where we could rake up a bag from about three square yards. He could not grasp the concept of this at all and said he thought those were the best cockling sands in the world.

We spent a day or two, probably waiting for the next ferry, looking round the island and watching the men from the herring fleet which was in for the winter from Campbeltown. They went out every evening as dusk approached, at about 4-00 PM, to fish near one or two islands not far away. I was told that they went out at night because the herrings swam near to the surface in the dark so they had less chance of damaging nets on the rocky seabed. It was here on the quayside that I watched them repair a massive hole in a net. The hole was about as big as the area of the front of an average house and one or two men started to repair it but as others finished their various tasks they joined in until there were perhaps ten men working on the net.

I could not envisage how they could possibly end up at the right place but they did, right to the last mesh. The following year, when I was ill for a long time, I acquired a book on the subject and taught myself to mend nets. We could braid new nets and codge up torn nets but could never mend them properly. The secret is in the cutting of broken meshes so that having started to mend, one can carry on to completion without having to cut the working twine and start again. It takes some practice before one can do it proficiently but once mastered it is a handy skill for a fisherman to have.

Jack and I came home but were still anxious to find cockles. Earlier in that year as we were bringing our equipment back from Silverdale, Jack, Father and I had set off with a tractor on a wagon, searched for and found a small bed of cockles in Scotland. We rode along the north side of the Solway and looked at several inlets past Kipford and Kirkcudbright, then up to the Isle of Bute, crossing from Wemyss Bay to Rothesay, leaving the tractor on the mainland.

On Bute, all we found were a few very large cockles in a tiny sandy bay, some of which were over six inches in circumference. We were told that there were never any small ones so the likelihood was that they grew somewhere in the sea and were washed up. On the way back we stayed the night at Largs where we went into The Anchor pub for a drink and mentioned what we were looking for. A man who looked like a boatman, wearing a peaked yachting cap said: "If you go down the road three miles to Fairlie and walk out a few hundred yards you will find plenty of cockles -you could probably fill a bucket." We remarked that we were looking for something like thirty tons a week. His jaw dropped. The two barmen were called Sandy and Jock whom we were soon to know quite well and the names were memorable because Sydney Bland and I used to play a cornet duet called Sandy and Jock. Not many years later I was playing the same duet with Stephen and my nephew, Tony.

At first light next morning we went down to Fairlie, which was on our way home, and went out to look at the cockles. There certainly were some cockles but we were not sure whether there was the quantity available to make the job viable. There was no great lot so we decided not to work them at that time. Eight months later, as we came home from our trip to the Hebrides, we thought over the project, trying to work out all the things which could go wrong and the expenses involved. Me, being the world's greatest pessimist, assessed everything at its worst and still came up with the answer that we could indeed make money from those cockles. The only advantage in being a pessimist is that when one views things at their blackest they have got to turn out better than expected.

•

It was on a Monday morning, (that sounds like a Flanders and Swann record) about ten days before Christmas 1963 when Jack and I set off to Fairlie with a tractor on one of Kershaw's wagons. We arrived at lunchtime and unloaded the tractor from the wagon onto a car-lift in a garage and later parked it on the shore at Fairlie. The next thing we had to do was to find lodgings. Seeing a B+B sign outside a house called Clover Cottage which was virtually just across the road from where the tractor was parked on a piece of waste ground, we approached the cottage. A lady (Mrs Henderson) was in the garden so we asked if she could offer accommodation. She said that she was fully booked but her daughter, who was there at the time but lived at Largs, could accommodate us. We later went up there and discovered that the daughter, Grace Thomson and her husband, Joe, lived in a very nice flat over the Trustees Savings Bank in the centre of Largs and had a spare room. We stayed there for nearly three months at a price of £7 per week each for bed, breakfast and evening meal, which was nearly a week's wage for an average manual worker but it was very nice and we were treated as part of the family. Their daughter, Carole-Anne, was about eighteen months old or maybe less than that. The last time we visited them she was a solicitor. The Anchor pub was only twenty or thirty yards from the flat so we soon got to know Sandy and Jock very well

After arranging the accommodation we went out cockling late in the afternoon and although there was only a short time before dark I think we got about eight bags. By this time we were working with bags of about 90lbs. We then set about looking for men to work for us, making enquiries in the town and at the labour exchange without much success. Someone suggested that we should go to West Kilbride, a small village about five miles south-east of Fairlie, because there were reported to be unemployed men there. We duly went there and recruited two or three men to start early next morning. We loaded the wagon with ten tons and came home for Christmas. Knowing what Scotsmen are like at New Year we didn't think it worthwhile going back until it was over. When we did go back we soon had about twenty men working for us and were loading two or three wagons per week. We took it in turns to drive the wagon down to Flookburgh where Kershaw's driver met us with an empty wagon and he took the load on to Scarrisbrick.

When the tide is high at around noon, one cannot get out to start gathering cockles until say 3 pm. so in winter there is not much time to work before it is dark. Likewise, in a morning the tide is coming in just after daylight so not much time again so we used lamps to work in the dark which we had never done before.

I think we were making about a hundred pounds a week clear after deducting money for lodgings and diesel etc. when, for instance, the wage for a daytime process worker at Glaxo was about twelve pounds per week. The Scottish workers had previously worked on the construction of Hunterston Power Station, on the shore at the south end of the small crescent-shaped bay in which we worked and were the roughest men I have ever encountered. The job only went on for three months because, although the cockles were a good size they had a very poor meat yield and the Dutch were starting to come on the market again. Whilst they were scarce, Kershaws were glad of them and we had an excellent winter. I look back on this time in Scotland as a very good period in my life, not only financially but as a pleasant experience. In the last few years, men have travelled around seeking and working cockle and mussel beds but it was unheard of in the 1960s.

Just before we left Scotland, I went down into Kent and Essex to look for more cockles. On the south side of the Thames there were none but on the north side below Leigh-on-Sea, off Shoeburyness, there were plenty but the local fishermen had them tied up through an ancient charter, or so I was told.

For us it was now back to shrimping, and what a come down in financial terms. Fishing has always been that way, good periods but seldom more than a few months, then long poor periods or even months with no income at all. If there are cockles, one can usually make a steady living and that is particularly important through winter when shrimps have left the bay.

•

In the spring of 1963, after the cockles at Silverdale finished, Bob Dickinson and his cousin, Jack Butler, (both related to me – our grandparents were siblings) started to try to catch whitebait which had never been done before in this area. The Morecambe boatmen had been catching it for a few years and my father had tried ten years earlier but without much success or enthusiasm. The Morecambe men caught whitebait in nets which had twenty foot square mouths and were set under the boats while they were at anchor in deep water when the tide was well up. They could catch on both ebb and flood tide. We obviously could not operate in that way so another method had to be worked out.

Bob and Jack made nets which were similar to those at Morecambe but on a smaller scale, that is, with two long beams on which to fasten the net top and bottom with a rope down each side with which to control the depth to which the mouth could open. The length of the beams was probably about eighteen feet. The net started at the beam with a mesh of four or five inches, decreasing to a very fine size at the cod end. These nets were staked out on the sand using two strong iron bars, one against the ebb tide and one against the flood. They set them in various places and obviously learned a little as they went along, but that year they did make quite a bit of money from whitebait. The next winter all the fishermen were catching whitebait but this was at the time when Jack and I were in Scotland.

The following year, 1964, at the time that I was ill with brucellosis, Father and my brother-in-law, Jack Rowlandson, started to try to catch whitebait. It was then that I went out with them and made the dramatic recovery from brucellosis about which I told earlier in the book.

Father had gone two or three times to the nets which were set near to the Leven channel and found that the meshes were white with whitebait struck in (jammed in the meshes) but the strong tide had pulled one bar out of the sand thereby turning the net round and releasing the fish. We strengthened the anchorage, (we only had two nets then) with the result that we caught 900 pounds of whitebait in two tides the next day. This was the first time that we had caught any quantity. This type of net was difficult to hold against a strong tide but was also cumbersome to transport around so it was soon replaced by a net without poles which could be rolled up to transport and, more importantly, collapsed into a shape with less resistance to the incoming tide which is almost always much stronger than the ebb. Even so, in bad weather, and/or strong tides, the six feet long iron bars could be pulled out of the sand and the nets lost.

In the 1960s and 70s good quantities of whitebait were caught from time to time and it was something of a replacement for cockles as a winter job although very unreliable. The fish come and go without any pattern or recognised season. I think it is safe to say that whitebait has been caught in every month of the year whereas when we first started it was thought to be only a winter job. Many times we have gone to nets twice a day for weeks, catching almost nothing and other times there have been great quantities and we've had to dump it because the factory could not freeze it all. There were sometimes a dozen or more men with up to half a dozen nets each and there could be two or three hundred pounds in each net which simply had to be tipped out on the sand and left. At a push we could freeze 2000 pounds but with that quantity of wet fish in the freezer it took more than a day to freeze solid so we couldn't fish the next day. Whitebait was packed in one-pound blocks and placed on freezer plates which was quite easy. By the late 1980s the markets were demanding I.Q.F. or Individually quick frozen product so that one could pour out the required amount in the kitchen when cooking, just as one can with frozen peas from the supermarket. We could not produce this satisfactorily. We could only put a few thinly on trays and when they started to freeze a little, stir them up from time to time to prevent them from sticking together or to the tray. There was no way that we could process any quantity like this nor was the finished product satisfactory.

The last time whitebait was caught here was from the 7th to the 21st of May 1990 in which time I caught a considerable amount. After that the 'cockle moss' (a plankton type of very tiny weed) came into the bay, as it does every year, and bunged up the nets, making the job impossible. No doubt whitebait had been in the bay earlier than that so if I had set the nets a few weeks sooner I would have done really well. It was very often a frustrating and difficult job because over the years I lost probably about a dozen nets through strong tides or high winds thereby incurring quite a large expense. Then there was the time, in the mid-80s, when a young man called Michael McClure and I were catching whitebait off Bolton-le-Sands when we arrived at the nets at midnight we found that out of twenty-one nets that were set, seventeen had the cod-ends cut off. This was done by jealous fishermen from Morecambe. The cod-ends or tails as we call them are of small meshed nylon and very expensive so again this cost us a considerable amount of money to replace them plus the time to stitch new cod ends on as well as one or two tides of fishing missed.

I remember going with Margaret's brother, Noel, in the 1970s, to nets which were set close to Chapel Island and had caught a fair quantity of whitebait but they were too small so we had to dump it. As I remember it, they were about 1½ inches long when they needed to be at least 2 inches. I did a rough calculation and said: "I have tipped out and left on the sand this week, whitebait to the value of the price of a new car." This was after having previously made virtually nothing for several months. I have pictures of whitebait nets

A whitebait net. As the tide ebbs and the end poles touch the sand, we see that it is just a large funnel

from that week and have shown them in my talks for forty years.

When a number of fishermen were catching whitebait, there had to be a quota or rationing system when catches were good because of the limited freezing capacity, therefore the only time one could make a good bit of money was if one could catch some before everyone else got started. When looking through some of the documents of Flookburgh Fishermen Ltd., I came across an item in the minutes of a meeting which says that a limit of 100 pounds per man per day or a maximum of 500 pounds per week was put into force one year in the 1970s. Although I have learned that one should never say never, it would certainly appear that the job is now finished so far as catching and marketing viable quantities because of the inability to freeze them in the way the markets demand.

In the 1980s and 1990s there were some good and some very poor seasons of shrimps but in those years there were never the amounts that we saw in the 1950s and 1960s.

There have only been two reasonable years of salmon in the last three decades and those were 1988 and 1989. Memorably good years were 1949, 1959 and 1966 (that is in the Leven). In the Kent, almost all years were good until the 1990s when numbers seriously declined. Since the arrival of farmed salmon the price is less than half what it used to be in real terms. Before licences were issued in the rivers Kent and Leven we used to catch nearly all our salmon on shallow bars in the rivers with a long-shafted garden fork with short, sharpened prongs. This of course was illegal; in fact it was illegal to take salmon here by any method.

Licences were issued in about 1954, to allow the fishermen to catch salmon with a lave net and this is the only legal method in our estuaries. Six licenses were issued for the Leven Estuary and eight in the Kent. It is much easier to catch them with the net than with a fork and also leaves them unmarked. With the fork there was always at least one hole through the fish.

I think it was in 1978 that there was a terrific run of salmon in the river Kent when the netsmen did extremely well. One day the eight licensees, between them, caught a hundred fish on a bar in one tide. Similarly, the most fish to be caught on a bar in one day in the Leven estuary was in the early 1970s when fifty were caught on a bar on the west side of Chapel Island – thirty in the early morning tide and twenty in the afternoon. Almost all of those taken in the morning were caught in the dark in the headlights of a tractor. The fish came down on to a very shallow, fast flowing bar, and as they were forced to turn and fight upstream they splashed. Those splashes shone quite spectacularly in the headlights. To catch this number was most exceptional. Usually, if one or two fish were caught it was considered to be a reasonable day and six would be a very good day.

I suppose it was in the late 1950s or early 60s that I designed the folding lave net. Until that time we carried a fixed-frame net which could be awkward, either in a cart or on the tractor. I had seen a man with a lave net in the Severn estuary who had a folding net in the shape of a Y, the arms of the Y being held apart by a short piece of wood which the man removed so that the net folded when it was being carried. I used to spend quite a bit of time in the smithy watching the blacksmith and can remember being there and trying to work out how to make a frame for a lave net which would fold up but have all its parts integral. This proved to be a surprisingly difficult problem. It looks so simple now when we are used to seeing it but it took many days to work out.

Through the years I occasionally had what we considered to be good days when I came home with ten or more fish which would include small sea trout and grilse. Likewise there have been times when I have gone out day after day for up to a month looking for salmon and caught nothing. On one particular day in the late 1950s, Father and I had pulled a boat from where we had previously left it, anchored at Skelwith rocks, up the channel to Greenodd to catch flukes with a flue net. It was a large rowing boat in which we also carried a draw-net (seine). On our way back down we remarked that there must be very few salmon around as we had not seen one leap all day. When we arrived at Procter's Point, to the west of Low Frith Farm, where there was always a deepish hole in the river he said; "Let's have a go at drawing, just for curiosity to see if there are any salmon." On the first pull we landed eighteen salmon and exactly doubled that figure with two more sweeps. This was with an old cotton draw or seine net which was nearly rotten and certainly had many tears in it. I believe that if we had we been in possession of a decent nylon net we would have caught hundreds of salmon on that day.

I have been prosecuted six or seven times in my life for illegal fishing and all except one of these occasions involved salmon fishing in one way or another. The exception being the bringing ashore of unriddled shrimps in which instance I was in court with half a dozen others. This is not a record of which I am proud but most of the incidents happened whilst carrying out my normal job to the best of my ability which meant doing as much as I thought I could get away with. On only one occasion was there actually fish involved, the other offences relating to fishing with wrong gear or at the wrong place. Looking back now I see that it was daft because there was certainly no great financial incentive, just the thrill of catching salmon.

On the last occasion that I was booked, I had some nets set to catch sea bass on the east side of the river Kent but half a mile east from the river channel almost halfway out between the river and the salt marsh in front of Carnforth. I used to go to those nets twice almost every day, which meant crossing the River Kent during the night regularly as well as the day tide. It was a Sunday afternoon and I had simply gone across to escort a large party of cross-bay walkers on a walk for the charity, Cancer Care. If it had not been for that walk I would not have been on the sands that day. I rode past the net, not intending to stop but saw that there was a small salmon in the net. When I went to pick it up I thought that it looked odd because it was just caught by its mouth and was lying on the sand but there was no impression of the shape of the fish in the sand. They usually flap around a little as they settle on the sand, thus making a depression the shape of the fish. There was also the fact that it was stiff. I wondered why it was stiff. If it was fresh that tide, it should still be soft and supple. If it had been in from the early morning tide, the birds would have pecked at it or there may only have been bones left. In spite of this, I put the fish in a box to take home.

Four hours later when I had taken the walkers to Grange and arrived back at the end of the road at Holywell, Humphrey Head, the bailiffs were waiting. One of them stopped me and said: "Where's the fish", indicating that he knew that there was one. His companion came along to the tractor and the first bailiff said: "Can you identify this fish?" After looking in its mouth, the reply was: "Yes." They had been out to the net before I got there and planted the fish in the net with a piece of silver paper or similar in its mouth to identify it.

They deliberately chose a Sunday to set the trap because one is not allowed to catch migratory fish under any circumstances on Saturdays or Sundays. If it had been a weekday it would have been impossible to prove that I didn't catch the fish legally. I landed up in court at Lancaster and was fined a hundred pounds and about three or four hundred costs against me. When I went to court I had been retired five months. I pleaded guilty because it was an offence to bring home salmon on a Sunday and in any case who would have believed the true story. There have been several cases lately of police officers and others being suspected of involvement in fraud, conspiracy or other crimes, who have suddenly retired and therefore could not be prosecuted. Should this rule have applied to me?

Having mentioned the Cross-Bay Walk, perhaps I should add that for more than thirty years I escorted groups of sponsored walkers across the bay for various charities. The numbers of walkers varied between 100 or, on a couple of occasions, as many as 250. Some of the walks were from Hest Bank to Grange-over-Sands, a distance of about 8 miles, and some from Silverdale to Grange which was a leisurely stroll that took no more than an hour and a half. The old traditional route across the bay was from Hest Bank to Grange-over-Sands then overland to Flookburgh and, if so desired, the following day across the Leven estuary to Ulverston.

•

In June 1966, I and a group of fellow workers from the Glaxo factory walked directly from Hest Bank to Ulverston, crossing the rivers Kent and Leven. We did this just for the challenge. We had to cross the Kent two miles out from Hest Bank as early as the ebbing tide would permit and walk briskly the nine miles or so from there to the Leven before the next tide flowed in. The total distance was fourteen miles. Three or four miles of that walk were through what we call caff sand. Caff is the local dialect word for chaff, so caff sand is soft chaff-like to a depth of maybe six inches but hard underneath. There were some aching legs at the end of it. We were pleased to come ashore close to the Bay Horse pub at Canal Foot, Ulverston where friends were waiting with liquid refreshment.

•

I'm sure it would be true to say that in the salmon season, for every time I came home with fish there were about five or six days with nothing. In nearly fifty years of fishing I could certainly count on the fingers of one hand the number of years when I have made any money from salmon but it is a pleasurable and sporty occupation if there are some fish running. As long ago as 1959 at a time when the shrimpers were making a reasonable living in the month of May, I had given up that particular job to try to catch salmon. I had caught a couple of salmon early in the month so I thought there could be enough around to make it worthwhile. I stood in the channel with a lave net almost every day for a month without catching anything. Jonathan Butler had gone from Allithwaite to Canal Foot, Ulverston, to stay with his son, Alfred, for a few weeks. (Alfred was a fisherman and guide across the Leven sands.) He could see me standing in the channel, a mile from shore, so he walked out and stood with me for a while. During the general conversation he said to me: "Tha's gitten salmon fever." What Jonathan said was true and I realise now that I was afflicted for the rest of my working life. Luckily things did improve later in that season as salmon became quite plentiful in July.

•

My father said that he did not remember there being mullet in the bay when he was young and yet there were great shoals of them in the 1970s and 1980s. In the 1950s and 1960s we used to catch odd ones or perhaps half a dozen in the nets which were set for flukes but we often threw them away as we didn't know where to sell them. It may have been the late 1960s or perhaps 1970s when we started to catch mullet in quantities and were able to sell them. In very warm weather mullet come out to the very edge of the channels, probably because the water is much warmer where the sun heats through it and particularly when the tide creeps back on to the warmed sand. At low water and just for perhaps an hour of the rising tide, as it comes over the heated sand, the mullet swim around in just a few inches of water and can be seen - sometimes so shallow that the dorsal fin is above the water. We then shoot a long net round in an arc, paying it out off the back of the tractor to surround as many fish as possible and drag them out. As the net is being pulled to shore, some fish jump over the net, whilst others try to swim round the ends. They are extremely lively and fast swimmers so it is certainly very sporty. In the 1970s and 1980s there were times when there were large shoals to be seen but this was, as I have stated, only on the hottest of days and mostly when the tides were low.

There have been catches of nearly a ton but the most I caught, along with another person, was about eight or nine hundred pounds. The fish are tangled or gilled in the net and are often difficult to remove so it is almost impossible to remove hundreds of fish and have enough time for another drag and in any case it would have to be in a different place because on being disturbed those left simply disappear into deeper water. If great numbers of fish are caught in the net, the only option is to haul the net on to the tractor and remove them at home. Since the 1990s there have been boats continually drift-netting up and down the channels day after day until there are few mullet or bass left. In fact I rarely hear of anyone catching mullet or even trying to catch any.

I suppose it was the 1980s when we started to catch a few sea bass and found that they were almost ten times as valuable as mullet and there was always a ready market for them. In 2008 and 2009 I caught more bass than I ever caught before I officially retired. Most of the sea bass were between two and four pounds in weight but in September 2007 I caught one that was 11½ pounds. In the 1950s, the licensees in the Kent used to catch a few salmon around Easter time and certainly some in May but now no one even tries until June or July as it has proved worthless until that time in recent years. Salmon fishing here is now a sport or recreation rather than a job and for me it has always had a fascination. I know several anglers who go fishing for salmon and it seems to become a complete obsession; they can scarcely speak about anything else. I suppose that was how I was in a way but perhaps not so extreme that I had no other conversation. When I was young I even used to dream about salmon and looked forward with eager anticipation to the next season although very few years have lived up to expectation, especially in the Leven where my licence applied for forty years. I was allocated a licence in the Kent in 1994 after fishing the Leven for all those years. The last year in which I took out a licence was 1997, after holding one for about forty-four years or from the time they were first issued.

*

Our grandchildren when they were young liked to go out fishing with me in summer. One day in July 1989 when Ryan and Tim, who were only about six years old, came to a baulk net with me there was a grilse of about six pounds in weight, swimming in front of the baulk in a pool which was, I suppose, a hundred yards long and ten inches deep. I said: "Go and catch that salmon," thinking they hadn't a hope in hell of catching it. They went with Tim's small butterfly net that had a mouth of only about eight inches diameter but soon were shouting that they had caught it. One of them had placed the net over the fish's snout and the other grabbed its tail and dragged it out of the water. I was most surprised because I know that without a lave net I would have had great difficulty in catching it. I wish I'd had the video camera that day, it would have made a nice little item in the library of film I have collected on the various activities in fishing or a section in the lads' videos of which they have had their lives recorded periodically from birth.

*

The main occupation of all local fishermen since WWII has been shrimping. It is my belief that without shrimps there would now almost certainly be no full-time fishermen in Flookburgh. There have been, as I have indicated before, good periods of cockling and musselling, but these have been spasmodic whereas one could, up to now, guarantee to catch a few shrimps every spring from about the 20th of March until late June and good quantities from the end of August until mid November. In the 1950s, 1960s and early 1970s I could borrow money from the bank to buy a brand new van or car, pay it off by Christmas and still have enough money to keep us through the winter. I'm fairly sure one could not say that today.

For the first time in living memory there have been cockle beds on all the shores around the bay. There have been cockles on the sands off Aldingham, Bolton-le-Sands, Flookburgh and on the sands south of Heysham, known as Middleton Sands. Some of the young people now seem to think that this will carry on and that the rich pickings from cockles will continue. I think it is a temporary blip and that shrimps will always be the mainstay.

Because the cockles have been bringing good prices there has been a great invasion of cocklers from various parts of the country and even gangs of Chinese who are brought here by gangmasters. A licensing or permit system was introduced by the fisheries authority but anyone could apply. The last information I had said that over 700 permits had been issued by February 2004.

In the afternoon of the fifth of February 2004, twenty Chinese, including three women, were drowned as they were trapped by the tide at about 8.00 pm. They had been taken out about a mile and a half from Hest Bank and left to rake up cockles but the people who took them out left it too late to bring them back. Stephen, myself and two people who worked for Stephen were out there on that afternoon but were back on shore at 5.45 pm, at which time it was almost dark. We expected that the Chinese would be brought off soon after but it didn't happen and they were cut off from the shore as the tide came up a channel which was a few hundred yards offshore. There was a fairly strong, perhaps force six, south-westerly wind blowing and the sky was heavily overcast but visibility was reasonably good. Any experienced fisherman who had consulted the tide tables and carried a watch would have had no trouble in getting back to shore in the dark. The trouble was that the people who took the Chinese gang out on the sand had no real knowledge of the sands or tides.

My son Stephen and grandson, Tim, left home at five o'clock next morning to search for bodies - they found six before daylight. Stephen and I were among the many people summoned to give evidence in Preston Crown Court at the trial of the gangmasters. There were some heavy fines and a jail sentence handed down to people held responsible for that tragedy.

The cockle beds were closed in May 2008 because the stocks were almost depleted. It was hoped that there would be new sets or spats of young cockles but none have materialised as yet. Great quantities of tiny cockles were spawned in the summer of 2009 but they all died through reasons unknown to me. The autumn of 2009 was extremely wet and some people are saying that was the reason for the death of all the young cockles. If that is true, it is a new one for me; I've never heard of that in all of my 83 years. Throughout my lifetime, and perhaps never, were the cockle beds closed by the Fishing Authorities until about the year 2004.

Now, in 2016, the beds have been closed for eight years and it looks as though they may open this year, not because of any great quantity, but because there are just a few large cockles that will almost certainly die if left for another year. Having said that, I can now say that a good quantity of cockles spawned in last summer and, if they survive, will probably be ready for harvesting in 2017. I believe that until the powers that be enforce the use of riddles so that the small cockles are left to grow, cockle fishing in Morecambe Bay is almost bound to be spasmodic.

•

Many times I have said publicly, either in the press or on television, that far fewer shrimps are caught than was the case thirty or forty years ago. Not everyone agrees with this so I will now try to show what the difference is between the present and those earlier years.

On either the last night of September or the 1st of October, in about 1955, a Saturday, I was in the Hope and Anchor pub with my cousin, Colin Jones, when I remarked that I was going shrimping at 11pm that night so he said he would come with me. The state of tides and time of year were perfect for good catches. We went a long way down the west, hoping to catch big shrimps. There were very few in that particular area so we came back up, probably a mile and a half north to a small hod or channel that I knew about. In this hod there were so many shrimps that we filled the cart to capacity in about an hour, half of that time being spent trying to fit them into the cart. We stacked the boxes round the side of the cart and tipped shrimps loose in the middle. Eventually we had loaded so hard that the cart was piled high, and the horse, (old Bob) could hardly drag it. In fact we could not get the net along the cart for the homeward journey. It was early Sunday morning when we arrived home and we boiled and riddled for about six hours. At that time we brought all our shrimps home unriddled and we only had a hand riddle and a coal-fired boiler. They were not very big shrimps but nice quality when riddled so we had something like ninety quarts or 130lbs when peeled, and a huge pile of riddlings (small shrimps) to be dumped. This catch was with a horse and cart and one 14ft. wide net.

In the autumn of 1958 I was working over on the Furness side, down near Newbiggin, along with uncle Bill Butler and a couple of other fishermen who lived over there. (There were no part time fishermen over there at that time). I remember the year because it was at the time that Princess Margaret opened Cartmel School. The main channel was less than a mile from the coastal road and shrimps were very thick (plentiful) and were a good size. We used to go out and load up with up 70 or 80 quarts day after day whatever the tides were like. Sometimes on neap tides the channel was very deep so we could only trawl along the edge on a fairly steep bank. The horse could be in four or five feet of water just a few yards in from the edge of the channel. We were by that time using mechanical riddles at home and I had made one which in normal times was far too wide in the mesh but I used this to make the shrimps into cobs as we used to call big shrimps. We could of course work both tides in the day if we wished – and very often did.

I think it was the spring of 1957 when my father and I first went shrimping in the Mussel Hollow. It is, or was, close to the mussel scars off Rampside or Whitehall, down off the Furness peninsula at the place where I earlier told the story of losing a trailer and gear on the telephone cable. Nobody had ever been in there with a horse and cart because it was considered unsafe through the presence of gooey boulder clay into which horses could sink. If there is a covering of a few inches of sand over the clay it is usually safe. When we first went there it was the spring season and not much good for shrimps in that region but when the autumn came it was a different story. In the month of August, when the weather was warm, calm and sunny Father went in there to give it another try. With those conditions, one would have thought it most unlikely that there would be any shrimps in a still, tideless hole but he caught fifty to sixty quarts of big, clean shrimps in little time. I was working at night as I thought it would be cooler and better in that warm weather. Setting off in the evening at about 9pm, I naturally went into the Mussel Hollow anticipating a good catch. There was virtually nothing! The next day, because I believed there would be no shrimps over there, I told Father he might as well take my spare horse and go shrimping from Flookburgh. (I had a horse at home and one over on the Furness side). He remarked that he might as well go over there again and take a chance. A few hours later he rang home and said: "Light both boilers", i.e. his and mine, so that the shrimps could be boiled more quickly before they died. (Shrimps have to be alive when they are put into the boiler or they will not peel). He had loaded up again. I could hardly believe it because at that time if one could catch a lot of shrimps through the day, one could always catch some at night or vice versa.

From that time we caught good quantities throughout the autumn, even though at least fifteen men went over there to work in what was a quite small area of water. I know this was 1957 because early one fine morning in that autumn, whilst it was still dark, I had just finished shrimping and had come out of the channel in which I had been working and was making my way to the coastal road where my horse was kept. By chance, I came across my father who was taking flukes, plaice and a few cod from his nets. This was a baulk net that was set out on the sand just a few hundred yards west from the channel where I had been shrimping - a mile out from Moat Farm, Aldingham. He kept stopping from his work and looking up to the sky. I asked him what he was looking for. He said: "A Russian satellite." I had not thought of such a thing or perhaps did not know it was coming over this way but it was in fact the historic Sputnik, the first man-made object ever to be launched into space to orbit the earth. It was launched on the 7th of October 1957. I can't remember if either of us saw it.

One of the things which I often think of and which dates back to the 1950s and 60s is the fact that when we were travelling home with boxes full of shrimps, either in a cart coming up the bay or in a van coming from the Furness side, when one hit a bump or any roughness, the shrimps on top of the boxes would start to jump around as if the whole lot had decided in an instant to move. The noise was quite loud, like the sound of rustling of crinkly paper - or of heavy rain. This would only last for perhaps, at most, fifteen seconds but there would then be shrimps scattered all over the van or cart unless the boxes were kept covered. I have not seen this happen, so far as I can recall, since we worked with horses. Is it the fact that we work with tractors or that we no longer catch the large, crisp, clean shrimps that we did then?

When we started shrimping with tractors, shrimps were plentiful every autumn, so with two nets one could often come home with huge amounts, although catches, even then, varied tremendously. Throughout the spring of 1971 there were hardly any shrimps at all, so bad in fact right down the west coast that there was a news item on the subject in which I appeared on the BBC Television's Northern News about the situation. We could catch about a bucketful or, put another way, something like six pounds of peeled shrimps per day which was hardly worth going out for. That being so, as I have written later, in the chapter on boats, I spent quite a bit of time learning to sail. When the autumn season started, things were little better but in October there came a period of southerly winds, sometimes strong and sometimes just moderate but which continued for a couple of weeks. Shrimps came into the bay in good quantities, from whence I know not, but over the following month or more I regularly caught between sixty and a hundred quarts of big shrimps in a place called The Goldmine.

On Monday the 2nd of December of that year, as the season here was declining, I took a tractor to Southport where there were tremendous amounts of shrimps. On the first day there I caught about fifty quarts which was much less than the other twenty or so fishermen because it was a completely different way of working for me. The next day, having learned a little, I had about ninety quarts. On that first day one man said that he had run out of boxes and therefore had to come home early. I remarked that it would never happen to me, but it did, and on more than one occasion.

On the Friday of that week, the 6th of December, my nephew, Mitchell, came with me to Southport. It was about four o'clock in the afternoon when we started trawling which was of course just about dark. It was a calm, fine but rather misty evening, and as we started to trawl we could see shrimps jumping out of the water in front of the nets. I was using two fifteen-foot nets straight behind the tractor in not much more than a foot of water. Within a few minutes both nets contained good quantities. There were so many shrimps that Mitchell just walked along beside the nets and lifted tail or cod-end out of the water every few minutes until he could see that we had as many as we could manage to empty into boxes. We loaded up with as many as we thought we could transport home. It took us some time to stack everything so that we could get the nets along the rear mudguards. I think we had about 12 boxes and some in the nets as we came back to base which was at a village called Banks, just to the north of Southport.

There were stacks of boxes on the backboard and on the front mudguards of the tractor. We travelled home with the Morris 1000 van packed solid with boxes and with sacks stuffed in every space down the sides, so much weight in fact that we broke a spring on the van. They were all good clean shrimps and we had 150 quarts, or about 225 pounds of peeled shrimps, which was by far the most I have ever heard of in this village in one catch. I recently worked out that if one were to catch that amount now, the gross value would be in the region of £2000.

Three weeks later, on New Year's Day, my friend, Alan McDougall, came with me to Southport when we caught 90 quarts, finished boiling at about eleven P.M. then went down to Ravenstown Club for a few pints of beer. I only went to Southport when the tides were ebbing well and not even then if there was wind from any westward point because being on the edge of the open sea it could be very surfy and in such conditions one cannot usually catch shrimps. Perhaps I put in 50% of days until the end of January or just into February, after which I finished with the best ever season, after having made practically nothing until October. There had often been good seasons at Southport but this particular year was exceptional. I went there again the following year but there were very few shrimps and there have not been any really good seasons since that time.

One night in December of that year, because the tides were too low for working at Southport, I went shrimping down the west here and came home with between 70 and 80 quarts, it was an exceptional catch for that time of year in this bay. On that evening I set off from home at about 7 pm and arrived back at 11 pm. This was at the time when shrimps still came out to the edge of the channels at night.

One of the main factors in this business of comparisons is the size of shrimps. We seldom see the very large shrimps which were common in the autumn seasons of thirty or forty years ago when one could catch several boxes of shrimps out of which one could occasionally end up with almost

Trawling for shrimps with a short rope between tractor and trailer;
the rest of the long rope lashed to the trailer   (1986)

100% after riddling and cleaning. There were, even then, great quantities of small shrimps at times, obviously, hence the good harvests which followed. When working among small shrimps, one can often end up with perhaps only 10% of the catch after riddling. This is often frustrating and hard work, hauling in great quantities then manually riddling away a large percentage. Legislation was brought in to enforce the riddling of shrimps out in the bay so that the small ones returned to the water thereby preserving stocks.

When I started shrimping we only had "tuppence ha'penny" riddles. This meant that two old pre-decimal pennies and a halfpenny together would just neatly pass between the wires. I only knew one person who owned a larger size and that was a man called John (Gog) Hodgson; he had a thre'penny riddle.

Occasionally, when we caught a great lot of shrimps, Father would send me down the street to borrow Gog's 3d riddle. After a few years we were all using 3d riddles. The difference in size was virtually imperceptible to the eye but it did make a difference to the amount of shrimps that passed through so that the remainder were more even sized and therefore faster to pick. Later on again we started to use slightly larger meshed "thre'pence farthing" riddles and this has been the norm from the mid-1960s to the present day.

Live shrimps, a crab and a tiny plaice

The practice in former years when working with the horse and cart, certainly until the late 1950s, was to just "crab-riddle" the catch whilst out in the bay and bring all the shrimps home, that is to put them through a larger riddle whereon the shrimps fall through and things such as crabs or flatfish remain in the riddle to be thrown away. All of the catch of shrimps was brought home, boiled and riddled afterwards. Eventually we realised that we were wasting time just sitting in the cart whilst fishing and also for at least another hour and a half when travelling home so we started to riddle the shrimps as we caught them and, if necessary, on the way home. This was a matter of expediency of course rather than preservation of stocks as later by-laws were meant to do. It did save time as it meant we had fewer to boil and most of the work was done. When the shrimps were cooked they only needed a quick shake in the riddle to remove a few more small and to sieve out small pieces of fish that remained in the catch and were broken up in the cooking.

Cooling of shrimps after boiling was traditionally done by thinly spreading them on hessian sacking. It was perhaps in the late 1950s that we made wire mesh trays for this purpose. Eventually I started to cool them by putting them into a net bag and dipping them in a bath of cold water. After washing they had to seep for at least a couple of hours to remove excess water but after this treatment they were cleaner and nicer to pick. Mechanical riddles came into use when tractors were first used for shrimping. Although we riddled what we could out in the bay, the great quantities caught at times meant that there was no way one could keep up with the riddling. Unlike working with the horse, one could not riddle whilst travelling home and to stay out there and riddle would often result in the shrimps dying, therefore rendering them worthless, they must be alive when put into the boiler otherwise they will not peel.

The smaller meshed riddles of earlier times meant that there was not so much waste. People picked shrimps that would be considered too small these days. Even so we did, at times, catch large shrimps, particularly at night. In short, shrimps that are peeled now are generally bigger than those of fifty years ago but only because they are riddled using a wider meshed riddle. To pick a quart (1½lb) in an hour used to be exceptional in the 1940s and 1950s. Now, two pounds per hour is common. I can remember the day, in the1950s, when Jim Benson shouted to other fishermen as we headed out across the sand with horses and carts: "Audrey Dickinson's picked a quart in't hour today." Earlier in this book I have written that the most I have known anyone pick in an hour was three and a quarter pounds or just over two quarts. This was achieved in about 1975.

Size does matter, and particularly with shrimps, so far as picking them is concerned. Most of the people who pick shrimps regularly will accept whatever comes along, knowing that the person who caught them did the best he could on that day. Some people however could be rather selective, and if shrimps were small they would tend to have other pressing duties to perform. On one occasion, the aforementioned Jim Benson went to Ravenstown on his bike with a couple of tomato baskets of shrimps to be picked On arrival at a certain house, the lady, slyly eyeing the shrimps hanging on the handlebars and noting they were small, said: "I'm sorry I can't do any today, I'm doing the washing." Jim went home rather disgusted with this response and reported to his wife, Mary: "There's (sic) people washing today who've never washed in their lives." (tomatoes came from the wholesalers in wooden boxes or baskets with handles and held about twelve pounds. Lots of them came to the local men who hawked fish, fruit and vegetables round the countryside with vans).

•

In mid-November 1965 there was a rather prolonged period of hard frost. Shrimps disappeared, as they are wont to do in cold weather, and all the fishermen, including me, gave up and settled to do other things for the winter. I started working at the Glaxo chemical factory on Monday the 20th of December in that year by which time the weather had become very mild again.

On the previous day we went up to Distington in West Cumbria to see all Margaret's family and to deliver Christmas presents. When we returned in the evening we found that Thomas Butler from Newbiggin on the Furness side had brought a good quantity of big shrimps to see if we would buy them because he had hardly any pickers. I was rather perturbed by this as I knew that I had to start at Glaxo at 7am on the following day and finish at 3pm which was just the time for shrimping. I went to work that day but on the following day I went straight down the coast road after finishing the shift at Glaxo and caught a good lot of shrimps. This continued although it was at a difficult time with Christmas upon us and naturally no one wanting to pick them. We got picked as many as we could and put a lot into the fridge until the festive season was over. I carried on shrimping after Christmas as much as Glaxo shifts would allow. The main encouraging factor was that they were such big shrimps and I can remember old Tom Butler, known as Lile (little) Tommy) saying: "Thou's gittin' as many as thou's hed all this back-end." That was true, although this was about New Year and unheard of for us to catch shrimps like of that size and quantity at that time of year.

In the mid-1970s I was shrimping a long way down the west side, not in the Leven channel but in a hod or channel that was dry at the top end. This was at a time of year when shrimps would normally have gone but I was still doing very well, working alone and mostly through the night. This particular channel was quite narrow and I could work with the trailer hooked to the tractor or with just a short rope between tractor and trailer which is much easier than using a long rope. With that short rope I could shine a light from the tractor to see when the trailer came to the water's edge when I pulled it out. I was surprised that no one else came because fishermen in the same village usually have a good idea what the others are catching. At the same time as this I had some stream nets set for flukes away over on the east side of the bay, opposite Silverdale village so I had to go right across the bay to these after finishing shrimping. On the morning of the 23rd of December I had set off from home at about 3 am, caught about 45 quarts of shrimps which was quite exceptional at that time of year, then went to the stream nets, a journey of several miles to the east, where I collected four boxes of flukes. As I was about to leave for home, just as the first glimmer of daylight was appearing in the eastern sky, I could see something lying on the sand about 100 yards behind the nets. On investigation I found that it was a 19 pound salmon in perfectly fit condition. This had proved to be a very profitable morning and just in time for Christmas.

It was just after this, around the New Year, that I saw a most incredible tidal bore. There had been a terrific storm that had wreaked havoc at Morecambe, tearing up the promenade wall and flooding the whole sea-front area which I'm sure will be remembered and well documented. After the damaging storm, the weather cleared and the wind swung round to the north but was still quite blustery. I went to the fluke nets to find that they were badly shaken and damaged, it therefore took some time to straighten some and remove others which were too badly damaged. I was still there when the tide broke nearly a mile to the south, like a great white wall of water probably a mile wide and four feet high, roaring like a mighty waterfall with spume blowing off the crest in the very cold strong wind. I often see a tidal bore but have never on any other occasion seen anything like that. This spectacular event was caused by the fact there was a very high tide coming in and a strong northerly wind blowing against it. I wish I could have filmed it, it would have made a nice contribution to the film which I am trying to compile about all our fishing methods and different aspects.

These have been just a few examples of very good periods but I could tell of many extremely bad times when I have gone for weeks catching hardly anything - whole winters when there were no cockles so I didn't make a penny for four months or more. The main thing I wanted to indicate was that there were far more shrimps in general pre -1980 and that one could, with hard work and determination, make a lot of money (relatively speaking) in a short time, which seems no longer to be the case. The markets are now volatile, particularly since the company Flookburgh Fishermen Ltd. closed down. To sum up, I will say that before 1980 I often took more than 100 pounds of peeled shrimps a day and sometimes 150 lbs. to the Flookburgh Fishermen's potting factory. In the last few seasons in which I worked full time, say the early 1990s, I considered 60 lbs. to be a reasonable amount to take in and that would now be considered a good catch. Fishing has always been a fickle occupation in which I believe it was easier to survive in the past when life was simpler and expenses less.

The autumn seasons of 2012 and 2013 were disastrous so far as shrimping was concerned - catches were minimal. Stephen, along with his son Tim and Lynn's son, Matthew, were shrimping and occasionally I used to go down to the boiling shed to see how they had fared and I would say, quite truthfully, that I used to catch more than the three of them together were catching. In 2014, they took the tractors and all their gear onto the north side of The Solway and worked there because there were practically no shrimps and what there was were very small and didn't grow.

Surprise! Surprise! Right from the start of the 2015 autumn season the men caught good quantities of shrimps. By the beginning of September they were catching more shrimps than I had ever seen. Best of all, they were lifting only shrimps. When shrimping, one usually catches lots of crabs and very often great heaps of seaweed. At this time, it was only shrimps – very rare indeed.

On the 2nd of October I went with them just for the ride out. It was a morning of thick fog that didn't clear all the time we were out there. I rode on Tim's tractor as we trawled down the channel using a long rope between the tractor and trailer. Matthew was a hundred yards or so behind us and at times, because of the fog, we couldn't see him and we certainly couldn't see the trailers which were two hundred yards or more out in the channel. On the first trawl, both lads had about ten boxfuls each. We went back and did the same again with the same result. Stephen was working in the same channel but a little further north. He had the trailer hooked up to the tractor so was trawling in shallower water but still had good catches. Total amount lifted that day was over fifty boxes which was more than I'd ever seen. About a quarter of those shrimps were too small so they riddled out but it was still a very good result. Those sort of catches continued through September and October. Why that quantity after a dearth for several years?

*

Stephen came out fishing with me from a very young age. He first went shrimping, driving a tractor himself, in May 1964 when he was nine years old. Although I was there with another tractor along with several other fishermen, I know now that it was ridiculous, he was far too young. I remember the day so well because it was just a week or so before I was taken to hospital with brucellosis. When he was a few years older and was at Cartmel School we quite often went shrimping with two tractors. Sometimes I would be waiting at the school gates for him coming out and off we would go and often came back with very good catches.

Throughout the last twenty years or so that I was fishing I was usually the first to try to catch shrimps in the early spring. I found that I could often catch a good lot of shrimps as they first appeared in the bay after their winter migration; this was usually about the twentieth of March or whenever big tides occurred around that time. I have started as early as the tenth and occasionally it could be just into April. The best tides were early mornings at the height of the flood or spring tides - starting to trawl just as the first glimmer of dawn was showing. As I had not been in the channels for several months, I knew they had inevitably changed so I would go out on a trial run, setting off from home about mid afternoon which would be about five hours after high tide. I would catch a few shrimps but more importantly, look at the layout of the channel and assess where to start trawling when I next turned out. This would be early in the morning a few days later when there was an hour or more of daylight in which to work the last of the ebb tide. This meant leaving home at about 5am to arrive at the chosen starting point to trawl at first glimmer of daylight. The tide would be flowing back in at that point by about seven or seven-thirty so there was only time for a couple of drags.

I remember one particular year when I had done just that. I always prepared the tractor the previous evening, ready to jump on and quickly away in the early morning with as little fuss and noise as possible so as not to disturb the neighbours. On this occasion, when I was about to set off, I looked at the three boxes which I had placed on the tractor the previous evening and thought I might need another if there happened to be a lot of rubbish such as crabs or seaweed with the catch. As it happened there was a stack of four boxes jammed one inside the other so I just threw on the four of them. This proved to be a very lucky move. I trawled down quite a distance then pulled out to discover four boxfulls of clean shrimps in the nets. I went back to the starting point and trawled down again, pulling out just before the tide was due to return and this time there were five boxes. If I had taken only the three boxes that I had originally thought to do I would have been unable to cope with that amount of shrimps. With four boxes I could just possibly have managed. I could have filled the four on the first drag then if possible struggle the last lot on to the trailer in the nets.

On another occasion, in 1975, I had not started shrimping but my friend, Ben Woodhouse rang from Morecambe to tell me that he had been shrimping in the Kent channel with his boat that morning and had done quite well. I decided to give it a try the next morning, which happened to be Good Friday, the 28th of March. It was early morning setting off, in fact, just about the optimum time as I have described. The weather was very cold with a fresh east wind but I was determined to go. Although there was only a glimmer of dawn as I travelled a long way down the west, following the edge of the channel until I came to a shallow bar where the water ran, as always at such places, very fast. This was the first trip out since the previous autumn and the channels had changed completely over the winter so I had no idea just what the layout was. On reaching the end of this bar, the channel dropped into an ideal stretch of water in which to catch shrimps. That morning I caught what was a very large amount of big shrimps for that time of year, in fact, a good catch for any time of year, over forty quarts or about fourteen stones. The thing that really bothered me was the fact that on the following day, Easter Saturday of course, we had to go sixty miles north to Cleator Moor to a wedding. This meant that I couldn't go shrimping that day after having done nothing all winter and now had the chance to make a bit of money. We went to the wedding and no doubt enjoyed the day. The following morning, Easter Sunday, I arranged for my friend, Alan McDougall, to come shrimping with me. We went with two tractors and really loaded up with shrimps; we filled all our boxes and travelled home with some in the nets.

•

The price of shrimps increased slowly over the years but in fact this increase was much less than the rate of inflation except for one mad year from about August 1990 until the following summer when the price shot from about £3.50 per pound to something like £6.50 at the peak. This was fine whilst it lasted but when the bubble burst it was a shock. That £3 extra had been all profit and with that we had raised the price of picking by twenty pence per pound. Although the price of picking was probably due to go up, when the price of shrimps did collapse it fell to a lower level than we had previously received so in a way it was a double whammy. When the price was up there were virtually no shrimps taken into Flookburgh Fishermen Ltd. because that company could not afford the prices being paid by foreign buyers. After the price fell we paid members of the company £4 per pound and non-members a little less, which, as things turned out, was probably too much on both counts. The company was sold in 1995 because of the fact that there were only three members still fishing, all the others having died or retired. Three of us could not put enough product through to make the profit necessary to pay the running expenses. The company served its purpose well and owed me nothing.

•

There have always been plagues of various things such as jellyfish and seaweed that arrive in tremendous numbers and may come in any particular year or may not. Every year in the 1940s, 1950, and 1960s there were vast numbers of Moon Jellyfish which usually come in May. They are about two inches or less in diameter and through the summer grow to a maximum of about the size of a saucer - perhaps six inches. These are transparent or perhaps translucent, greyish in colour with four purplish-blue round marks near the centre. They have very little sting except if they touch tender parts such as the face or arms where they cause a slight irritation for a few hours. They sometimes come in such quantities as to make it nearly impossible to fish with nets at all whether shrimping or using set nets. When they did arrive in huge numbers the staked nets were piled up with them as the tide went out and many times were knocked flat and great holes gouged along the back side of the nets as is caused by any obstruction to the tide. I suppose it was the early 1970s when, surprisingly, they didn't appear. At that time I read in a newspaper about a great number of jellyfish on a beach at Redcar in Yorkshire and assumed, rightly or wrongly, that these were ours, having made a wrong turning somewhere. From that time forth there were none at all until June 1991 when quite a number came but stayed only a few weeks and even then only a small fraction of the quantity seen in earlier years. In 2009, there were great numbers again but they came in early June and had gone by the end of the month. The odd thing about this particular species is that there are always twice as many on the afternoon tide than on the early morning. One would think that with an almost inert object which appears to just drift, that with conditions and tidal currents equal on both tides they would float in and out of the bay in equal numbers on both tides. This is certainly not the case so one has to assume that they in some way made a decision as to where and when they travel. Jellyfish do swim but there is no way that they can swim against the fierce local tides which can rise more than ten metres and flow very swiftly.

Large transparent pearl-coloured jellyfish, which we call Cowkytes but I believe they are Barrel Jellyfish, come into these waters almost every year but in 1989 they came in millions, first showing up in mid-May. These can weigh up to forty pounds and can demolish rows of nets. This species again have only an irritating sting when touched on the underside but like most jellyfish have no sting when picked up by the bell or dome-shaped topside. Prior to 1989 I have many times seen perhaps thirty in a 200 yards-long net but I see from my diary that on the 25th of May 1989 there were 44 in a net, 71 on the 26th and on the 28th I wrote "Thousands of Cowkytes." There were up to twenty between each pair of stakes or iron bars which were four yards apart. They were lying on the sand everywhere. When the sun shone they were like mirrors glinting, sometimes from several miles away. I could go out from Sandgate, look west across the estuary, and see them shining in their thousands on the shore between Ulverston and Bardsea, as well as those which were scattered all over our sands. By this time it had become almost impossible to set nets out on the sands except odd occasions when the tides were very low so that not too much damage was done to the nets. Surprisingly, shrimping wasn't much affected because in the water those particular jellyfish are floating so the nets mostly pass under them but one did catch some. They remained in the bay, and at many other places along the west coast, until late autumn. Since that time there has been one other year when fair numbers arrived but nowhere near like those seen in 1989.

Several types of really nasty stinging jellyfish come into our waters at times. The worst of these, the Lion's Mane, is of a deep beetroot or burgundy colour. They can be a foot or more across, and have long, slimy, tentacle-like appendages on the underside which contain the sting. We usually see some of these in summer and autumn. In one year, which I think was 1988, there were considerable numbers. I had up to nine lots of nets set at any one time in that summer and there were often thirty or more per tide in each net. I was badly stung nearly every day in the process of taking out flukes and generally tending the nets. Bits of the slime would fly around when shaking out seaweed or would stick to the nets after having shaken out the jellyfish so I would also come into contact with this when handling nets to move them to a different place. This sting was bad enough on the hands, but on the face, particularly around the eyes, it was extremely painful and lasted five or six hours. This is just one of the many unpleasant aspects of our type of fishing. There are many others with which one has to contend.

•

In 2006, when I set some nets to film and record the baulk net and stream net, I caught two jellyfish that I could not remember seeing before. I might have seen them but when one is fishing for a living, one throws them out without taking any particular notice of them. I sent a photograph of those two jellyfish to the Natural History Museum in London to see if they could identify them. The reply was to the effect that they were probably young Lion's Mane but: "What a pity our jellyfish expert has just retired."

During the 1980s and early 1990s I campaigned quite vigorously against the spread and increase of nuclear pollution, pointing out that every fisherman who had died in Flookburgh since 1976 had died as a result of cancers of various kinds. My father was the first, then Alan Benson, Jack Butler, Leslie Butler and lastly, Tony Wilson. I had articles published in the press and made several appearances on television about the subject. When I wrote to the health minister of the time, the reply was to the effect that yes, unfortunately one in four or 25% of people these days can be expected to die from cancer. Here, among fishermen, at that time, it was 100%. The trouble is that however strong the circumstantial evidence of the cause of these deaths it is impossible to prove the case. In 1989 the father-in-law of a friend of ours was in Australia and happened to hear that the Perth News was closing down so he bought the very last publication of that newspaper, simply as a keepsake. When he opened it he discovered a story, with photograph, in which I was featured with the story about the cancers. This item was first published in The Observer in London.

•

On an October day in the late 1980s or early 90s I caught a lot of flukes at Plumpton Viaduct. Being reluctant to waste them, I decided to keep them alive in cages. I had some wire cages in which I successfully kept flukes alive to be collected by Manchester University. I brought the flukes home then put them in cages in the beck on Sandgate shore so that I could keep taking out a few to sell. When I went back after a couple of days, half the flukes were dead. I removed the dead ones and took out a few of the live ones to use. After a few more days I returned to find half of those remaining were dead and that most of those still alive had red ulcer-like sores on them about as big as my thumbnail. I reported this situation to various officials in the fisheries department at Lancaster and to a person at Northwest Water. I was told that the water in the beck was checked periodically and was always of an acceptable standard and that: "Fish kept in close proximity do develop strange habits through stress." Many times I had kept fish alive in cages with no ill effect whatsoever. I asked if we could have the water analysed. They said that would be too expensive.

I thought about this incident for several years then I saw a programme on television which reported on a similar situation in America where fish had died in their millions and mostly with the same sores as I have described. Fishermen and others working in those waters had become seriously ill, often with permanent disabilities. The problem was eventually proved to be caused by a bug that is washed into rivers from farmland and outfalls from farms. I am certain in my own mind that this problem in The Beck at Sandgate was the same as that in America where the people affected had great difficulty in convincing anyone that there was a serious problem.

Incidents and Accidents

There have been numerous incidents down the years, some heart breaking with the loss of tackle or tractors, and some frightening but all part of a job which, by the sheer nature of it and the environment in which it is carried out, must inevitably lead to accidents. The first incident about which I write, and of which I have memories, did not directly involve any local fishermen but a large trawler which came aground in the bay.

Snow in Cumbria (then Lancashire) in 1940

In January 1940 there was a tremendous blizzard which raged for nine days, stopping all road and rail traffic and which, as I well remember, left snow piled up to the tops of the hawthorn hedges. Father was working at the army camp and from there they could hear the ship's siren blowing all day on the 26th of the month, which happened to be Father's birthday. Visibility was about forty yards in the howling wind and snow but because the siren continued to sound on the following day the Commandant of the camp, (Brigadier Gover) consulted with Father to see what could be done to ascertain the source of the sounds.

At two o'clock in the afternoon, Father and Tom Wilson set off walking down the sand in the blizzard with visibility still varying from twenty to forty yards they headed in the direction whence the sound was coming. Both men were experienced fishermen who knew the bay very well. With some difficulty and in fading light they eventually found the ship, the Impregnable, about four miles out and, as I remember it, in a S.S.W. direction from what is now the Lakeland Leisure Park, or in the general direction of Blackpool. The crew were amazed, relieved and delighted to see two human beings because they had no idea where they were. They had already been battered by three rough tides and another was due in a few hours.

There had been some problem with their navigation system and had simply drifted into the bay. They were completely lost and of course had not seen any land since running aground. Over the next few days the fish from the hold, said to be worth £400, was carted to Flookburgh by horse and cart. The crew of twelve stayed with families in the village for a month. The skipper and the ship's cook stayed at our house. The ship had come aground on a high tide and in a south-easterly gale so they had to wait for the next set of high tides to float the ship - which occurred a month later.

The skipper, Kenneth Thompson, said afterwards that when he saw Harold and Tom Wilson approaching, he was so relieved that he would gladly have given them a thousand pounds if he had been in possession of that amount. I made one trip to the ship when they were carting water out there and bringing fish back, and I vividly remember being amazed at the sheer size of the vessel. The 86 feet long steam trawler was Fleetwood based at the time but Kenneth Thompson, one of a family of eight trawlermen, came from Lowestoft at the outset of war because it was too dangerous to fish on the east side of the country. I recently discovered that the ship was taken to Ostend to be broken up in 1957.

The trawler, Impregnable. (Jan. 1940)

In January 2008, when telling two of my friends about the incident, they said it should be written up and recorded. On the 4th of February 2008 I emailed the story and a picture to the BBCs North West Tonight programme. They were quite enthusiastic about the story and next day sent a reporter, Peter Marshall, with a camera. On the same day, Martin Lewis came to record the story for Radio Cumbria. Peter filmed me for over two hours and Martin recorded about 15 minutes. The result of all that was two or three minutes on television at 6-55 pm. and four minutes on Radio Cumbria at 8am The granddaughter of Kenneth Thompson saw the piece on TV and phoned the studio. We were then united on Radio Cumbria, me here at home and she from her home in Cleveleys. It turned out that her sister Janice had a holiday home in our street. On the 16th of February, Alison and Janice visited us at home and we had a very pleasant hour exchanging memories.

I remember the incident quite well and had already written about it when, in the summer of 1994, Dick Taylor of Southern Lakeland Nurseries gave me nine letters which were sent from Iceland by my father to his uncle, the Rev. Canon Samuel Taylor, with whom my father had been friends since boyhood. In one of the letters dated 26/1/45 (again, his birthday) he describes this incident in detail. Incidentally, from his letters it is clear that some of my father's time spent in Iceland was very traumatic because of the remoteness of the outposts. He reported that some men had to be removed because they could not stand the isolation.

•

There is a steep hill in Main Street, Flookburgh, only a hundred yards from our house. On a day when there was snow on the ground, my father and I set off up the hill on a tractor with the intention of tending to some whitebait nets that were set in the Leven Estuary. We had climbed more than half-way up the hill when the tractor, whilst the wheels were still turning in the forward direction, began to sledge backwards down the hill. As it picked up speed, we both jumped off. It eventually dropped back onto a patch of clear road where it regained traction and set off up again on its own. It travelled almost to the top of the hill then ran at forty-five degrees into a wall on the right side of the road. It stopped there with the wheels still churning on the snow. There were some trees growing at the side of the road so we took a tow-rope that was already fastened to the front of the tractor - put there for emergencies on the sands or for towing off on cold mornings - and tied it to one of the trees, switched off the engine and left it there for several days until the snow thawed.

Sometime in the 1970s I was shrimping in a channel called The Goldmine when one of the shrimp nets became stuck, with the result that the rope with which it was fastened to the trailer snapped and the net was left in about ten feet of water. There was a buoy attached to the net, so in the evening, when the next tide had ebbed, Stephen and I took a small fibreglass dinghy out to try to recover it. When we arrived at the edge of the channel there was still quite a strong tide running and about fifteen feet of water, hence no sign of the marker buoy. Whilst waiting for the flow of water to decrease, I rowed out to the region where the net was left, ready to pick up the float if and when it appeared. At a distance of perhaps two hundred yards I saw what appeared to be a small dark object of about two or three feet square, floating on the perfectly calm glassy water - not protruding above the water but at surface level. Just for curiosity I went to investigate. When I got to within a few yards of the object it moved and the whole area of water became a boiling mass.

Whatever it was, it certainly was gigantic and left the water over a quite large area in a turbulent state, just like the scenes we see on television around the great whales as they dive or surface. On thinking of it now, I cannot remember it breathing or blowing through a blow hole, so whether it was a whale or not I could not be sure but it gave me quite a shock to be so near in a tiny rowing boat. I should have thought it was at least thirty feet long. I would describe it as it says in the bible of the great animal that swallowed Jonah: "A Leviathan of the deep."

On a beautiful day in May during the 1980s I set off with a video camera to do some filming of birds on and around Chapel Island. As I went into the hill a hundred yards from the house the tractor had a fuel blockage and stalled. It was stopped in gear but there were no brakes on the vehicle so as I put my foot on the clutch, the tractor ran back down the hill. I released the clutch and the tractor stopped with a jolt with the result that the camera shot off the rear of the tractor and broke. I decided to carry on to the island to look at birds' nests. About half a mile from the island I came across a whale lying on the sand, still alive and breathing through the blow-hole. I knew it could not last long in that warm sun and the next tide would not reach it, even if it did survive that long. I touched it several times and considered what to do but there seemed to be no answers. The nearest water was almost a mile away so there was no way of moving it that far. The whale was, so far as I can remember, all black, perhaps seventeen or eighteen feet long and weighing several tons. I was so disappointed at not having the camera. It was a once in a lifetime occurrence that I would have liked to have recorded on film to add to the collection of pieces of local interest that I have accumulated. The whale died and lay rotting for several weeks. The very next day I went out to the island again to tend some nets and found a small marine mammal about five feet long, either a whale or a dolphin, I really don't know what it was. It was alive so I picked it up, placed it on the back of the tractor and deposited it in a deep pool at the island. When I went out on the following day I found it lying dead only a few hundred yards north of the island. Thinking about it later, I realised that it was almost certainly the calf of the whale, which obviously could not survive without its mother.

•

One spring morning in the late 1950s I set off with a horse to go shrimping to the Kent Channel. The weather was calm and hazy and looked as if it might come in foggy. The channel was at that time coming round the shore at Grange and Kents Bank, swinging south-east towards Bolton-le-Sands then going past the end of Morecambe Central Pier. I decided to go over Pigeon Cote Lane at Humphrey Head so that I could travel the half mile or so across the sand to the edge of the channel and follow it down to where I wished to start shrimping then back up to that spot on the way home if fog did come down. I arrived at the desired place and had only been trawling a short while when Jack Butler and Bob Dickinson arrived, having come via Humphrey Head point. We trawled a long way down so that when we finished we were not far from the top end of Morecambe.

We set off for home in the general direction of Humphrey Head Point but didn't hurry, just talking as we came. The incoming tide was a very high one and the weather was still hazy with visibility probably half a mile or so. When we arrived at a shallow channel which was not far from Humphrey Head and which dried out at low tide, we found that the tide had gone up past us so we couldn't make it to Humphrey Head Point. Bob panicked suggested we should try to gallop through the tide. I thought he would have no chance of getting through because the tide, apart from getting rapidly deeper, spreads out over the sand at an extremely fast rate and can, if the ground is flat, spread faster than one can travel through the water. I quickly explained that I had come over Pigeon Cote and if we hurried we could just beat the tide. Jack Butler, who lived in Allithwaite, was on his first trip with a new horse and knowing that there can be a very nasty muddy route to the rocks behind Humphrey Head he asked whether I thought it would be O.K. I said there was a patch of quite deep mud but we now had not much option but to go that way. The three of us came ashore safely but it was sheer luck that I had gone out via Pigeon Cote because if I hadn't I don't suppose we would have dared risk coming in that way and would have been in a predicament. There's no doubt we could have walked ashore at several places between there and Kents Bank but could not have got the horses off the sands.

On another occasion I had gone over Humphrey Head via Pigeon Cote Lane with my big horse Bob. On arrival at the edge of the rocks I thought that the sand looked to be sound enough so I didn't get off the cart to test it but drove the horse straight out. Old Bob was soon striking down into sticky mud about eighteen inches deep. There was no way that I could turn him round because I felt sure that the horse would fall on turning as he could only just pick his feet up high enough to clear the surface so I let him struggle on. The river channel was only a few hundred yards out from shore so I thought if we could get to there it should be fairly hard. Bob ploughed his way through but was absolutely exhausted by the time we got onto firm sand. If he had gone down in that I have no idea how he could have been recovered because the whole area was a quagmire. It was an experience which dogged my mind for a long time and one which I would not wish to repeat.

In October 1982 I went out from Aldingham at 2 pm and crossed a channel almost a mile out from Bardsea to go shrimping on the east side of that channel to where we had been most days for a month or so. Alf Butler and Michael McClure also came across but went to another channel further east. It was raining with a moderate breeze from the northeast. I had one drag down the channel and caught one box of shrimps but by then the wind had increased and turned to due south, the sky darkening and a mist coming in. I went back to the top to start trawling again by which time the wind was at storm force and visibility less than a quarter of a mile. The wind kept increasing until the water was white with surf and spray blowing off it - an absolute hurricane. I decided to try to pull the trailer out of the channel and go home. As I turned the tractor out onto the bank, water was blowing across the sand where it should have been dry and visibility was then down to hundred yards or so plus the fact that it was very dark. The trailer came to the water's edge but the waves rolling up the channel docked the wheels into the sand and were pounding the trailer. It was extremely difficult to pull the nets to the trailer into that wind and I almost abandoned the lot. I did eventually recover all the gear and set off up to re-cross the channel but had difficulty finding the way as there was water blowing across the sand and visibility was very much as in fog.

When I arrived at the place where I should have crossed the channel, I found that the wind had pushed the water back up so that I could not get across at that point. There was just one possible crossing place upstream where I did eventually cross to my own side and to safety. I knew that Alf and Michael were still on the other side somewhere so I waited by the edge of the channel, wishing they would be coming as the water was still deepening. When they did arrive, Michael had all his gear but Alf had lost his trailer and nets when the towing rope broke whilst trying to pull it out of the water against the wind. We stood by the tractors and Alf, who was then, I suppose, in his 60s said: "I've been out in all sorts of conditions but have seen nothing like this." Michael left his tractor to walk to us and as he did so the tractor started to move backwards, blown by the wind. This had been a purely local phenomenon. We found that many large trees were down on the coast road but in Flookburgh they said there had been a strong wind but nothing like that. Later that afternoon, Alf took another trailer down the coastal road ready to use the next day and found that the storm had abated and the water receded again. The next day there were reports in the local paper of damage on the Furness Peninsula and a newspaper reporter had phoned the weather station at Eskmeals to see what strength they had logged and they said that; "Yes, there had been a quite strong wind of around 45 miles per hour. Having previously been out in winds which were known to be 70 mph, I know that on that day it was nearer 145 mph than 45, but certainly over a hundred. Alf spent some time over the next day or two looking for his trailer but he did not recover it. Of all the bad days and gales in which I have been out it was the only time that I have ever seen water come back into the bay when it should have been ebbing. Water was pushed a mile or more up that channel and raised the level by about five feet.

On an autumn afternoon in about 1979, I set off shrimping with two tractors. The man driving my other tractor was not a fisherman so he was absolutely reliant on me. We travelled south for three or four miles to cross the Leven channel then went westward for another two miles over a quite difficult route because it was a maze of small gutters and patches of shallow water which meant we had to meander. After arriving there, we set off trawling down with long ropes between tractor and trailer, he a few hundred yards behind me. As we trawled, I could see what looked like a fog bank in the distance, straight ahead, in the direction of Blackpool. I thought, or perhaps hoped, it might remain down there as there was no wind. However, it soon rolled up to us and when it arrived it was so thick that I literally could not see more than ten yards; it was some of the thickest fog I'd ever seen. As it enveloped us I could taste and smell chlorine. I turned to pull the trailer out of the water but the difficulty in fog is that one cannot tell when the trailer has arrived at the water's edge. I guessed the distance and, luckily, when I followed the line of rope back, found that the trailer was there at the right place, almost at the edge of the channel. I then hooked the tractor to the trailer and set off back up the edge of the channel to look for my companion. After travelling some distance I realised that I must have gone past him. I was then panicking as I knew that he certainly could not find his way home and wasn't too sure that I could. I did eventually find him and we hooked up his trailer and headed upstream to try to find our tracks for home.

By sheer chance I found the tracks and tried to follow them but, as I said, it was difficult terrain through patches of shallow water and a meandering route (I didn't have a compass). When we arrived at the main channel, almost two miles east from where we had been trawling, I was very relieved because, although we were still more than four miles from home, from there I knew the whole of the sand as well as I know the layout of my own village. We made our way home safely but it was a nasty experience, especially in the company of a man who knew absolutely nothing of the sand. If it had happened at night I suspect we might not have made it home. Fog is always a problem, even on familiar ground, but if one is on unfamiliar ground it is extremely difficult.

Almost certainly the worst incident that occurred because of fog took place in November 1958 or 59 and involved Uncle Bill Butler, his son Leslie and I. Uncle Bill and I had been shrimping a few times in a channel which ran from above Silverdale down past Morecambe where the river Kent had previously been running and we had done quite well. We were pleased with this as the season was well on and shrimps were becoming scarcer so we decided to take our horses over to Bolton-le-Sands to work from there. The river channel was then running close to Humphrey Head so to fish in this other channel one had to cross the main channel and then travel probably more than two miles east or south-east. Les and I set off across with the horses on a bright moonlit night at 2.30 am. of all times, when neither of us had ever been across to that shore before. We went past Humphrey Head Point and soon encountered Tom Wilson and his son Ted (real name Harold) who were at some stream nets on the edge of the river Kent. We exchanged a few words with them, saying what a nice night it was and so forth, then carried on.

Having crossed the Kent we headed in the direction of Bolton-le-Sands, talking quite happily as we went. It must have taken us the best part of an hour to cross the sand between the main channel and the one where we hoped to work during the next few weeks. We were nearing the far channel as the moon went down but at the same time a thick fog came down, as dense as I have ever seen. Before we left home we arranged with uncle Bill to come round with a van to collect us from Bolton and he said that he would walk out onto the sand when he arrived there to find a route to the shore. Les remonstrated with him, saying that there was no need to come out as we could manage well enough, but used rather stronger language than that. Just before the fog came upon us I had seen Bill's torch flash on the other side of the channel so we knew he was out there. After that time, as well as the fog, it was absolutely black dark. I was leading because Les had no idea where to go. As I drove the horse into the channel with the intention of crossing to the east side, I found that it was too deep. I came out of the channel and travelled upstream some distance to try again but with the same result. Luckily I had a compass and was used to navigating by it. The fog was so thick and it was so dark that, although Leslie's horse was as close to the back of my cart as possible, we could hardly see each other. After several attempts I did manage to find a place where we could cross. Bill, who could hear the sound of the horses wading through the water, kept abreast of us on the other side. Soon I could hear him shouting so we stopped to listen, only to find that he was saying; "Don't come across here, the sand is too soft." We then had to move still further north until he did find firm sand but by that time we had no idea how far north we were.

139

We headed out towards land and eventually reached the salt marsh, not knowing where we were except that we were somewhere between the north end of Silverdale and Bolton-le-Sands. We had no idea how to reach land because we didn't know where there was a track through the marsh. We considered things for some time but knew we had to move because the tide would come over the marsh and yet there was, as there usually is, a cliff more than two feet high all along the edge of the marsh and it was still two or three hours before daylight.

It was decided that I should set off across the marsh, eastwards to the shore and try to determine just where we were. To walk over that marsh at any time is difficult enough but in darkness and fog it was nightmare. Because of the deep pools and gullies, one has to constantly change direction so there I was with a compass in one hand and a torch in the other, wandering over the salt marsh. Every time I negotiated an obstacle I had to look at the compass to set a course again. Eventually I arrived at the shore, and, luckily, at a place where there was a farm right on the edge. There was a light on because the farmer had just got up to milk his herd. It was just after five am when I knocked at the door. When he opened it I said: "It might sound a silly question but can you tell me where I am?" I then explained our predicament. He said that I was near Carnforth and that we should make southward for perhaps a mile and a half to where we should, with some luck, find the track over which he travelled with a tractor to tend and move his sheep. Now I had to find my way back to the two men who were a mile or more out across the marsh, again by the compass. Luckily I found them fairly quickly by heading in roughly the right direction and then listening for their voices. We wandered along the edge of the marsh until we arrived at the track and into the lane at Bolton-le-Sands.

If we had not been experienced fishermen and used to navigating by compass or had not taken a compass, we may well have been drowned. On the other hand, if we had been on familiar territory we would not have had much difficulty but it still would have been unpleasant in fog so dense. As we were travelling home along the road it was just coming daylight and we saw double line markings in the middle of the road which were the first we had ever seen and were, as I seem to remember, only experimental. It was only in the 1950s that we started to use compasses installed in carts. They were about 6" in diameter and came from lifeboats which were broken up at Ward's, a ship breaker's yard in Barrow docks. They were luminous and were set into a hole carved in a board and the board placed loosely across the front of the cart and could be removed when not required or could be put on another cart.

•

One morning in the 1960s, I set off with my horse, Bob, to go shrimping out east. It was well before dawn but a fine moonlit morning as I made my way over what was known as The Bad Road across West Plain saltmarsh. The cart either hit a bump or a large pothole, of which there were many, whereon the cart tipped over. The horse was left lying in the ground and I was inside the upturned cart. My brother-in-law, Jack Rowlandson, and one of our friends were following down the track just a short distance behind and came across the disaster. I heard one of them say: "Where is he?" I shouted: "I'm inside the cart." They then eased one side of the cart up a little so that I could escape. One of the shafts of the cart was broken so my fishing trip was at an end. I went home then decided that, as my father was not going out that morning, I would commandeer his horse and cart. I went out to the west and, although late in setting off, arrived home with quite a good catch of shrimps.

*

Not long after we started working with tractors and long ropes between tractor and trailer I was travelling out on the sand in the direction of Morecambe and going quite fast with the trailer at the end of two or three hundred yards of rope and running at almost parallel with the tractor. I had not noticed that the trailer had turned slightly towards the tractor thereby allowing the rope to become slack. As the trailer slowed down and the tractor took up the slack it gave the tractor an almighty jerk, which almost overturned the tractor. As it suddenly lurched up on to two wheels, I was thrown off the tractor. I lay on the sand and watched as the tractor roared on, balancing on the two right side wheels for perhaps a hundred yards. As it righted itself, it turned slightly to the right and proceeded to travel at speed in a circle of about eighty yards diameter around me. On every circuit that the tractor made I was in the path of the rope which was at that time still heavy wire rope almost an inch thick and still fastened to the trailer. I had to jump over the rope several times as it came round. Eventually the tractor straightened up and set off straight towards Grange. I had visions of it going up Grange shore and perhaps hitting someone or landing on the promenade or perhaps veering off and hitting Humphrey Head rocks. I need not have worried. When the rope tightened, the trailer was at right angles to the direction that the tractor was moving and the effort of pulling the trailer round from the static position stalled the tractor. As I was sorting things out, my uncle Bill Butler, Harry Shaw and Matthew Couperthwaite came on the scene with horses and carts on their way to the shrimping ground. They, having seen something of the action but from a distance of half a mile or so, enquired what had been going on. It was difficult to explain! Still, that was a lesson learned and soon after this we started to use a short rope between the tractor and the trailer when travelling back up the side of a channel for another drag or from one channel to another. With the use of the short towing rope the long rope trails behind between the tractor and trailer, the drag on the long rope ensures that the trailer never comes alongside or ahead of the tractor but is pulled along at one side and slightly to the rear.

•

On the 7th of September 1985 I was shrimping alone in the Goldmine on a wet and quite windy Saturday morning. Having finished shrimping, I was running the long rope up the edge of the water when two fish boxes blew off the tractor. I stopped and ran to pick up the boxes but on looking round I could see the tractor going down. It was well and truly stuck so I had to leave it and walk home having left everything except two riddles, which I carried.

The tractor with axle torn off

As I set off to walk I could see two tractors a mile away, coming out of Lancaster Channel. I waved my oilskin coat but they had their backs to me, sheltering from the weather. Having walked all the way home in that weather in oilskins and thigh boots, I was shattered. Being probably more than two hours late in arriving home, I kept wondering why Margaret had not sent someone to look for me. It was not until I arrived home that I remembered that she had gone shopping to Barrow. The next day we went on a recovery expedition with two or three tractors and several men but in pulling the tractor out we tore off the front axle and did other damage. Obviously it was also full of seawater and sand. As we arrived at the marsh on our way home, Mitchell put his great foot in a box containing a fairly expensive camera. The box tipped up, thus depositing the camera into a pool of dirty water. The photographs came out all right but the camera was ruined.

•

In the spring of 1970, at the time that I was putting the finishing touches to the house, 63 Main Street, concreting paths and so forth, I got up on Easter Sunday morning and considered whether to go to church or go shrimping. No one had started shrimping at that time so as it was a beautiful sunny morning I decided to give it a go. I went quite a long way down the west and started trawling. Having trawled for a while, I pulled out near to where a small channel or gutter came off the sand into the main channel in which I was trawling. This channel was called West Dyke and had formerly been a large tributary where we caught shrimps but had slowly filled up. As the trailer and nets came to the edge of the channel I was away out on the sand and crossing this small channel, which was only a few inches deep. As the tractor went into this bit of water, it dropped off a brack or small cliff, only about ten inches high. This was no surprise nor was it anything unusual. I could see exactly what it was like as I approached it.

Unfortunately the draw-bar on the tractor was rather low so that when the rear wheels dropped into the stream, the draw-bar stuck on top of the brack, thereby literally jacking up the rear wheels off the ground. The tractor stopped with the front wheels in the fast flowing, although only a few inches deep, water. This flow of water rapidly scoured sand from around the front wheels until it was almost down to the axle. The tractor was well and truly stuck. I set off to run home, hoping to return with other tractors for a recovery before the tide came back. It took me an hour and a half to reach the Ponderosa caravan site from where I rang home for someone to come and collect me. By the time we gathered up two or three tractors and equipment and travelled back to the doomed tractor the tide was just covering it. We pulled it out the next day. That was the punishment for going to work on Easter Sunday, which I would not normally do.

*

I essentially gave up fishing on Sundays in the early 1970s, not for reasons of religion but simply to have a free day. I did occasionally go if circumstances were such that it was really necessary; particularly if it was just a short run to some set nets or the odd shrimping trip if I could be home and finished before lunchtime. This often meant that I had to go out alone at midnight on Sunday or some unearthly early hour in order to have shrimps on Monday whereas everyone else had caught theirs on Sunday afternoon.

On the 20th of December 1976 I went to some stream nets two miles south-west from Sandgate and almost didn't make it back. I had been working these nets, which were on a ridge between two channels, for about a month and doing reasonably well but flukes were becoming scarcer so I had set a net over by Lancaster Channel, over in the east, a day or two earlier just for a trial. This had caught rather more so I decided to move the lot over there. On Sunday afternoon, the 19th, I was going carolling round the farms with Flookburgh Band so Stephen went to the net out east. It being an extremely cold day with a strong east wind and the tractor's battery being doubtful, I put a brand new one on to try to ensure he made it back safely. I intended going to load the long length of nets in the west at about 3 am next morning but when the alarm went off it was blowing a gale from the east so I decided to stay in bed. By chance I woke up again at about five o'clock and the wind had dropped so off I went. It was a very cold dark morning with no lights showing round the bay. I pressed on and knew that by the time I had loaded most of the nets and stakes the tide must be near but was determined to have them all, although, having been in the sand for a good while, the stakes were extremely hard to pull out.

Whilst I was working, the tide came rushing through the nets. I jumped on the tractor and set off for home but there being no lights showing anywhere, I only had the direction of the flow of the water to guide me. Unfortunately the tide does not always run in the same, or rather the opposite direction from that on which it goes out so I headed a little too far west. At the time I set off, the water was already over knee deep so it was hard going for the tractor which, after only about two hundred yards, air-locked due to restricted flow in the fuel line. This had occurred several times before when shrimping but I had soon bled it up and set off again. If I had dared to stay two minutes to bleed it, things would have been all right but I was on a ridge between two channels and knew that I must be moving if I was going to survive. The water was already more than two feet deep as I jumped off and started to run whilst throwing off my clothes, first oilskins then boots, jumpers, in fact all except jeans and a T-shirt.

As I struggled through the water, which was soon up to my waist, I was breathless but knew that I had to press on. After about a quarter of an hour I was out of the water and onto sand but I could hear the tide running up a channel which came up past Cowpren Point where the river Leven had been the previous year and had left a quite deep 'old spot'. I kept jogging on although there were pains in my chest through exertion and complete exhaustion. I beat the tide to Cowpren Point where I rested for a while to recover, even though I was freezing cold, then walked to Canon Winder farm from where the farmer, Michael Philipson, brought me home in his Landrover as daylight was beginning to show. It was just before eight when I arrived home and would have liked to have gone to bed but I had to start organising things to try to recover the tractor when the tide ebbed again. As things turned out, I might as well have left it.

We went out, at about 3.30 in the afternoon as dusk was falling of course being Christmas week. We took two or three tractors. Alec and Tony Hornby came with their big Muirhill four-wheel drive machine - a rare thing on farms then. When we arrived at the site we could not see the tractor. It soon was spotted upside-down with just about a foot of one back wheel showing, the rest being under the sand. Luckily I had a nylon rope of about three inches diameter and thirty yards long which had come from a steamer on Windermere. Alec Hornby set his tractor's stabilisers down and we fastened the rope to his front loader and the other end to the wheel of my tractor which was above the sand and he slowly lifted the bucket of his tractor. To my amazement, the tractor began to rise out of the sand. Due to the tremendous tension on the rope and the stretch in it, as the tractor came up it was catapulted several yards and as it did so the new battery came adrift and shot through the air, breaking on impact. That day I lost a hundred stakes and iron bars, a dozen stream nets, a pair of waders, oilskin coat, trousers, jacket, jumper, some tools, a tractor, and of course my new battery. I reckoned nearly a thousand pounds worth, almost the price of a new car then - just through stupidity.

I need not have gone to move the nets at that time and in any case I was too late in setting off. As I was working I knew that the tide was due and could have left some of the stakes until another day. On the other hand, if the tractor had not had a fuel blockage it would just have been another day's fishing. The tractor was packed full of sand and although I worked on it for many days over the winter, trying to clean it out and repair it, when I had it running again it went one mile down to West Plain Marsh where it seized up and was scrapped.

When I was in the water on that morning I thought that there was no way that I could get out and that I was going to drown. Surprisingly, I was not afraid, just matter of fact thinking. My thoughts were that my father had just died in June, surely we were not both going to die in the same year. Then the thought occurred that I had in my pocket a bunch of keys which were for the boatyard and various other things. (more about the boatyard later) What would they who were left do without those? Certainly odd thoughts at such a time but I can assure you, absolutely true. If the same thing happened just a few years later I could not have survived it. Running or struggling in water is extremely exhausting. I certainly lost more money that morning than I had made from flukes or could have made in subsequent weeks and had all the work and stress of the incident.

•

One morning, probably in the late 1970s, I set off down the street on a tractor at 7 am but only got as far as Bill Robinson's house at 36 Main Street, when the tractor, which was travelling quite fast, took a sharp turn to the left and started to tip over. I was either thrown off or took a dive and landed in the road with a bang, injuring my right arm as I fell on it. The tractor carried on a few yards on two wheels then rolled onto its side, close to Bill's door. I was picking myself up but was very shaken and shocked when he came out to see what was happening. He invited me in, gave me some whisky or other spirit and a cup of tea. Tony Wilson and my cousin, Leslie Butler came on the scene with tractors so we pulled my tractor upright and off we went shrimping. When I arrived home my arm was swelled to double its normal size so at five o'clock in the afternoon I went to the doctor who said he thought it was broken so I must go for an X-ray.

This diagnosis was confirmed and a plaster was fitted from my elbow to the wrist but I kept on working although I wasn't supposed to. Three weeks later back for a check-up where a further X-ray showed another fracture that hadn't been detected first time round so the plaster was extended to include the thumb and most of the hand. Inevitably the plaster was wet every day therefore it disintegrated up to the wrist so I used to buy plaster of Paris at the chemist's shop and repair it. A few weeks later; back for another check-up, only to be told that there was a third break. I did not miss a day's work throughout this time whereas if I had worked for an employer I would almost certainly have been off for two months.

•

Soon after we started working with Nuffield diesel tractors, one developed a lot of play in the bushes of the front axle with the result that there was a lot of slack in the steering. Not having had any experience of renewing bushes I decided to replace the axle. I started to work on it after tea and finished it at about nine o'clock in the evening. I then thought that I would give it a run to see that everything was working correctly. It was then that I found that on turning the steering wheel to go left, the tractor turned right. With some difficulty I drove it to the Village Square but had the most awful time trying to get back home. I was desperate to go shrimping early next morning but had no time to change the axle back again. I thought that if I could get as far as the shore I would manage as there was plenty of room for error on the sand. I did go shrimping with the tractor as it was, and indeed carried on with it for several months and got used to it. Stephen was probably ten or twelve years old and he got used to driving it. One day as I took some shrimps to Ravenstown in the van, a car came out of Jutland Avenue, nearly colliding with me. I moved to take evasive action but having got used to driving the tractor with the steering the wrong way, I turned the wheel of the van the wrong way and nearly went through a hedge. I then realised the danger of getting used to the steering that way and decided I must change it back.

One incident which was particularly annoying was when I came home from shrimping out the east side on a very wet and windy Saturday morning in September circa 1980 and after boiling the catch, decided to have a quick run out to a fluke net which was set down the west, just to see that it was all right. When I drove off the shore near Redhill at Sandgate I drove into a great hole full of mud and quicksand which was so bad that I had difficulty in walking away from the tractor. It was only about a hundred yards from the bottom of the stony shore but the tide was coming before I could organise a recovery. I waited until the tide went out in mid-afternoon then tied about nine or ten fifty-gallon oil drums to it to float it out on the midnight tide. It is not easy to tie on drums securely with ropes because they slip as the tension is exerted by the rising tide and also there is stretch as the knots tighten. That very evening, Margaret and I were invited to Christine and Alan MacDougall's house for dinner so we had to leave earlier than we would normally have done to attend to the tractor. We had left a rope from the tractor to the top of the shore with which to pull it when or if it lifted. We went back at midnight when it was still a terrible night of wind and rain, having never eased all day. This weather was good in one respect in that it ensured a higher tide than normal, therefore giving more lift. A couple of drums had broken free but the tractor just lifted enough to free it from the mud. We were able to drag it out about twenty yards before it stopped and would not budge any further. Next morning, before the next tide came in, we went back and found that the tractor was stood on hard sand and simply needed towing away. It was only about a week later that Michael McClure went into the same place when he set off to take his tractor and trailer across the bay to Aldingham.

•

There is an episode on which I sometimes reflect and usually at these times I think how silly I was to embark on this trip. I was shrimping with a horse which was kept at Goadsbarrow Farm at the end of Leece Lane on the Furness Coast Road, as I did nearly every autumn from about 1957 until 1980. On a very foggy morning at about four am I went over there in the van, yoked the horse and set off out onto the coast road where, by chance, I met Alf Butler who was the guide for the Leven sands and lived at Canal Foot, Ulverston. We had a bit of a conference, the consensus being that it was too foggy to be able to work. It was still dark and although I could easily have navigated to the fishing ground it is impossible to work in still water in thick fog. If there is a fast flow of water it is as good as a compass.

The horse was only on the Furness Peninsula for the autumn shrimping season and this being nearly finished I decided that when the first daylight started to show I would take it home across the sands. I had a compass so I thought that if I could get to the Leven channel and cross it somewhere out from Aldingham I would wander up the east side of the channel then strike out north-east towards Flookburgh. I had not been in that area all of the autumn so I was not too familiar with the layout of the sand and channels. All went as planned and after crossing the channel I was coming northward up the edge of the water when I came across my father who was tending his stream nets. Knowing where I had been fishing, and should still have been, he said: "What the hell are you doing here?" I simply said; "I'm going home." I believe he thought I was barmy. He had come out over ground with which he was familiar, having travelled it day after day to his nets. This was almost certainly the same place from where he had taken 140lbs. of flukes from a net of twenty yards long of which I told in the chapter on Fishing Methods when describing stream nets. The reason for me setting off home on that morning was to spare having to go back on another occasion for the horse, thereby wasting another day. Looking back at it now I tend to ask myself the question -what difference would one day have made?

The mention of Alf's name reminded me of an incident which happened, probably in the early 1980s. Alfred and at least one other person were shrimping in a channel not very far out from Newbiggin village where a freshwater stream, known as Lennie Beck, (not sure of the spelling) flows from the shore. This stream is often treacherous with soft sand and mud, particularly in wet weather. The two men were working in that area and were crossing the beck when Alf's tractor went down in the quicksand. After trying and failing to pull it out, they resorted to the method described earlier – attaching large drums to the tractor to float it out on the tide. The tide came in and the tractor floated away up towards Ulverston. When the tide started to ebb it was obvious to Alf, who had been watching it through binoculars from his house at Canal Foot, thought it was going to float out to sea. He went out in his rowing boat, tied a rope to the tractor and proceeded to tow the tractor towards the shore. He was a modest man but after that he boasted that he was the only man in the world to tow a tractor with a rowing boat.

•

The final two incidents of which I will relate occurred exactly a year apart. Both happened on the 3rd Monday in November and on consecutive years. It was the afternoon of the 18th of November 1991 when I went shrimping alone down the west channel and had finished trawling at about four o'clock as dusk was falling. Having caught quite a lot of shrimps, I had pulled the trailer out of the channel to the edge and was coming back in to put the nets on and hook up ready for home. As I drove back, I pulled the towing pin out which released the long rope and as I arrived at the trailer I jumped off the tractor to lower the trailer's draw-bar whilst the tractor was still rolling slowly down the bank towards the water's edge. This was fairly normal practice for me. When the tractor reached the water's edge it was almost stopped, then started to roll forward again and within a few seconds it dropped into a deep hole only a few yards in from the water's edge. I ran and jumped on but was too late so while I was still on, it landed in five feet of water. It was a hole which I didn't know about even though I had worked there most days for the previous two weeks. I took a rope and waded in but the only place I could fasten it was round the top of a rear wheel, which was the only part above water. After putting the nets on the trailer I started to walk home via West Plain in almost darkness on a fine but cold night and into the face of a fresh east wind. When I was a few hundred yards from the point where the tracks from the east converged with those from the west near to West Plain marsh, I could hear tractors coming from Lancaster Channel. They were John Wilson and his son Michael who spotted me in the dim moonlight and came over to me. I explained the situation and they kindly offered to go and see if we could do anything. The tide was just starting to flow in when I had left the scene at least an hour and a half previously so of course when we arrived back there everything was well covered. The long rope was still fastened to the trailer so we pulled that out then went to tackle the tractor to which the other end of the rope was tied but, as I said, only round the top of a wheel. We moved it only a couple of yards when the rope broke. Stephen and I went out at about 2.00 A.M. with two tractors and heavy chains to try to recover it. It was a fine, cold, mainly cloudy but moonlit night.

When we arrived, we found that the tractor was just on the water's edge but down in a hole which the tide had scoured round it, even so it was a good thing that we had pulled it out a few yards the previous evening. I could see that the hardest part was going to be dragging it up the steep sides of the hole. We put a chain to it from each tractor and just managed to pull it out. There were now three tractors to bring home but only two drivers. A rope was fastened to the recovered tractor to tow it and it followed on its own all the way to the West Plain Marsh where we left it until morning when my brother-in-law, Jack Rowlandson, came with me to tow it home. I took the rocker cover and sump off, also removed the injectors and flushed the engine out from the top and underneath as I had learned from previous experiences. Radiator and all water pipes received similar treatment then put it all back and started the engine within four hours of arriving home. Once again, if I had ensured that the tractor was stationary before jumping off or if I had turned the steering wheel as I got off so that it ran along the edge of the channel, or even if I had left the rope on the tow bar, at least it would have come out when I went back with John and Michael the night before.

As I said, both happened on a Monday, the first was on the 18th of November and the next on the 16th because it was a leap year. I was shrimping again at the same place but this time it was a pouring wet afternoon. There were one or two gutters running into the channel down the steep bank which, with the rain, were very nasty. They were carved out like canals, with water teeming down into the channel -so bad in fact that I know that I should not have tried to cross them. Having already done so twice that day and wanting to catch the last possible shrimp, I thought I could do it again. I knew that when I had crossed the gutters I was on good level ground on which to pull out the trailer out of the water and prepare to go home. As I approached the last gutter I could see that the teeming water was carving a gorge down the bank but I thought I could edge into the channel and get round the bottom of it. As I tried to cross it, the tractor dropped into a gully two feet deep and only about three feet wide and couldn't rise out. This time the tractor was well stuck and the trailer, with three nets attached, was two or three hundred yards out in the channel. With the water pouring down the gully it soon dropped the tractor further down until it was hopeless. Again I was walking home, this time in daylight, albeit fading light of late afternoon. When I was perhaps three quarters of a mile from the edge of the marsh, some men who were working on a project to raise the sea defences saw me and picked me up in their Landrover and brought me home.

Stephen and I again went out at about 2 am on a recovery job and this time Tony Wilson volunteered to come along. By this time the weather had cleared but there was no moon so we had to look for things by headlights. The tractor was well down but the sand around it was fairly muddy or loose so with two tractors pulling, it came out. The next thing was to try to recover the trailer and nets.

We had taken a rowing boat so we went out with it and with much effort, because they had settled into the sand, lifted the nets on board, and rowed them to the side one at a time. Due to the fact that the night was fine with a light northwest wind, at low water the trailer was only in three or four feet of water so we could tell by feeling with an oar that it had settled down in the sand and was well stuck. The reason for this is that the tide scours sand from around any static objects which are on the bottom, dropping them down but then because of a slow ebbing tide it had filled the holes with sand again, thereby fastening it solid. We gave it a few pulls but with no success so we left it with some ropes and marker buoys with which to lift it on the afternoon tide. Stephen and I went back in the afternoon with some barrels which we fastened on at low water so that the rising tide would lift it out. As the tide rose, the body of the trailer was lifting slightly but only the body because the ropes were fastened above the springs and the wheels and axles were well and truly stuck. We hung around for perhaps two hours watching for a movement of the barrels which were being pulled almost under the water even though they had tremendous buoyancy. The strong north-west wind and rough showers were also helping to free it. We had a rope from the trailer out to a tractor on the bank and I knew that as soon as the trailer lifted it would swing out in an arc to the water's edge. The tide was only about two hours from high-water when it suddenly lifted and we were able to pull it out, hook up and come home with nothing lost but having caused a lot of work and again having to wash out the tractor's engine. On this occasion, even if there had been other tractors on the scene when I became stuck, we could not have pulled it out. A bit more care and the sense to come home without having to have that extra drag would have avoided all that.

•

In 1964 when I was in hospital suffering from brucellosis, Thomas Butler from Newbiggin, who was a second cousin and a couple of years older than me, rolled his tractor over on the sand about two miles out from Baycliff and was trapped under it. His uncle who lived on a hill overlooking the bay could see the tractor, did not know who it was but wondered why it had been stationary for a long period of time and yet no one could be seen near it. He sent someone out to investigate and they found Thomas who had been trapped for a couple of hours. He landed up in the same hospital as me but soon made a full recovery. If he had been in a position where he was not visible from the shore or his uncle had not been interested in what went on out there or if it had been dark, then he would have been trapped until the tide came back and drowned him.

One morning in about 1969, Stephen and I were due to go shrimping with two tractors. I got up at five am and just before I left home I woke Stephen and said that I would go to the fluke nets and he could follow on in about half an hour. I took the fish out of the nets and carried on to the shrimping ground but Stephen didn't arrive. I was rather annoyed because I thought he had probably gone back to sleep. On the way home I saw my father at his fluke nets, went towards him and asked if he had seen Stephen. He said; "Stephen is the luckiest person in the world." As he drove along the road to Sandgate Shore, for some inexplicable reason the tractor had suddenly swerved off the road, gone through a wall and over a drop of about seven feet into the field opposite Sandgate Bungalow. It dropped down close to the wall, still in the upright position. Why it didn't roll is a mystery. I feel sure that it couldn't be done again in a thousand attempts. He was unharmed except for bruising and severe shock. What might have been did not bear thinking about. He would be fourteen or fifteen years old.

As mentioned earlier, I used to go to Plumpton railway viaduct to work with a small boat in the deep holes on either side of the bridge. On one occasion, which was almost certainly in the 1960s, I was there late at night along with three amateur fishermen, Eric Wilding of Ulverston and two brothers, namely Myles and Bill Haddow. The brothers lived with their parents in a house which used to be at the west end of the viaduct but was later demolished. On the night of this incident we had been working with flue nets, trying to catch salmon as we did regularly every summer. The incoming tide was due back at the viaduct just after midnight so I left the scene to go home shortly before it was due. We were working at the south side of the bridge so Myles and Bill waited for the tide to drift them through the opening to bring them to the north side where they moored their boat. Having said that I am not sure whether Myles was in the boat or had walked up to the mooring to wait for Bill. The next morning at about ten o'clock I went up to Old Park and walked down to a net that I had staked out on the sand just a couple of hundred yards north of the viaduct. When I arrived there I could see several people, including policemen, walking about along the railway on the bridge. I approached them to enquire what was going on and was told that Bill Haddow had been drowned on the previous evening. For some reason unknown, the boat had capsized as the tide came in and he was thrown into the water. I believe he may have become entangled in the nets as they fell into the water. The brothers had built the wooden, clinker-constructed boat themselves and it was well known that it did not have enough freeboard so perhaps this was a contributing factor in the capsize. A catalogue of incidents, some avoidable, some inevitable and some tragic.

As sure as can be, as long as men work or play on the constantly moving sands and channels, there will be accidents. Thankfully, not as many these days as there were before the construction of the railway, when one of the main routes from Lancaster to Ulverston was across the sands. Drownings were frequent and many times it involved travellers in horse-drawn coaches who were all lost to the tide.

Horses

Again, on this subject there are countless stories that I could relate - as one might expect after the forty-odd years and around twenty horses that this chapter covers but I must select those that are most memorable. From about 1920 to 1939, Grandfather Jim Butler had only one horse. It must have been an exceptional animal because for years after it had departed, whenever a new horse arrived we were informed that it couldn't compare with old Tom. I remember the horse but I was only a small boy when it was here so I could not compare it with the other seventeen or eighteen that came along between that time and the demise of horses on our job. Tom was bought at Brough Hill horse fair when he was about two years old and was broken in by Grandfather and another local man.

After Tom's departure the next one on the scene was Paddy but strangely I cannot remember much about this one except that it was light bay in colour and didn't seem to be around very long – perhaps it was because Grandfather was then retired and my father went into the Royal Navy therefore there was no need for a horse again until the end of the war.

The first horse that my father bought when he came back from service in the Royal Navy was a big cross bred Clydesdale type of mare. It was always temperamental and on occasions kicked out at me with both hind feet when I was attending to it in the stable. One day as I was about to leave home to catch the train to school, a girl who lived in a house next to our field came and told me that my father wanted me to go up to the field. When I got there I saw Father and Uncle Jont standing twenty yards from the horse which was yoked in the cart but the cart was badly damaged. The horse had gone berserk whilst out on the sand and had become unmanageable. As anyone approached the horse it screamed and kicked. Uncle Jont was not a good horseman and was always somewhat afraid of this horse and the horse knew it. Father told Jonathan to go home as he was making the situation worse. We tried to unyoke the horse but it was impossible because it kicked and screamed as we tried to unfasten the harness. Eventually the front of the cart was completely demolished but the horse was still in the shafts and the body of the cart intact. We undid as many straps and chains as we could until the horse eventually struggled free from the cart. It was taken down to another field where it stayed until it was collected by a horse dealer to go for slaughter.

Horses vary so much in character that it would be difficult to describe them all; suffice it to say that some were so dim as to drive one to the point of exasperation whilst others, and one in particular, were so intelligent as to be unbelievable. They usually came to us in one of two ways - one was to buy a horse which was known and recommended, perhaps from another fisherman,

The other was to take a horse from one of several dealers who would usually give a week's trial. Some horses would take to the work straight away, some needed two men to train them for several days and would eventually settle down but some were no good whatsoever and were sent back. If a horse showed any sign of jibbing at all, that is refusing to pull, it had to be rejected. One or two people did accept animals of a doubtful nature with the result that they were always let down eventually.

Whilst I was in the army, my father bought a mare which proved to be not very good - a bit slow and weak. My horse, Tony, was seldom put in a pasture with the new one as it was known that the newer one, named Dolly, was apt to kick. Tony was a chestnut coloured light-weight horse, about 15.3 hands high, with white legs and a white blaze on its face. My father bought it for me to use when I left school and was reputedly sired by a thoroughbred stallion belonging to Dickinson's of Cark and in spite of being so light of build, was a calm, steady draught horse. One night, in the summer of 1953, because we were going cockling early next morning, they were both put in the field at the top of the hill. The next morning, whilst it was still dark, I went to the field and shouted for them to come but only one horse appeared. I kept shouting and was surprised and a little worried when Tony didn't come to the gate although I could hear him whinnying. After a few minutes I went up the field to look for him and found him standing by the far hedge with a front leg shattered where the mare had kicked it.

This was a devastating blow to us and although I couldn't bear to see the horse being shot, I had to drag the carcass down the field with another horse as the disposal vehicle was too wide to get through the gate. I shall never forget that experience. It was this mare which went down in quicksand in November 1952 when I was still in the army. Several of us (and as far as I remember all were of our family) were shrimping up near Ellwood Scar, a few hundred yards south of Chapel Island. When Father hauled his net he found that he had so many shrimps that he couldn't lift them. He shouted to me to go and help him to lift his shrimps onto the cart so I left my horse and walked the dozen or so yards to help him. When we had lifted his shrimps I turned to go to my own cart and saw that one wheel of the cart was going down in the sand. I shouted to the horse to move but with one wheel being about a foot or more down in the sand, instead of pulling straight forward it swung round in a semi-circle with the mired wheel at the centre and instantly tipped the cart over on its side with the result that the horse was thrown down in the soft sand. A good horse might have pulled straight forward when I shouted but this was, as I have said, was a lazy animal and rather weak. It was well stuck, and try as we might we could not free it.

Because it was in several inches of water I held its head up until the tide came. As the tide rose I had to lift its head higher and higher until just its nose was out of the water then as I thought it was going to drown and the men were shouting at me to leave it, the horse gave an almighty heave, rose up and was free. The cart was left in the sand but we dug it out several months later.

After I came out of the army I wanted a big horse which could walk fast and wade deep because it was often beneficial to be able to trawl as deep as possible and most of our travelling was at walking pace. We did trot quite a bit, especially on the homeward journey if the weather was warm and the shrimps were dying but cantering was no good because the action was too turbulent thereby spilling shrimps and making riding uncomfortable.

•

I think it was the summer of 1953, shortly after I came out of the army, when I was told about a big horse which was pulling landaus on Morecambe promenade so Father and I went to look at it. Old Blobs, as his then owner, Arthur Turner, called him, was dark brown but looked almost black in his winter coat. He was seventeen hands high, had legs with no more hair than a thoroughbred. He had a fine mane but a body as big as a Shire horse and was four inches more in girth, even when he was thin, than any of our other horses were when fat. Arthur said: "He walks for fun," and so he did, at about six miles an hour. Arthur tried to put me off buying him, saying that I would not be able to manage him and he wouldn't be a good shrimper but I took an instant like to him. I persuaded everyone concerned that this was the horse I wanted so Father bought it for me.

I met the train on which he came from Morecambe and immediately renamed him Bob. All animals, of whatever sort, have always been referred to as it rather than him or her but in Bob's case I usually say him because he was a friend as well as a workhorse. That probably seems a funny thing to say but I thought a lot of that horse from the day he arrived. He was certainly the most intelligent horse I have ever seen and seemed to know instinctively what was going on and also had a built-in sense of direction. I could hardly believe how fast he could walk and whereas we often used to walk alongside the cart on the sand, it was difficult to keep up with this horse unless hanging on to the back of the cart. This was always his pace without having to be driven. To keep horses moving at a good walking speed one usually had to be continually driving and chivvying but not Bob, he walked as fast as he could all the time. The downside being that he still went at that speed up and down what was called the bad road over West Plain Marsh or round the rough track at Sandgate shore, with the result that it was a most uncomfortable ride and broke several wheels. The only time he caused me any trouble was when I put him into a hay-making machine which he would not pull at all whatever action I took. For shrimping he was the ideal horse, quick and tall plus the fact that when he came out of the water when finished fishing he was off as fast as he could walk, as straight as a die, either up the side of a channel for another drag or towards home.

One of the most important things to look for when buying a horse for shrimping was one with a good stride, one that, when bringing the hind foot forward, placed it down in front of the mark where the fore foot had been. The further forward the better. If it brought the hind foot down short of the place where the fore foot had been, it was said to be a paddler. Think of David Suchet and his portrayal of Poirot; there is a good example of a paddler.

Looking for a dark coloured horse at night could be a long job if it didn't come when called. Bob just had a small blaze of white on the face, otherwise was completely dark brown so all one saw even with a torch was a white patch if he was facing the right way. I just used to stand at the gate and shout but if he was at the other end of the field it was a while before he arrived but I always knew he was on his way. From the time that he arrived in Flookburgh I always kept a few cow-nuts or a crust of bread in a paper bag in my pocket and gave him some every time I went for him so that he would always come when I shouted. This was handy when going to fetch him from a big field whether in daylight or dark and proved to be a blessing one summer's day.

Uncle Jont, Father and I were cockling with two horses which were unyoked and feeding. Suddenly they decided to leave us and go home. I set off to catch them but as I got near they went faster, as is often their way. After about a mile I did get near enough for Bob to hear the noise of a paper bag from which he was used to receiving snacks but which, on this occasion, contained my lunch. He stopped and I caught him and the other horse followed. At the time that old Bob arrived we were cockling, and for this work he was no better or worse than any other because there were plenty of good steady draught horses in Flookburgh. It was when shrimping that he excelled.

Father had some trouble with Bob because they had a sort of mutual dislike of each other. Only four months after leaving the army I was recalled for fifteen days of re-training which was mostly spent on manoeuvres on Salisbury Plain. When I returned home I found that my cart was broken. On enquiring what had happened, Father said: "It was that bloody old horse of yours." I have forgotten just what had happened but no doubt the horse had played up in some way. Some time later when I was away for the day there was another incident so I told him it would be best if he did not to use my horse again.

There was one other rather nasty incident at West Plain when we were on our way out cockling. As we arrived at the gate that leads onto the saltmarsh (where there is now a cattle-grid), Father ran ahead to open it and as he held the gate open, the horse went past him and grabbed him by the chest with its teeth. I could see that he was in considerable pain all the time we were at work but it was not until we arrive home and he stripped to the waist that we saw all the teeth marks and a great blue bruise in a circle of about five inches diameter. This was the only time I ever saw the horse display any ill-will against a person but it illustrated a fact which I already knew, that there was some animosity between them - probably because Father at some time had lost his temper with him. For me, that horse would do anything I asked and many times we, that is the horse and I, got into difficulties in quicksand or deep water etc. but he never let me down.

Bob, my favourite horse for shrimping

One night, in the autumn of 1953, seven or eight horses and carts were coming home from shrimping in the west at about 10 pm on a very nasty dark wet night. We hadn't picked up our tracks from the outward journey but were wandering home, looking for anything that we recognised to indicate exactly where we were. We knew that we were heading in roughly the right direction but not just how far east or west we were. There were great numbers of concrete poles still left from wartime and we should have seen one or two of those but as it was so dark and visibility so bad we thought we had maybe passed by some but not seen them. (thousands of these poles were set up to prevent enemy aircraft from landing).

The river Eea, which we have always referred to as The Beck, ran straight out from Sandgate towards Bardsea. We were heading for Red Hill but were obviously too far west and went past it. I was leading with old Bob in the shafts but stopped when we came to the edge of dark-looking piece of water which I didn't like the look of. John Hodgson (Gog) said: "Go on, it's nobbut a gutter." I urged the horse on, whereon it plunged belly deep into the beck. In this area,

157

The Beck was always soft and treacherous so we never went near it. As I turned the horse westward downstream I shouted to the others: "Don't come in, it's t' beck." As the horse struggled on through the water and mire I knew I couldn't get back out at that point because we had plunged off a brack or cliff of about two feet high so there was no way the horse could climb back up, especially in that darkness. I also knew that if the horse went down in that place it would drown so I kept urging him on downstream for a while but dare not go very far or the horse would tire. After heading downstream for a hundred yards or so I turned south towards the river's bank, hoping that it was not so steep, which, luckily it was not so the horse clambered out. All the other men had been standing on the edge helpless to do anything but thinking that I had no chance of coming out of the situation with all intact. Gog said: "Thou's the luckiest man alive." If he hadn't said: "Go on," someone would have walked forward to see what we had encountered and the incident would not have occurred.

Arthur Turner had several horses and landaus plying their trade on the promenade at Morecambe and sold a number of his horses into Flookburgh for fishing. One of his drivers was a young man who I will call Tom, although not his real name, who seemed to be Arthur's right-hand man and was always there when any horse-trading was carried out. When Arthur made a statement he always called upon Tom to confirm it. One would go there and say something to the effect that you were looking for a horse. Arthur would say something like: "Horses are in short supply at present – not many coming into Heysham docks from Ireland so they're fetching high prices." He would then turn to Tom and say: "Isn't that right Tom?" Whereupon Tom would say: "Aye that's right enough." It was always the same patter. At the end of one fishing season I decided to sell one horse rather than keep two all winter so off I went to Morecambe to see Arthur. After a short spell of general conversation and banter, Arthur, assuming I had come to buy a horse, went through his usual spiel about the high price of horses. I then said: "That's good because I've come to sell one." Arthur's face fell.

•

We used two types of cart, an un-sprung or block cart, which was the traditional farm type for carrying heavy loads such as when cockling. Then there was what we always called spring cart, (I suppose that really should have been sprung carts) on which were fitted light, tall, trap wheels and springs on which the bodies of the carts were raised as high as possible for going into deep water. The latter were mainly for shrimping or any job where there was not usually a great weight to be hauled and lightness and speed of travel were more important because from the time we left home until arriving back we were on the move, either trawling or travelling.

Wheels from horse-drawn traps and milk floats became scarce in this area so I brought them from various places including some from near Lands End where I picked them up when we were on holiday. They were transported the 400-plus miles in the back of the Morris 1000 van with Wendy and Stephen sat on top of them. Jack Rowlandson and I went to Newcastle and into Northumberland and brought home a large van full. I bought some in Yorkshire when I was in the army after I saw a potter or gypsy-type man driving a horse and trap through Catterick. I followed him on my motorcycle and found that he lived at Bellerby a few miles away and that the family often came across traps, with the result that I bought several sets of wheels and some harness from them. The Nicholson family were typical potters or travelling people but lived in a house in Bellerby. I went to the house several times and even dined with them on one occasion. The patriarch was Joe Nicholson. Several years later I was out in the countryside of North Yorkshire or perhaps the southern end of County Durham when, just by chance, I met Joe. As he was a long way from Bellerby I asked what he was doing in that part of the country. He said he was born up there and had come back to die on his home territory.

Until about 1953 everyone used tall wooden wheels with iron hoops or tyres, strong heavy ones on the block carts for obvious reasons and light trap wheels on spring carts. It was at the time that we had the great quantity of cockles in 1953 that we started to fit pneumatic tyres on block carts which we believed would make it easier for the horses pulling heavy loads of cockles. We were lucky in that the smithy or forge (now 58 Main Street), where the horses were shod, carts were mended and all manner of repairs were carried out, was only a few yards from our house. Jim Shuttleworth, who lived at 65 Main Street, a big, strong man and well on in years, was the blacksmith when I was a lad but the business was taken over by his assistant, Bert Rowlandson, who lived in Ulverston. He was also a big strong man with brawny arms and hands as big as shovels. Bert told me he had served his time to joinery and was quite handy at all necessary repairs, whether woodwork or iron. There had also been another smithy down Market Street where the trade of blacksmith and farrier was carried out for probably more than a hundred years. This closed in the 1930s or 1940s.

•

One night, near midnight, my cousin Leslie Butler and I were shrimping a long way down the west at a time when shrimps still came to the edge of the water at night. With this happening it meant that when a stretch of a channel had been trawled it was finished for that night. We soon realised that someone else had gone down in front of us so we put the nets on the carts and set off to trot further down onto clear ground in front of the other two who were Brian Shaw and Jim McClure. Whilst we were trotting as fast as we could, Bob hit a soft spot, stumbled, fell and was stuck in the quicksand. We got the horse out but a shaft was broken. I took the horse home and Les carried on shrimping, towing the cart home when he came. Unfortunately Bob had pulled a shoulder and from that time on, leaned to one side as he walked which was a nuisance, as I then had to drive all the time to keep him straight. I persevered for nearly a year, then, reluctantly, decided to replace him.

I went to see Dick Long, another dealer at Morecambe, who had just bought a very big strawberry roan horse from somewhere up on Tyneside. The horse had harness marks still showing so I thought it must be all right. We did an exchange deal and Dick did the transporting by wagon. I set off shrimping with the new horse along with Brian Shaw with whom I had always been friendly, he driving his very good grey mare, Peggy. As we went round the shore at Sandgate, the horse stopped a couple of times and then again probably a mile offshore, which already gave us doubts. When we were trawling in about three feet of water it stopped and refused to move whatever I did. After running out of options, we put a rope round its neck and dragged it out of the water with old Peggy. It stopped again whilst we were coming round the shore on the way home, by which time I knew it had to be returned to Morecambe.

That night I rang Dick Long and explained what had happened, whereon he said in his voice with a speech defect; "Did you twy witing a fiew undw it." I replied that I hadn't thought of that. I asked if I could have my own horse back but he said that Bob was already slaughtered and had gone to feed the lions at Blackpool zoo. At this news I was devastated but after quite a long conversation I found that this was not true and we did exchange back although he charged me £22, which was more than two weeks wages to most people. During the time that I had Bob, he suffered from colic two or three times and had to have a day or so off work but on the last occasion he was in agony. The vet was an old man and absolutely useless. I wished afterwards that I had called another vet, even though I know that the outcome would probably have been the same, but I would have been satisfied that everything possible had been done. He died after having been ill for about three days and I was as bereft as I would have been on the death of a relative.

I have spent some time telling about this horse because I had such affection for him and oddly as it may seem, he was more like a friend. When I reflect back to the days of shrimping with horses, it is usually Bob that I think of.

Whilst I was writing this out by hand many years ago I saw a programme on television about the famous show jumper Colonel Harry Llewellen who went to great lengths to explain his close relationship with his horse Foxhunter on which he achieved fame in the 1952 Olympics. He said that Foxhunter was a friend as well as a working partner and that they had an understanding. I knew exactly what he meant. On the other hand I felt sorry for the Duke of Edinburgh who has been driving horses all his life but said that: "Horses are the most stupid animals on the face of the earth." Perhaps that was because he had grooms to look after the horses and only came into contact with them on driving days.

In the late 1950s, when I was shrimping twice nearly every day, I needed a spare horse to give old Bob a tide off so I bought Charlie, a flea-bitten grey, that is grey with flecks of brown in it. This horse was only about 15.2 hands and was not a very good horse for our job but was a real old slave, doing everything asked of it. One day, Stephen, who was probably only about two years old, was with me as I brought it from the field down near Canon Winder and I put him on its back to ride home but it suddenly set off and left me, with Stephen still on board. He only rode about fifteen yards then fell off, luckily landing on the grass verge and was no worse, except for being a bit shaken but it could have been serious.

There was an incident when, being led into the stable, Charlie bumped his face into the end of the skell boose or partition, splitting an eyelid wide open. Another time I was going down Moor Lane, or what we call The Mile Road, in the moonlight at about 4 am when he saw something in the road and bounced across to the west side and down into the deep drainage dyke. Having gone halfway down, he put a foot on a piece of corrugated iron sheet which made a loud clang whereon he backed out again. The whole incident lasted only a few seconds but was almost a catastrophe. Charlie spent a couple of autumn seasons across on the Furness side at Tom Butler's place at Newbiggin and on one occasion, when I had been shrimping through the night, I came off the sand and onto the coastal road at Aldingham Church as first light was showing, at about 5 am. As we approached the S bend at Seamill, Charlie gave an almighty leap which left us cross-way in the road. In white letters of about three feet high across the road was written the word 'SLOW'. The horse had been almost on top of the writing before it saw it. I was sitting in the cart, but up on the side, nearly asleep, and was almost thrown out of the cart and onto the road.

One day, back in the 1950s, on a day of gale-force west wind, there were probably ten horses and carts coming home from a channel, the top end of which was only about a mile or so south of Humphrey Head Point and all had good catches. Jim McClure and I had trawled up the west side of the channel in the flood tide and absolutely filled the nets with clean shrimps. That side had not been trawled that day because there were many patches of quicksand. We already had a good quantity before we lifted these so we dragged them into shallow water and invited one or two other men such as old Will Cowperthwaite and Jack Stephenson to take some but even then we had to dump some after keeping what we needed ourselves. The track up the saltmarsh was in a very bad state then and one of the gullies, which is no longer there because the track was re-routed, was probably eight feet deep and muddy at the bottom, caused by carts constantly churning through. First in the line to arrive at the gully was an elderly man called Jack Hutton who lived in Allithwaite and fished for just a couple of years with his piebald horse. As he lurched into the bottom of the trench, the cart tipped over, with the result that the track was blocked for quite a long time until we could sort him out, plus the fact that his shrimps were scattered in the mud. The next day as we approached the same place, Jack was again first in the line. I said to him: "Let me go through before you, I don't want to be held up today." I went through first and as the horse bounced into the bottom of the gully with me sat on the forrend, both shafts snapped off and Charlie simply galloped away dragging the shafts whilst I was left sat on the cart with shrimps scattered all around. The horse was eventually sold back to Dick Towers at Morecambe from whom I had bought it.

About two years later I again bought Charlie to relieve Bob of some of the work, just as a spare horse for the autumn and mainly because at £45 it was the cheapest horse I could find. Again old Charlie bumped into the post at the end of the skell boose or dividing partition between stalls, lacerating its face. It was only then, after owning the horse for two years altogether, that I realised it was almost blind. The reason for the sudden leaps was that it did not see objects until it was nearly on top of them then took sudden evasive action.

One evening I received a phone call from Dick Towers asking me if I could tell him how he could contact God. I replied to the effect that there were no Gods in Flookburgh, only some people who thought they were. He was in fact trying to contact John (nicknamed Gog) Hodgson, about a deal with a horse.

Another horse which I bought from Dick Towers was a very nice bay of 16.2 hands and only four years old but surprisingly staid for such a young animal. It was with this horse that I went across to Bolton-le-Sands through the night with Les Butler when we hit thick fog and on which I have written extensively in the chapter headed Incidents and Accidents. Having taken the horses to Bolton-le-Sands, we had been working from there for only a week or so when we realised that we were having to travel a long way north on that shore in order to cross the channel in which we had to work. We decided to move the horses up to Silverdale. To go fishing from there we had to cross a salt marsh of at least half a mile in width. It was easier working from Silverdale rather than Bolton because at least we were entering the channel at the top and working down it, which was more convenient.

On a fine, moonlit morning just after Christmas at about 5 am, Uncle Bill Butler and I were crossing this marsh and arrived at the seaward edge where there was a nasty looking gutter. I ran ahead to see that it was safe to cross. As I was returning to the cart, my horse moved up to Bill's cart and touched it in some way, which startled it. The horse bolted and careered across the marsh which was a maze of potholes and deep gullies. As it went I could just see it in the moonlight, bouncing over and through great holes. It was galloping round some obstacles and through others, obviously terrified at the noise it was making. There was one time when the cart went for a good thirty yards on one wheel as it made a great arc at speed. It then headed towards a large cliff-sided channel which was about eight to ten feet deep. As I tried to follow it I knew that this was the end one way or another. It galloped to the edge and stopped. I went quietly up to it, speaking as I went and took hold of the reins to lead it back to Bill. The horse was still terrified so after some discussion we decided to bring the horses home. The very next day I went to set some stream nets near to Chapel Island with the same horse and it gave no trouble whatsoever. I eventually sold the horse to another fisherman, Tom Robinson, who later told me: "It has plenty of energy" but added: "It always will have because it never uses any."

Another incident with this horse occurred down at Philipson's farm at Canon Winder when I used to keep it there to go shrimping. The field is adjacent to the shore so I could leave the cart there, go to the field with the van and go straight out on to the sand. I went out all of that autumn, night and day, wandering all over the bay, alone because all the other night shrimpers went from West Plain. Working by the compass on bad nights I could, and did go anywhere. I suppose it must have been about 5 am when I arrived back at the field which runs from near Red Hill to the farm. I was unyoking the horse from the cart when Frank Philipson was bringing the cows in to milk.

As the horse saw the cows coming towards us in the moonlight, it reared up and fell down on the ground but as it came up again the shafts were at right angles across its back and all chains and straps dead tight so that I couldn't loosen them. The horse was ready to bolt and I certainly could not have held it if it had done so. I shouted to Frank to come and help, which he did. Eventually we got the horse out with very little damage but narrowly avoided a calamity. Frank was a good horseman who had worked with horses on the farm all his life.

•

I think it was 1960 when I went with Jack Stamper, a well-known horseman and landau driver from Morecambe, to look at a horse down in the Fylde area. It was at a farm belonging to Arthur Gardner, a horse dealer and breeder who also showed Shire Horses. Arthur said he had seen this horse, which he said was three years old, in Ireland, pulling a tinker's caravan and had bought it there and then. We yoked it up and walked it round a bit until after only a short time I was convinced it was all right and bought it. Tinker was piebald but predominantly white and at that time very slimly built and completely docile.

Wendy with Tinker,
Stephen & Mitchell assisting

It was Good Friday, about the 15th of April, when Tinker arrived, just as we were preparing to set off to Keswick to stay with Nana and Gag for the weekend. We came home on Easter Monday. On the Tuesday morning, Father and I were due to go cockling at about 9 am to get four hundred-weights which was probably as many as we could gather then. I had harnessed the mare and brought her out when Father came out of the house. On seeing the horse he said: "We aren't taking that thing this morning, it'll nivver git there an' back." I insisted that we did take Tinker which we did, taking our time over the four or five miles to the cockle beds, gathered the cockles and set off home.

Tinker plodded away on the return journey but was distinctly jaded when we arrived home. When the blacksmith, Bert Rowlandson, saw the horse he insisted that she was only two years old. This was almost certainly true because in the next couple of years she shed several teeth and filled out into quite a strong, sturdy horse with some hair around the fetlocks of which there was none when she first came. She proved to be the most super-docile and kind horse imaginable with which the children could play or bring from the field and was a pleasure to work with and a fine looking horse. We have a photograph of Wendy bringing Tinker from the field (they were the same age) and this mare is also featured in the film Moonsmen. Although I bought two other horses after Tinker, she was kept after the others had gone. In the last couple of years she was kept mainly as a pet from which we bred two foals, both sired by a thoroughbred stallion. The first, Sambo, was piebald and was born on the 22nd of April 1966. The second foal was called Lightning because he was born in a thunderstorm on the 11th of May 1967. He grew to be a big fine bay horse and went to hunt with the Vale of Lune pack.

In February 1962, just before we started cockling at Silverdale, I decided to go to Ireland to try to buy horses, simply because they were scarce in England and I had been informed that there were still thousands over there. I met the Triggs brothers near the Pier Head in Liverpool to discuss the sale of cockles to them then after several pints of beer I boarded the ferry. I landed in Dublin at perhaps seven or eight o'clock on a Monday morning to find snow on the ground. I had no idea where I was going or where to look for horses so I just started to walk into the city and along the north side of the river Liffey. By asking questions -to whom or what kind of people I cannot remember but I was soon directed to the house of Joe Cooper, a horse dealer. Joe was a very nice man who bought horses for the Continental meat trade, travelling round horse fairs buying whatever horses he could. He said that he was going to a fair on Wednesday and that I was welcome to go with him.

Having a full day free the next day, I decided to hire a car and ride out into the countryside to look at horses and assess the situation. Driving south, I came to a small town called Athy, where I saw a nice looking bay horse in a field, whereon I made enquiries as to the owner and whether it was for sale.

Somehow, and mysteriously, a couple of men appeared who said that they did not own the horse but assured me that they could sell it. I enquired whether it was broken. They said they did not know but would soon find out. We went into the field to catch the horse, an event which in itself proved to be something like a wild-west movie scene. After several unsuccessful attempts we drove it into a barn that was in the middle of the field and where the horse was absolutely wild or terrified. As we tried to corner it, it was rearing up, with fore feet scrambling up the walls in desperate attempts to escape. I certainly thought we were wasting our time because on this showing, if we did catch it, how would we ever get it into a cart? My companions were unperturbed and persevered until we did catch it and proceeded to harness and yoke the horse.

Having yoked it, we drove it around for a while and it settled down surprisingly well with the result that I bought it and left instructions for them to send it via Dublin to England. It certainly was a nice looking horse of about 16.2 hands and four years old.

It seems strange now looking back that everything was done so vaguely and on trust. I cannot even remember anything about where I stayed or in what kind of accommodation in Dublin. The main thing I remember is that everyone with whom I came into contact in Ireland was extremely kind and helpful. If I asked for directions of a person in a car, they invariably insisted on taking me to my destination.

On the Wednesday morning I was travelling down the road with Joe Cooper in his Volkswagen Beetle on our way to Kilkenny horse fair. Joe told me something of his business and how he had sent thousands of horses to The Continent, making an average of £5 per horse, which then was half a week's wage to a manual worker. I'm fairly sure that he told me that he dispatched an average of 200 horses per week - the figure of 200 is certainly correct and even if it was per month it was a lot. The one fact which has been indelibly etched on my mind is that he pulled out a wad of notes which he told me was £3,000 and that he always left home with either £2,000 or £3,000 and travelled round several fairs, buying strings of horses and moving on to the next fair leaving some boys to handle and move the animals. Now, if we consider that the price of a new car was about £600 and that we paid £500 for our house in 1955 and sold it for £1,600 in 1966 we realise that £3,000 was a great deal of money something like the value of three small cottages in Flookburgh and a figure I could not imagine to be possible considering that at the time I was earning precisely £8 per week.

On my first visit to Ireland there was a campaign in the English press, particularly the Daily Mirror, for a ban on the shipping of live horses to Europe for the meat trade because they were crowded into holds on ships to be thrown about in rough weather and many horses died in transit. An abattoir was built at Tipperary for the slaughter of horses but was standing empty then I was there because dealers were reluctant to change their habits. To end Joe's part of the story I would just like to add that in September 1967, when Margaret and I went for a holiday in Ireland, we called on Joe, only to find that the horse trade was finished and he made his living hiring out old horse-drawn vehicles to film companies etc.

At Kilkenny fair I did not see any suitable horses but met two brothers from Limerick who were into a different trade - that of riding horses and ponies. They were going back south and invited me to travel with them, saying that there were more of the type of horse in which I was interested in the south of the country. This time we were off to Limerick in a Hillman Minx.

Unfortunately, from the time that I disembarked from the boat I was suffering from influenza which took the edge off the trip but, being away from home, just had to soldier on. The brothers, whose name I have forgotten, took

166

me to their home where I met the family which included another brother involved in the business but who was not very well with a chronic illness. They took me to an hotel to stay although I would probably have chosen a small guesthouse. Nevertheless, they collected me by pony and trap at eight in the morning and off we went to either Cork or Waterford, I can't remember which but I drove the Hillman as we went to look at some ponies and also visited some racing stables. As we travelled, they told me about their business which was mainly in nice ponies for riding and show work, most of which came to England and if I remember rightly, were shipped to Bristol.

The horse dealers that I had known in England were mostly looked on suspiciously and were sharp characters. These brothers were absolutely straight businessmen who told me that they would rather send a doubtful horse to slaughter than sell it to a customer. Their house, called Gary Owen, was just a few hundred yards east of the cathedral with a tall spire which could be seen for miles over the flat plain of the Shannon region. It was Lent and Ireland being a strong Catholic country, people were going in and out of the cathedral to Mass, some obviously on their way to work and in their working clothes.

One memory which stands out is that of a funeral with a hearse drawn by two black horses adorned with black plumes on their heads, something which I had never seen before nor since, except in films. Limerick was busy on market day and one could see old ladies dressed in long black clothes and with shawls over their heads, driving donkey carts loaded with vegetables from the surrounding countryside. One got the impression that they were many years behind the English lifestyle which meant that there were still good numbers of horses around and this was the reason for my being there. I know that since then, things have moved on dramatically in Ireland.

The brothers either owned or knew of a horse which was just outside Limerick in a field on the outskirts of Shannon airport so off we went to look at it. It was four years old, black with a white blaze down the face and white on both hind feet, was just about seventeen hands high but looked thin and gangling. It seemed so friendly and kind that I took an instant like to it and although I cannot remember giving it a trial in a cart, decided to buy it and we settled on £70. They said that they would dispatch the horse from Waterford which was rather awkward because the other one was due to sail from Dublin. I left Limerick by train for Dublin to catch a boat home, having thoroughly enjoyed my time in Ireland in spite of being ill. I was able to arrange with the people at Athy to have the first horse sent to Waterford from where both horses were dispatched to Birkenhead. It was an episode in my life which I look back on as a pleasant and interesting experience.

Don Keith, a local livestock transporter, was taking a load of cattle to an abattoir in Liverpool a few days later so he agreed to collect the horses, for which he charged £11. When we arrive at the pens where the horses were waiting, we found that they had not been fed since arriving in England, or perhaps since leaving Ireland, and were absolutely ravenous. Both horses proved to be very good workers although completely different in character.

Wading deep with Black Bob (1962)

Only a day or so after they arrived I went shrimping with the big black horse, which I called Bob, and found that he went straight into the water as though he had done it all his life. Shortly after this he went out to grass for a few weeks and came back in nice condition with a shiny jet-black coat. He was a good workhorse which I kept for a few years although shortly after having bought these two, horses were disappearing from the scene. Bob features with Tinker in the film Moonsmen which was made in 1964, and is also on some slides which I have used for talks for fifty years.

The bay horse was completely different in that I had to spend some time getting it used to things and especially traffic. It was as though it had been out in the wilds and had not seen any everyday life such as vehicles and normal activities. I had to walk it round the village to see things and in doing so it soon became used to them. For instance, one Saturday morning I took it down to a local haulage company's depot on Moor Lane (the building which we later bought for the boats business) where all the heavy vehicles were in for the weekend and were being washed and generally serviced. I was driving it on long reins as though breaking in and at first it would not go near the place. It gradually went closer and I asked them to start some engines, at which there was more fun and games. Eventually it settled down and was no bother in traffic at all so that was how quickly it became accustomed to things.

My father's cousin, Tom Butler, at Newbiggin over on the Furness side of the bay, had a horse for many years but it died suddenly so I loaned him the new Black Bob, to which he took a real liking and begged me to sell it to him. I refused to sell it, offering him the brown one but he had heard about me driving the horse around in breaking gear so suspected it of being difficult. In fact it was a very good horse and after settling down to strange sights and sounds became a very fine workhorse and could jump. I sold it to a man whom I met at Cartmel races and he later sold it to Tony Dickinson, the racehorse trainer, for use by his son Michael. He was only a boy then, but became a jockey, and later, a famous trainer of racehorses. The family lived in Cark until perhaps the 1950s.

Harold with Darkie, Mitchell on top

One of the saddest episodes involving our horses was when, in 1959, Father's horse, Darkie contracted lockjaw or tetanus.

We went to Kirkby Stephen to look at this very fine 16 hands black horse and after driving it round for a while, Father bought it. This proved to be an excellent horse. It was docile, a very good worker and quite nice mover. Father really liked Darkie and I'm sure it could have lasted him for years with better luck. Unfortunately it contracted lockjaw whilst pasturing at the ex-army camp, before the site was bought by Dan Latham to make into a duck farm, now the Lakeland Leisure Park. Father doted on all his animals whether horses or dogs and Darkie was no exception so he was devastated when it died after about a week of suffering.

169

After Darkie died, Father replaced it with a really poor horse - on the small side and weak. How he came to buy such a poor animal I have no idea. He went out from Sandgate shore one morning and headed westward from Red Hill. On entering The Beck, which was often soft, the horse went down in quicksand. He walked half mile or so to Canon Winder Farm for help, whereon several men went out with a tractor to assist. They released the horse after a long struggle in which they ended up hauling it out with the tractor but the horse was injured in a shoulder and walked lame for the rest of its life.

•

There have only been two horses drowned in the bay in my time and both belonged to the same family. The first was fairly new to the job and belonged to Uncle Bill Butler who, along with his brother-in-law, Herbert Benson, had gone to some fluke nets well down in the bay. Whilst they were tending the nets, the horse, still yoked in the cart, was standing on its own as the two men worked their way along the net taking out fish. An oilskin coat was hung on a stake where one of the men had placed it and it was flapping in the wind thus frightening the horse, which bolted. Bill followed the horse as best he could as it went eastward or south-east until it crossed a channel which ran north to south down the middle of the bay. The channel was then very shallow but a big tide was due shortly so he had to abandon his effort to catch it. Nothing was ever seen of this horse or any equipment again, which was most unusual as most things eventually wash up with the tide.

The other incident involved Bill's son Leslie and a horse which had always been doubtful. It was a light bay with white legs and face and very much like a light riding horse. He was shrimping down the west with quite a number of others in a deep channel which even before this event was called The Graveyard. I had previously worked in this channel but at the time of this incident I was in the army so it was between 1951 and 1953. We had to cross the channel then trawl on the far side in a stretch of water which was very deep by our standards so one could not get back to our own side without travelling up to the original crossing point. Human nature being what it is, we usually worked on the far side until the last minute and then dashed up to cross again just before the tide arrived. This was why a fisherman said: "This will be somebody's graveyard" and the name stuck. On the morning in question, as the tide was starting to flow in, they were about to leave the channel to go back up to cross to our side when the horse jibbed and refused to move. Leslie stuck with it until the water had become so deep that he had to leave the cart. By this time it was too late for him to run up the other side to cross the channel at the shallower place so he had to swim across. Brian Shaw waded his horse in as far as he could from our side to meet him and Leslie scrambled into the cart, exhausted. The next day they found the drowned horse over on the Furness side of the channel and recovered the cart and harness.

Virtually the same thing happened to Geordie Shaw, in the same place but two years later, when his horse stopped and wouldn't budge. Someone drove another horse alongside his and picked him up. This horse had previously shown signs of jibbing and had let him down which, as I said in an earlier part, always happened with a doubtful animal. The horse was left to its own devices and we all stood on the bank at our own side of the channel and watched as the tide flowed in. The horse swam round in circles because one of the pulling chains had become unattached. In the end we didn't want to watch the horse drown so we came home and left it. Father and I had been home an hour and were boiling our shrimps when the horse came galloping down the street. In its desperate struggles the harness must have broken or in some way become unattached thereby releasing it. The amazing part is how it came to find its way to Sandgate and home when it could have gone anywhere. The place where the incident happened was at least five miles from shore. The cart was seen several times, the last sighting being just on the north side of Plumpton railway viaduct with part of one wheel showing above the sand but it was never recovered. I look back on the times spent working with horses with the thought that perhaps they were the best times, but was pleased to have moved on to tractors because of a severe allergy to horses which began when I was in my early teens. To look at the film Moonsmen and at photographs in the albums brings feelings of nostalgia, memories of a lifestyle long gone and of people with whom I worked, some of whom were fine men and great characters.

The Boats Business

I had worked and messed about with rowing boats from being a boy but had never sailed, although, for years I had wished to but did not have enough money to buy a sailing boat and did not know anyone who sailed. It was almost certainly 1971 when I decided to take the plunge and buy a sailing dinghy. I say 1971 because it sticks in my mind that I was thirty-nine years old. Although we were probably the worst off financially that we had ever been, I thought: "It's now or never" and bought a Firefly dinghy in March of that year. As chance would have it, there were hardly any shrimps that year until October so most of the time it was hardly worth the trouble to go shrimping so I had plenty of opportunity to learn to sail. I took a small book from the library and learned the basics from that, although I know now it would have been much better and quicker to have gone with someone who could sail. Even the experience of learning to sail, although sometimes difficult, frustrating and even scary, was a pleasure and I wished I had taken it up earlier.

When buying the first boat I had no idea what I wanted or even what the options were so, after much deliberation but not having seen many choices, I bought the Firefly. I soon discovered that the Firefly is not an easy thing to sail and certainly not a family boat. It was a very nice boat, in excellent condition – all varnished mahogany. I kept it for a year, then bought a GP 14 which was ideal, two feet longer, more stable and with seating for crew or passengers. To sell the Firefly, I advertised it in the magazine Yachts and Yachting. The book came out on a Thursday and from the first day the telephone kept ringing with replies. I promised to sell the boat to a man at Chatham and said I would deliver it but then we went off for the weekend to see Margaret's family at Distington. I was soon sorry to have sold the boat so quickly because when we came back, mother said she had sold the boat to a lady at Northwich in Cheshire. Unfortunately I had not told her I had sold the boat. I probably thought there would be no more calls. There were many replies from people who would have come and collected. This put me in a predicament, as both customers were extremely anxious to have the boat. I then went back to the man who sold me the first one and bought another from him. My nephew, Mitchell, and I set off with both boats, one on top of the other, one to Cheshire and one to Kent, towed by a light blue Mk.2 Ford Cortina that was bought brand new in August 1970 and cost £900. The response to the advertisement led me to think that there must be a market for second-hand boats - or was it just for Fireflies? I bought one or two more boats and sold them fairly quickly. Now it was turning into a business – a business about which I knew nothing but had to learn quickly.

When I started to buy a few boats, the problem was where to keep them so I asked a lady in our street if I could rent her small barn, which I did for a while, but this only held two or three. There were some in the barn and some in our yard. Boats do take up a lot of room. I think it was 1974 when we bought the building down Moor Lane from the haulage company which transported our cockles twenty years earlier.

The building was a hundred feet long and about thirty feet wide but within a year or so I was filling it to capacity with boats -especially in winter when I used to buy as many as I could, ready to sell when spring arrived. One thing I realised when I was looking for my first boat was that there was nowhere that one could go to look at a selection of sailing dinghies as one would if for example, when looking for a car. There were several places where one could look at speedboats or even sailing cruisers but no sailing dinghies. At first it was only sailing dinghies and I found that I could sell virtually any kind, but especially the popular class dinghies such as GPs, Enterprises, Mirrors etc. It was a seller's market and when Easter was approaching I advertised in various papers as far away as the Manchester Evening News and the boats sold like hot cakes. Many times I would be out shrimping early morning then off to Manchester or Carlisle buying boats from adverts in their regional papers. For the first few years I used to dash down to Grange station nearly every Friday morning at around 7 am to buy the Westmorland Gazette, Lancaster Guardian, Cumberland News. If there was anything interesting in any of them I would be phoning by 8 am or they would be gone, or at least someone would have claimed first chance. If there was no reply, one had to try all day to catch them when they first arrived home. That was the way the market was at first and remained that way for a few years.

At the start of the business, one could travel to London and back for £10 so the reverse also applied and people would travel here from as far as the Midlands. I once travelled to Winchester to buy a boat, which must be more than three hundred miles from here but it was a nice run via the Cotswolds. On another occasion, Mitchell, came with me to a small village called Lee, near Illfracombe, to buy a GP 14. We were playing in the orchestra at Flookburgh opera on the Saturday night, which was also the night that the clocks went forward. We set of at about 5am, having had the usual session in the Rose and Crown after the show so we only had a few hours in bed. There was quite a bit of snow down the M5 from Birmingham to Bristol and only one lane open on each carriageway so it was fairly slow going. I had seen the boat advertised in Yachts and Yachting and phoned the man who described it as in excellent condition but I was worried in case it was not worth the trip. We arrived at the house at about 12.30 pm and after a few minutes we went to look at the boat which was in the garage under a cover. I can remember saying: "This is the moment of truth." The man whipped off the cover in a flash and revealed a boat which was absolutely immaculate -just as brand new. What a relief! The distance we covered that day was 740 miles and arrived home late in the evening.

It didn't always work out as well as that. There was the time that I travelled to Doncaster, again to buy a GP14. It was so poor I could have cried; it was amateur built and badly finished off and looked awful. After much deliberation I bought it at the lowest price that I could negotiate - which I always did anyway - and hoped that with some work on it I could recoup expenses. One thing I soon found out was that boats sell by their looks. A nice smart boat, even if it were much older, would sell more quickly than a newer one which was a bit rough.

Occasionally I would buy boats which had not been used for quite a long time and could be just dirty or untidy. Having had some experience I could see that with a good clean or varnish they could be very nice and the transformation could be dramatic. I liked to buy boats which were in good condition, well equipped and ready to sell with no work. Obviously, even in these cases sometimes there were small repairs to be done but mostly just tidying up. I always drove a hard bargain, so much so that Margaret very often would not come to the houses if she was with me but it had to be done that way because in any deal that is where the profit lies. Several times I had boats which were not easy to sell but have come near to selling and would have sold if I could have come down in price another twenty or thirty pounds but couldn't. I soon found out that if a boat was purchased at the right price it was already half way to being sold.

The business went very well for a few years and I enjoyed dealing but I had to learn everything from scratch. There were times when I travelled to look at boats and made up my mind immediately that I saw them that I was going to buy did not let the seller get that impression. Nobody in our family had ever been in a business of buying and selling anything; we had always knocked out a living by sheer physical hard work so I had to learn about dealing and about boats.

On one occasion a lady rang me, wanting to sell a small cabin boat of the type which I call a day boat. It was Christmas time and almost certainly Boxing Day when, having nothing to do, I decided to look at the boat. I called on my good friend, Peter Thompson, and asked him if he would like to come for a ride out, which he did. The boat, which was on a housing estate in Kendal, had a good trailer and 6 HP Evinrude motor and the whole outfit was in absolutely showroom condition. The lady, whose husband was also there, said; "It's our son's boat but he's moved away and we just want to be rid of it." Peter looked at me with incredulity. I had already more or less decided that I would buy it but still gave a bit of a sob story about it being the wrong time of year to be buying boats, which it was, but soon paid £600 and off we went. I feel that I should qualify that a little and say that by driving a hard bargain it did not necessarily mean that I made a huge profit but did mean that a sale was easier.

The boat was first sold to a doctor who had a caravan on a local site. He traded it back a couple of years later and took out a sailing dinghy in exchange. It was then sold to a man at Milnthorpe and came back twice after that - each time making a small profit. By this time I was dealing in anything which would float and was fairly easily transported, from inflatable dinghies to small sailing cruisers.

This was the first time that we had any spare money around, in that there were a lot of cash deals, especially for small stuff such as trailers, which were always one of the best selling lines. Anchors, life-jackets, spare sails and chandlery which came with boats could also be sold. Some boats were also sold for cash so on the whole we had more disposable money around when dealing in boats. Even though the cash went through the books, it felt easier to spend than cheques through the bank.

There is one story about cash that I think is worth relating. I bought a leather jacket from a shop in Barrow for just under £50 and paid for it in £1 notes. The salesman said: "You must be a taxi driver." I asked why and he replied that the only people who pay in pound notes are taxi drivers or Chinese (from the takeaways) and I can see you're not Chinese. Several years later, on a day when there were some motorcycle races on the nearby aerodrome, a man called in the boat shed and bought something for £450 and paid the lot in one-pound notes. I could see he wasn't Chinese so I said jokingly: "You must be a taxi driver," he said; "Yes, I am, but how did you know?"

All of my life up to the point where I started selling boats I had to graft hard with my hands for every pound I made, now I was making some by simply wheeling and dealing. I can remember turning one or two boats over for £10 profit if they had come in as part exchange. Margaret would question whether it was worth it. I replied by saying that only a year or two before this, in 1971, I had worked with a pick and shovel on the Kendal by-pass for £13 a week and just on the final week I took home £20. Everything in life is relative.

Stephen once came with me down into Gloucestershire, around Painswick and Cheltenham, where I had advertised for Mirror dinghies. I bought four, of which we brought home three and left one to be collected later. We had loaded the last one onto the roof rack and were ready for home when I slammed the boot lid down and snapped off the key in the lock. Unfortunately it was also the only key we had for the ignition. This was a Mk.3 Cortina and it was about 5pm but we were told that there was a Ford garage only half a mile or so away so we went there to have a key cut. On arrival back at the car we found that it would not fit so had to go back again. It was checked and re-cut but the same thing happened again. Eventually another key was cut and this time did work but at one time it looked as though we were in for a night's lodgings in Cheltenham.

Our stand at the Lakeland Rose Show in 1978

On one occasion, Margaret and I bought an old touring caravan especially to go on holiday to Wales. We spent a week or so in North Wales, moving up and down the coast, then at the end of the holiday, sold the caravan to a site owner and bought four boats, one of which I sailed on the Menai Strait while on the holiday. We brought three home and left one in Chester for a day or so. It was a regular occurrence for me to buy a boat whilst on holiday on the south coast or wherever, use it for the holiday then bring it home to sell and, so far as I remember, always made a profit.

There are two such stories, one when we were staying at Holimarine, Burnham-on-Sea in Somerset and one perhaps only a year later at Looe in Cornwall which was definitely 1976.

I had been catching whitebait right up to the very morning that we left home and was really tired, so for a couple of days all I wanted to do was sleep. We usually went away in early June and on this occasion we were packed and prepared to go as soon as the whitebait finished. One morning father and I went to the nets near Chapel Island and found that there was almost nothing but small jellyfish in them. We brought the nets home so now we were ready to go on holiday. On arrival home, at 6 a.m, I woke the family and said: "Right, we're off." On this occasion only Lynn came with us.

I was tired but after resting up for a couple of days after we arrived at Burnham, the next thing I wanted was a boat because the site was adjacent to

176

the sea. I bought a Yachts and Yachting magazine and found there was a GP 14 advertised at Dorchester, which is about ten miles from the south coast. After ringing the man, off I went. The boat was brand new and although he had built it himself it was very nicely finished so I bought it. I thoroughly enjoyed sailing it for the ten days that were left of the holiday. Every class dinghy has to be built to very precise measurements and have a certificate to that effect in order to qualify as a racing boat. This one had never been measured so I made arrangements to have it measured at Windermere. It took a good half-day to do the numerous measurements. I had wanted to call Lynn Linda when she was first born but lost the argument; nevertheless I sometimes called her Lindi-Lou. I called the boat Lindi-Lou, which I thought was bound to be unique. Perhaps a year later when I was in a boathouse at Lakeside looking at another boat, I noticed a very old but beautiful motorboat with the name Lindi-Lou. The man said it had been called that for all of its fifty-odd years.

In 1976, father had died on the 10th of June and having done what we could, set off on holiday to Cornwall a few days later. This particular summer is now looked back on as 'The Long Hot Summer' but even so it broke for a couple of days as we went south with a caravan to Hayle, near Penzance. It was a nasty drizzly night as we pulled onto the site which made it look unattractive. After a day or so we moved eastward along the south coast and eventually to Looe, to a site called The Three Bs, where again I was looking for a boat and particularly one which would fit on the roof-rack. When looking through the ads in a local paper I saw a boat called a Skipper 12 advertised at an address in Plymouth and went to look at it. I had sold several of these boats so I had an idea of its value. We settled a price then he told me there was a trailer and an outboard motor with it. Knowing that the trailer was worth at least £40, I wasn't going to leave it so I took the boat, trailer and motor back to the site.

After sailing it in the sea at Looe for the holiday I bought a hacksaw and sawed the T-shaped trailer in half through the main beam so that it would go into the caravan to take it home. On arrival home, at 8 pm. I took the trailer out of the caravan and welded it back together immediately, even before we unpacked the car. Stephen came home shortly afterwards and said that someone had just been on the phone asking if we had a Skipper sailing dinghy. I rang the man back straight away and he came up from Haydock and took the boat that same night at 11 pm.

One winter I had stocked up to capacity with boats as usual, including seven Mirror Dinghies, but when the season for selling started I was surprised that they were slow to sell, whereas there had been a time when there was a waiting list of people wanting them so that when a boat came in I used to ring the next person on the list and they would come and collect.

That particular year it took the whole of the season to sell them. This proved to be the start of the downward trend and after that one could see an ad for a boat for sale in a local paper and wait a week before replying and find that the boat was still for sale then possibly make an offer. I then had to be choosy as to what I bought and even then could be stuck with it. The number of boats for sale in all papers increased so that people had lots of choice where at one time I had the monopoly through collecting boats nationwide. I could see that the bubble

Lynn on a Skipper dinghy at Looe in 1976

had burst! After a few more years we decided there was too much hassle and work which involved most weekends. We thought, probably correctly, that if we sold up we could receive almost as much income from the interest from capital as we were making with all the work we were doing so we decided to sell. I advertised a closing down sale and most of the stock went, except for a great amount of small stuff. The building was sold just after Christmas 1988 and so I was back where I started - just fishing.

I enjoyed that period of my life, including the dealing and preparing boats for sale. It perhaps sounds as though it was all straight forward and all deals were very profitable when of course they were not. Boats were not too bad because one could look inside and out to assess their condition and value but engines are more difficult. I bought engines which were supposedly worth hundreds of pounds, only to find when I got home that they were scrap but there was no way of testing them where they were bought. The law said that as a dealer I should know about such things so there is no comeback on the seller.

Music

Music has been one of my greatest pleasures from a very early age. I used to enjoy singing at school and in the church choir where I first encountered part-singing. In the choir there were a couple of tenors and several good bass singers, including my father.

As WW II was coming to an end, Flookburgh Band was reformed, many of the players having been away in the armed forces. My father had played a cornet in the band for many years so I was inclined to follow in his footsteps but he didn't teach me. I, along with several other youngsters, had my first lessons in 1945 from Septimus (Sep) Benson, a fisherman who had been the principal cornet player before the war. I then thought Sep to be an elderly man but he was in fact about forty-seven years old and aged only fifty-three when he died. Shortly after this Mr Jack Jacobs came from Barrow to teach us and to conduct the band.

The first engagement at which I played was the Remembrance Sunday parade at Grange in 1946. We marched from the British Legion Club, which was then up The Fell, to church for the service, then to the cenotaph and back to the Crown Hotel for tea and a concert for British Legion members. Tea was actually a good meal which I suppose could be called High Tea.

After a few years the tea venue was moved to the Commercial Hotel, now The Commodore. On that first engagement I was extremely proud and excited. Joe Moyle, who was then chairman of the band, and his wife, had altered a uniform to fit me so there I was, marching in the band as a second cornet player, a dream come true. I was soon playing in the front line because there was a shortage of players. We played several concerts each year and attended our first contest at Kings Hall at Barrow in 1947 playing a piece of music called The Pride of the Forest.

Sidney Bland was principal cornet player from about 1946 until 1970 and for most of that time I played next to him. As I progressed to being a reasonably proficient musician, I wished that just for once I could take over as principal cornet on a concert. Through the years Sid and I had played duets on dozens of concerts but I hoped that I might one day play a solo. Sid very rarely missed a rehearsal or a concert so it was only when he retired that I was able to take the top seat and play solos on a regular basis. I retained the position for about ten years until firstly Stephen then my nephew, Tony, took over, both being excellent musicians.

There have been four generations of Mannings in the band, Harold, Stephen, Tim and me and now only Stephen plays, and then only occasionally when work permits. Seven of Joan's descendants have played in the band and four are playing at present. A total of twelve of my relatives have played in

Flookburgh band since it was formed. At a contest at St. Helens in November 2001, my nephew, Tony Rowlandson, was awarded the trophy for the best soloist of the day and the bass section of the band, consisting of three of Joan's grandsons, Neal, Lee and James, along with our grandson, Tim, were awarded the trophy for the best bass section – the lads were all still teenagers.

Flookburgh Band at the 21st birthday of Mr Hugh Cavendish
3 Mannings in the band. Harold, Jack and Stephen

It has given me much pleasure to see the younger generations become better musicians than I was and perhaps especially to have played duets in concerts with Stephen and with my nephew Tony, also to play and sing in ensembles with the three of them, the quartet being completed by Mitchell.

Starting with The Mikado at Grange in 1950, I played in orchestras for local shows at Flookburgh, Ulverston, Barrow, Kendal and Millom. Over the years, going back to the mid 1950s, I have played at local musical festivals and have won quite a number of competitions. I entered the South Cumbria Musical Festival several times in the Slow Melody and in the Air and Variation classes on the E flat base (tuba) and won a number of classes. This was particularly pleasing as I was then well into my 50s and a headline in the local paper read: "Veteran player wins at music festival." I have also sung at the musical festival, the first time in 1987 and in two classes in 1988. I didn't do much good in either. In that 1988 festival I did win the open class of the brass slow melody and was second in the Air and Variation class. Having said all that I must say that I also went on stage and played dreadfully several times through being unable to control the nerves. In the photograph, taken at Millom in the 1960s I was obviously playing a euphonium. On this occasion I gained first prize playing a quite lively piece of music called La Belle Americaine which all brass band players will know is quite testing in parts.

Sid Bland & I between matinee and evening show at Holker

At one period there were twelve of our family playing brass instruments. Two or three times in the late 1990s we entered the family class at South Cumbria Musical Festival and on each occasion we won by quite a large margin of points. We gave up entering the festival because it seemed unfair to other, perhaps less experienced, competitors.

The band had elected me as bandmaster and conductor in the 1960s but I would concede that I was not a good conductor so gave it up after a few years and concentrated on playing. Conducting, like most skills, needs to be learned and practised in order to become proficient.

I continued to conduct occasionally but it was when I took on the position of Musical Director of the Grange and District Operatic Society that I gained experience in conducting - this was about 1979. The first two shows I did were summer shows, sorts of revues, then operettas, The Maid of the Mountains,

The Merry Widow, and Calamity Jane in 81, 82 and 83 respectively, all of which I enjoyed very much. These main shows were staged in February and the summer shows in July.

One of my most pleasant memories associated with stage shows was when I was MD of Flookburgh and District Operatic Society. In 1983 the show was Oklahoma and we won the Oscar for the best local production.

That was a most memorable show. A few years later I was their musical director again for one year when the show was Annie Get Your Gun. I did not wish to have the job regularly because there was so much work and hassle over a period of about six months just to stage five or six performances, at a time when I was busy with other things, including trying to make a living. Sad to say – the society put on their final show in 2015 after being in existence for almost a hundred years.

•

I was principal cornet player for the South Cumbrian Retirement Band for sixteen years. I know that was no great honour but at least I was a soloist again. All the members are retired or semi-retired men and women who meet in Ulverston once each week to rehearse. In effect it is a very pleasant social activity for retired people.

The first contest at which I conducted Flookburgh Band was held in the Free Trade Hall in Manchester on Sunday the 17th of February 1985 where we came fourth. On Sunday 13th of September 1992 I conducted the band at a contest at Widnes when we were in the third section and playing a piece called 'Amaranth'. On the Wednesday before the contest I was in bed suffering from flu and had a very high temperature when Mitchell came up to tell me that our conductor couldn't come to the contest so I must take the band. This left just one full rehearsal which was on the next day. I felt absolutely awful but dragged myself down to the band room to take that rehearsal and another for an hour on the Saturday where I was still trying to find my way round the music score. I could sense that the players were rather despondent but I said that we would go in to the contest "with guns blazing" which we did -and came away highly delighted with second prize. We have been to London to compete in the national finals seven or eight times. The first time was 1960 and the last time was when we played at the Wembley Conference Centre on the 22nd of October 1994, on which occasion we were placed 7th out of twenty. The band again played in the national finals in 2007 and 2008. On those occasions the venue was the Harrogate Conference Centre.

Down the years I have played most of the instruments in the band, the exceptions being the trombone and double B flat bass. I have been conductor, chairman, was made a life member, and later, vice-president.

182

The inaugural meeting of the band was on the 4th of May 1909. We celebrated the centenary with a gala concert in the Victoria Hall at Grange on

Stephen & I after winning our respective classes at Millom Music Festival

the 2nd of May 2009 and on the following evening, a dinner for members, their partners and special guests. The concert was a huge success, the hall being full to capacity with about thirty people failing to gain admission.

I decided to retire from playing in Flookburgh Band at Christmas 2002, when I was seventy years old but the band is often short of players so I continued to play fairly regularly until Christmas 2015. With the fact that my health was starting to fail and having been a member for seventy years, I thought that was a good time to retire.

The band has been a big part of my life but I had come to the time when I felt that, particularly when rehearsal time arrived on Monday and Thursday evenings, it was sometimes a drag to turn out. There was nothing outstanding or extraordinary in any of my musical activities, in fact, the experiences I have described would be typical of those of many amateur musicians. Nevertheless, these were my experiences and a large part of the leisure time in my life. At the band's AGM for 2016 I was again elected as chairman, so my association with the band continues.

Epilogue

As I look back on my life now, my thoughts are that I have enjoyed most of it and would not change much if I had the chance again. Unlike William Wallbank, a local man of many years ago, who, on his deathbed was reputed to start saying to a man who was visiting him: "If I had my time again —" but was cut short with the response: "Thou's left it a bit late for that William." Yes, there were some parts which I could have done without but how many people would not say that? It has been a hard life but I have lived it virtually as I wished, that is, not at other people's dictate and most of my ambitions have been fulfilled.

Several of my friends and relatives who had worked hard all of their lives did not live to retirement age. A good example was my cousin, Leslie Butler, who was one of the most hard-working men you could ever meet. He said that when he retired he was going to do many things, including visiting South Africa where his wife came from. He died from cancer, ten days after his 65th birthday. I said that was not going to happen to me if I could help it. I intended to retire as soon as I thought it possible. I also worked tremendously hard – too hard sometimes, but always believed I would not have enough money to see me through. It would have been the same if I'd had ten times as much – that's how I was, always financially insecure.

In the early 1990s I started to have problems with my shoulder joints. Sometimes the pain was so bad that it was almost unbearable. I had to give up shrimping because I could not wind the long rope back onto the trailer and couldn't riddle the shrimps. For a few years, all I did was to catch flukes and try to catch a few salmon in summer but by then salmon were so scarce that it was useless. In fact, I made very little money in my last few working years.

Anyway, I did retire when I was sixty-five, and for a few years I did no fishing and didn't even want to talk about fishing. We had several holidays each year and visited many places we had always wished to see. It was at this time that I, along with others, levelled the cemetery. After perhaps five or six years, having done most of what we wished to do, I started to do some fishing again. I've had almost twenty years of happy retirement and have, until recently, been quite fit for my age which allowed me to carry out those activities - which is what I had hoped for.

If I were just starting out as a young man and knowing what I know now, I might choose a different career – but as what? I still don't know. I enjoyed dealing in boats and dabbling in property so perhaps I might go into that sort of line.

To the generations that follow me I would say, whatever you take on in life, give it your best shot and try to be contented with your lot. Most people,

\including myself, have seen others who have a nice lifestyle and may be envious of their position but we must accept that we all have limits to our capabilities and must recognise them. There's a saying: "The grass is always greener on the other side."

One of my father's most profound and memorable statements to me at a time when I had lost my tractor and gear - at which I was rather despondent was: "Anyone can smile when things are going well, you have to be able to pick yourself up and carry on in times of adversity." That is absolutely true and well worth remembering. All in all it has been a full, mainly happy and satisfying life.

In 2008 I was diagnosed with cancer of the prostate gland and was treated with radio therapy for which I had to travel the hundred mile round trip five days per week for seven weeks. In 2011 a large tumour developed in the back of my thigh. That was removed in Birmingham Royal Orthopaedic Hospital followed by another seven weeks of radio therapy at Preston. In 2013 a metastatic tumour from the one in my leg developed in my right lung and another one in 2014. Both of those were removed in Blackpool Victoria Hospital.

As though that was not enough, in 2015 I was told I had type 2 diabetes and heart failure. On my last routine visit to the oncologist at Preston the consultant said I was phenomenal, having come through so much and yet still being active. Bearing in mind all of that, I intend to make the best of the time I have left - however long that might be.

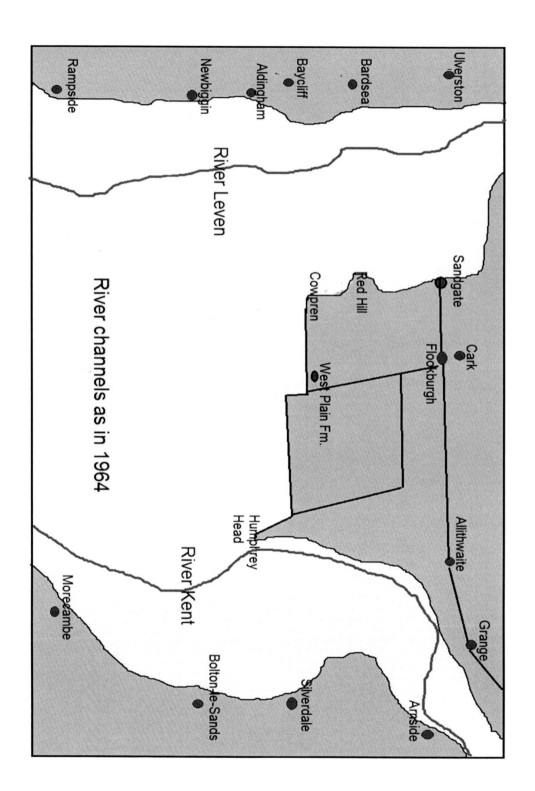

River channels as in 1964

Rampside

Newbiggin

Aldingham

Baycliff

Bardsea

Ulverston

River Leven

Cowpren

Red Hill

Sandgate

West Plain Fm.

Flookburgh

Cark

Humphrey Head

Allithwaite

River Kent

Grange

Morecambe

Bolton-le-Sands

Silverdale

Arnside

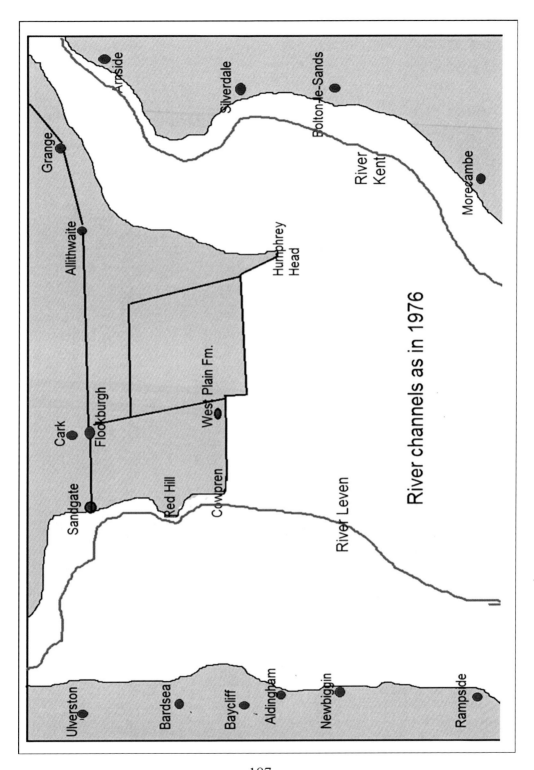

River channels as in 1976

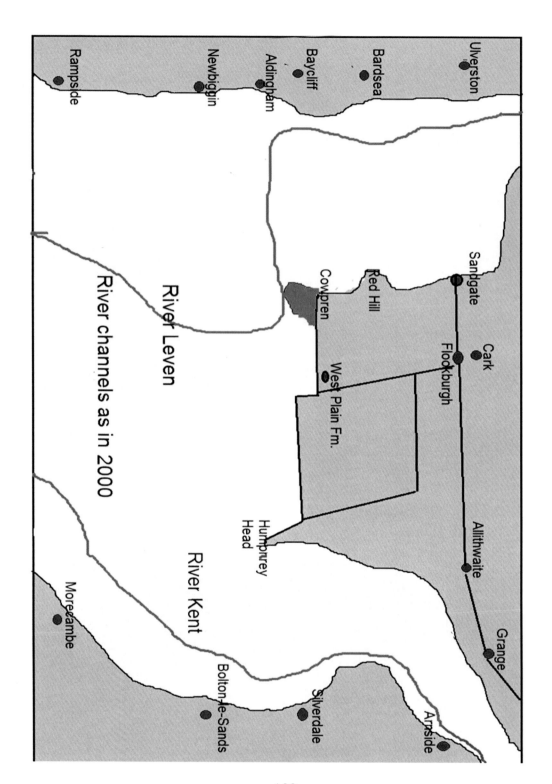

River channels as in 2000

River Leven

River Kent

Ulverston

Bardsea

Baycliff

Aldingham

Newbiggin

Rampside

Sandgate

Red Hill

Cowpren

Flookburgh

Cark

West Plain Fm.

Humphrey Head

Allithwaite

Grange

Arnside

Silverdale

Bolton-le-Sands

Morecambe

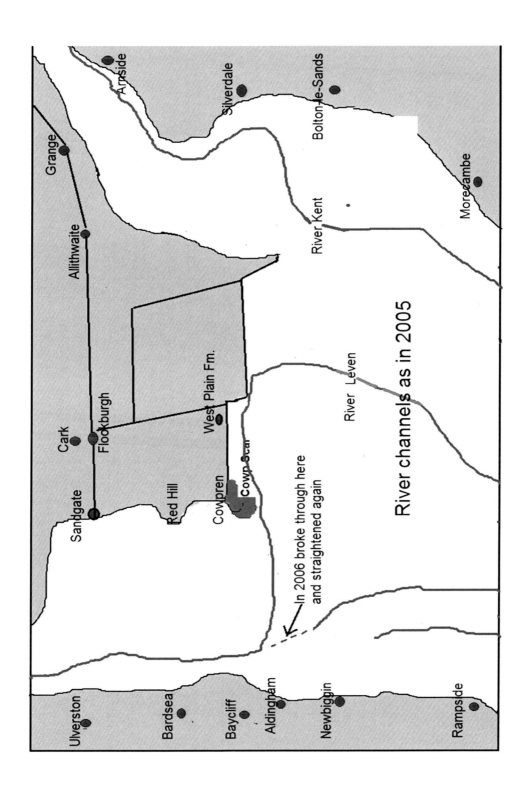

Arnside

Grange

Silverdale

Bolton-le-Sands

Allithwaite

Morecambe

River Kent

Cark

Flookburgh

West Plain Fm.

River channels as in 2005

River Leven

Sandgate

Red Hill

Cowpren

Cowp Scar

In 2006 broke through here
and straightened again

Ulverston

Bardsea

Baycliff

Aldingham

Newbiggin

Rampside

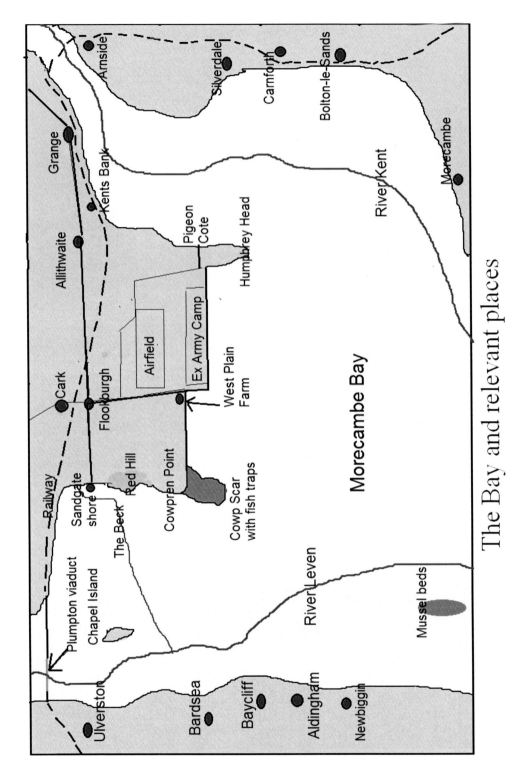

The Bay and relevant places

Family Tree

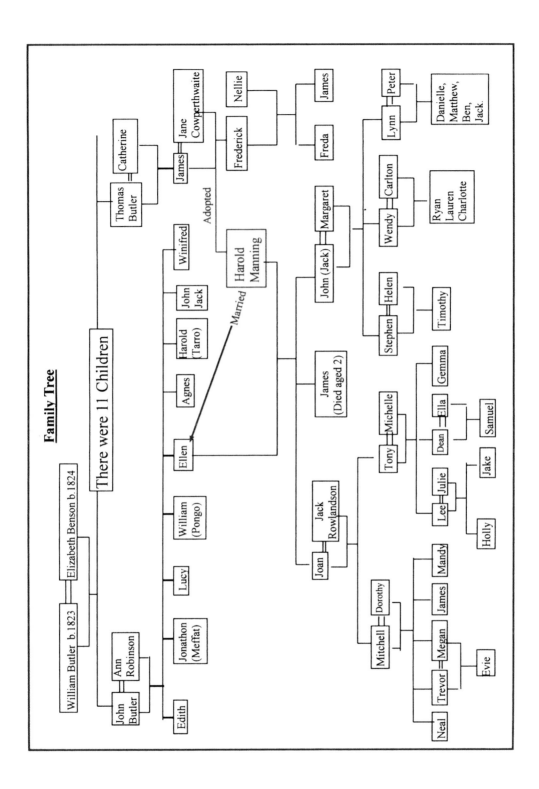

Index

192